JAFFER RAJPAR.

R H Nicklin (signature)

From Civilian To Sailor

WW2 1940 to 1946

R.H. NICKLIN

authorHOUSE®

AuthorHouse™ UK Ltd.
1663 Liberty Drive
Bloomington, IN 47403 USA
www.authorhouse.co.uk
Phone: 0800.197.4150

Published by AuthorHouse 04/26/2014

ISBN: 978-1-4918-9609-9 (sc)
ISBN: 978-1-4918-9610-5 (e)

Tutbury is a very small village in the county of Staffordshire and this is where I grew up, I was just like any ordinary teenage lad in 1939 and the world seemed to be a great place, we made our own enjoyment, mostly outdoor sorts. I left school at the tender age of fourteen on the Friday and started work at the local Glass Works on the Monday. This is where all my family from Grandfather downwards had worked over the years, it is a very warm job from Monday to Friday and not very well paid, but most families in those day's only just managed to make a living, and so my dear Mother was only too pleased to receive my first week's wages from which I received pocket money of half a crown (2/6 pence), two nights at the cinema, a trip to the nearest town on the bus, a few sweets and my 2/6 had gone. The living standards were very low and most houses were lit by oil lamps, all the cooking was done by the open fire place which was made of metal, the fire heated a oven on one side for the purpose of cooking all the food and on the opposite side was a small compartment for a water boiler, when you went to bed it was by candle light, milk was delivered to your house by the local farmer who used to come round with a big churn of milk on two wheels and measure out pints and half pints straight into your jugs. The daily bread was usually delivered by the local Co-op and most of the groceries came from a chap with a horse and cart, the streets were lit by gas light, a man was employed as a gas lighter, his job was to go around every night and light the lamps with a long pole then back in the morning to put them out.

The life of a married woman in those days was spent mostly at home, but some did work in industry as did the single girls. It was a very hard life and yet it was a happy life, even with few home comforts apart from your Radio or Gramophone. But over the years living standards began to improve and gas was the first thing introduced to most households and so came the gas lights, gas ovens and then the marvel of Electricity, very soon after, the wonder of Television for those people that could afford them but not many could. And then my life suddenly changed from working in a very old Glass works where I got the sack for larking about (to the annoyance of my Father but pleasing to my Mother) when I got a job straight away at another local factory, this was Nestle's Milk Factory where my two Aunties and my Sister worked, the wage here was a matter of a few shillings a week more than my previous job, it was a lot more interesting and clean, it was here that after a few weeks I found the girl of my dreams and my first love, this happened just by chance one day during the summer, I had just finished my lunch break and was returning to the factory from the canteen when the sun light caught on a window being opened on the top floor, and there she was smiling down at me, with her were two local girls known to me but she was a new girl who I had never seen before, but to me it was love at first sight and although she left the factory after a short time I could never get her out of my mind, and then a few weeks later I was out walking when we met and got together, from then on we began to see each other whenever we could, but due to her Father being very strict our times together were not as we would have liked, he only allowed her out four nights a week and then for only set hours, but she was the one bright thing in my life at that time and I was very much in love with her and everything seemed so perfect, we did manage to go to the local cinema once or twice a week but only on certain days, so on the days that I didn't see my girl friend I was always out with my mates, but at times it was very tedious especially when the dark nights came with nothing to do week in and week out, it was not the same as being with someone that you love very much, but this was the same for my mates who were always moaning and saying that they were fed up with this every day stuff, there was just nothing to do and the only thing to look forward to was a game of football on the local playing field and watching one of the local teams playing on a Saturday afternoon.

Then out of the blue it happened "War!" I was sitting in my grandmothers listening to her radio when there came a break in the program for a very important announcement, the Prime Minister was about to speak, and off he went but I wasn't interested in what he was going to say, but I soon woke up when I heard "CONSEQUENTLY THIS COUNTRY IS AT WAR WITH GERMANY," well I remember sitting there and my dear old Gran saying "Oh No! Not Another One."

THE KING'S MESSAGE
Sunday, Sept. 3, 1939

THE PRIME MINISTER ANNOUNCES
A STATE OF WAR
Sunday, Sept. 3, 1939

WAR DECLARED 11 a.m.

THE DAY of the WAR DECLARATION

But being just a lad it didn't really mean much to me and I suppose that I didn't realize the seriousness of it all. I knew that my Father had been a soldier in the last one because there used to be a big photo of him in his uniform hanging on our living room wall although he never ever mentioned the war to us, anyway war to most lads of my age meant two minutes silence on November the 11ᵗʰ, the parades to church by the ex soldiers, the service around the war memorial and the wearing of the poppies, also seeing the war films a few times at the cinema.

Anyway the next day all the daily and local papers were full of it, all men of certain age groups were being called up for service in one or other of the services and had to report to certain places named by the local authorities, it seemed as though everybody had gone mad, but to me and my mates it didn't mean a thing as we were too young to be called up. My elder Brother got his calling up papers after only a few weeks and had to report to some place in Derby and in no time he was in the Army.

Lots of things started to happen to change our way of life completely as we knew it, the 'Black Outs' came, no lights to be shown of any description at night so all window curtains had to be blacked out (we used to hang old blankets over ours), doorways darkened and street lamps were no longer lit at nights, all vehicles had to have lights blacked out to just a faint glimmer of light showing, even cycles were not exempt, they painted the glass on their lamps black and when it dried a little square was scratched off so there was just a chink of light showing, what a job it was trying to ride one at night. Then things began to move forward very quickly and the next thing that was to keep most families busy was the building of their very own air-raid shelters, people were urged to do this for their own safety by the government.

And so it was all hustle and bustle to get these shelters up, prints of how to build one were printed in lots of newspapers, and very soon these things went up in most back gardens, public ones were also being made but on a larger scale, the back garden one's were made of corrugated metal sheets bent over like a letter U, after digging out a fair sized hollow in the ground the U was turned upside down and planted in the hole and then banked up on the outside with earth and there you had a shelter with seats which also served as beds, this was because people often had to spend whole nights in them, although some seemed to be a bit rough they were perfectly safe, anything except a direct hit and they were certainly safer than being in a building that collapses from bomb damage.

Then the air-raid sirens, lots of the big factories had them installed on top of their buildings and the noise they made was terrible, at the beginning of the war they had practices so that the Air Raid Wardens could get people to run into the shelters as quickly as possible although some people did actually ignore them and just carried on into their homes.

Then 'Rationing' was the next big thing to come, it was really hard on everyone, everything that was edible was rationed, sweets, chocolate and all food stuff was issued by coupons only, people had to sometimes stand in long queues for almost everything, often having to make do with scraps at times to make a meal, quite a lot of the food had a substitute now but getting used to what we could get was what we had to put up with, "There's a war on you know" was the answer to everything and didn't we just know it. But the real Heroins of these hard and very difficult time's were our Mothers, just how they coped and what they had to endure is a big question and the worry that they must have suffered at times, 'they all deserved a medal was my opinion.'

It was really hard at first trying to get used to all these changes, but I suppose that some people never got used to them although after a while it slowly began to work, most of the factories went onto war work so your job changed completely, my girl friend was now working on bomb shell cases and doing twelve hour shifts days and nights seven days a week, yet they used to make lawn mowers, it was like that all over the country, people were being moved from job to job, but in certain industries lots of the workers were in what was termed as deferred jobs, this meant that the work that they were doing was important to the war effort and so although they got their calling up papers for the forces they didn't have to enlist.

Living in the country as I did I suppose we can say that we were lucky as we didn't have any of the targets that the German bombers would be looking out for, but the sight to meet your eyes on approaching a Town was something to behold, there were Barrage Balloons all over, now, these were great big Rugby ball shaped balloons, they flew overhead, their purpose was to deter the German Bombers from flying too low, they were anchored by a steel wire to a machine on the ground, search lights were another new thing that we saw occasionally but not so much in the country side as on the outskirts of the towns and they were manned by army personnel, and when the enemy planes appeared over head during the night the search lights would come on to try and pinpoint them so that the anti-aircraft guns could fire at them.

Well, the days passed by and the monotony for us lads got worse although I was still seeing my girl friend three nights a week and when I say nights I mean just about three hours as she had to be in the house by 9.30pm, so you can imagine what it was like and further more I don't think that her Father liked the idea of her going out with anyone, I am sure that he didn't go a bundle on me very much, I think that he wanted to pick someone that suited him.

This war had been under way for some months and the frustration seemed to get even worse, the pleasure of watching our local Football teams had now been affected as most of the lads who played had now been called up, so the usual stroll through the fields down by the river with my mates became more constant. Most of the conversations always turned to the war and the lads the of the village who had been called up, how they were making out, how fed up we were, other trouble's and moans.

And then it happened one of the lad's said that he had been thinking about volunteering for the Navy and this idea started a big discussion, it was handed about among the three of us while we were strolling along for quite a considerable time, lots of things were brought up and after a lot of thought we all agreed that as no one else in our village had yet joined the Navy then that is what we will do, I suppose that my first thoughts were that I would show my girl friend's Father that although I was still only a young man I was not afraid of going to war "Bravado" you might think! Well I suppose it was in a way but just like my mates I was fed up to the teeth with the life that we had been going through and we were all very determined now. I suppose that if I had been seeing my girl friend on a regular basis that I would have had to think a lot more about what l was giving up, but I could not see any change coming up so had no intentions of backing down now.

And so the very next day bright and early we set off for Derby and the Royal Navy Recruiting Office in Green Lane, I did say bright and early well in actual fact it was a very cold and wet morning on the 14th of March 1940 when we arrived. After giving our particulars to the Naval Officer on duty, stating that we wanted to Volunteer for the Navy, we were told politely that one of us could sign on right away but two of us are too young, however as I was so keen to volunteer as he put it and being seventeen years of age he said that there is nothing to stop me from signing on now but l would have to wait until they sent for me, and so I signed on for the navy on that very day, I didn't have to wait too long before I got my papers and sure enough they arrived on the 14th of May with orders to proceed to the Assembly Rooms in Derby that very day for a medical, I duly reported there at noon and passed my medical at the age of seventeen. After passing the test I was told to report to the Royal Navy section at the far end of the room where quite a few other lads are assembled, and after a short wait we are all welcomed by a Naval Officer who gave us a little chat and told us what would be expected of us as Naval recruit's, he then gave us our destination from Derby, it is Skegness and our Base will be Butlins holiday camp which had been commandeered by the Navy and was now a training camp, it was named as H.M.S. Royal Arthur.

Well, everyone thought eh? This should be great as each one is handed a travel warrant and we headed off to Derby train station, 'Skeggy here we come.'

After a short journey we are met on arrival by a chap in Navy uniform with a coach and after piling into our transport we are taken along the sea front at Skegness to our destination Butlins. On stepping out of the coach on to what we found out later is the parade ground we are all shuffling around wondering what to do next when a loud voice made itself heard above the noise "Get fell In! In columns of three's" and a little man appeared in a uniform that we found out later is a Chief G.I. Short for Chief Gunners Mate, he called out "when I call out your names answer <u>here</u>," when this was done he made a little speech starting off by giving his name and telling us that it was his intentions to make men out of us in a very few weeks. As groups we marched over to the Navy stores, as your name is called you enter and get kitted out with everything that you would ever need as a sailor and it all went into a kit bag, right on the end of the line we are issued with a paper which has the number of the chalet that we would be in, also our Official numbers which you keep the entire time that you are in the Navy, Mine was P/JX192801 the letter 'P' denoted that I am now a Pompy rating (Portsmouth) like some of the other lads, some have the letter 'D' which denoted Devonport, the letter 'C' is Chatham.

TRAINING AT H.M.S. ROYAL ARTHUR
1940 (BUTLINS HOLIDAY CAMP)

Our chalets are on the small side but just billeted two ratings which are comfortable enough, after settling in with all our kit, we all fell in on the parade ground and are given a talk to by the Chief who is going to be our instructor while we are training. Our first taste of the Navy is square bashing with a '303' Rifle, this in civilian terms is marching up and down with a rifle on your shoulder 'did they put us through it.' The art of rifle drill is doing all the marching, learning the naval terms, commands and orders while on the march, by the time we had finished that first day we were very happy to crawl into our beds at lights out only to be called out of them by a bugle call sounding out over a tannoy system at a very unearthly hour on a bitterly cold morning, a quick wash and into your uniform which had to look neat and clean, with boots blacked and shining, then dashing down to a big hall full of sailors for breakfast (this in naval terms is the mess desk). The food in the navy is pretty good but you have to eat what's put in front of you or you go without.

I paired off with a few other lads, there is four of us to be exact, two of us are almost locals and the other two come from Yorkshire. It is a great thing to have mates as it really helps you get through what is very hectic at times as it is a very hard life, entirely different altogether from the lives that we had been used to, but as mates we could help one another, help to grin and bear it, take the rough with the smooth as it comes, although I must say that I did see a few tears at times. There are nights when we get together, the big subject every time is our folks at home and how they are coping now that the German planes had started to bomb places more inland than before. My thoughts are always on my girlfriend and how she is coping, being up here on the coast and trying hard to cope with being so far away from her and home for the first time, I am really having a struggle.

And so it went on, I can tell you after a few weeks of this you really toughened up, I certainly felt a heck of a lot fitter, I also put on a bit of weight, It is an entirely new beginning getting used to this life and the routine of course became a lot easier as we went along, all the naval terms began to make some sense and the one that we like best is the "Going Ashore" one. Now even though this is only an establishment, you are leaving the ship Royal Arthur when you go through those gates, and so you are going ashore, this is the respite that we get when it is our turn, but only at night time and only in Skegness. The nightlife is almost nonexistent and in any case we had very little money to throw about, don't forget the 'black out' but it is a change just to be able to walk about freely, doing just what we want and 'Eye the girls' what few there are, though I am not interested because I have already got one back home who I am missing very much. Can you imagine though a sea side town in almost total darkness, just what do you do for enjoyment? No it isn't very exciting and we have to be back on board at a certain time (don't forget that I am still talking about a ship).

The days passed by and we are all looking forward to the day when the passing out parade is to be taken, I must say that our class is really looking quite smart now, the general idea is to be the best class on the parade ground at the passing out parade for your instructors when you march past the Captain on that final day. Now, I haven't said much about our instructor lately and believe you me we hated the little "B" when he first took charge of us he used to rant and rave swear and wave his arms about, also stick the butt of his rifle into yours if you wasn't holding the thing correctly, yet when that final day did come and we passed out, we really did put it together for him and was rated the smartest class on the parade, he said "Well done, you have done me proud," We all had a whip round for him and on the day that we left we presented him with a small gift on behalf of his class who all said then he was the greatest. Well, that was H.M.S. Royal Arthur and our training is now over.

From the Royal Arthur everybody was given different establishments and their official number, mine being a "P" I thought that I would be heading for Pompy but not just yet, a whole gang of us including some of the lads who were in our class at Skeggy headed for an establishment in Liverpool, yet another shore base H.M.S. Wellesley, one of my mates who also landed up on this draft is Walter Fudge and is one of the lads from Yorkshire. On our arrival we are taken down to a base very near to the docks and are told that this place used to be a Venereal Disease Hospital before the war, now what a place to be billeted in is on every bodies mind and quite a few expressed their feelings, but we settled in Ok. Training here we found out is entirely different from what we had experienced at Skeggy, not so much of the square bashing but a lot more of the naval type and by naval type I mean a lot more of the things that we would need to know about ships and the routines of a sea going warship, type's of ships and there uses in war time, parts of ships workings also lots of other things like how ships crews operate at sea, the watches "Port and Starboard," some shells and how they are made up and function, this is real seamanship and I must admit to myself who had never been near a ship of any description, living as I did right out in the open country, that this is going to be really something, all of this training on Wellesley is to make sailors out of even the rawest of recruit's. What is noticeable is that things are not as strict here as they were at Skeggy so that is a good thing for a start, one thing that we found very different is the march through the streets of Liverpool to the brand new Cathedral on a Sunday morning which had only been open a short time, that is where we headed for our Sunday services, but on the Royal Navy ships all church services are held on the Quarter Deck, that is on the after-deck.

I had my very first experience of a bombing raid after only two nights of being here in the big city of Liverpool, this happened when Walt and I were on shore leave, we saw the search lights come on and thought that it was funny because we hadn't heard any sirens, so we just carried on but it must have only been minutes before they did go off, almost immediately the ground shook and we both legged it to a nearby railway bridge that we had just passed as we had no idea where any of the shelters would be, anyway we spent almost two hours there just listening to the bombs dropping, luckily for us and half a dozen more people who had also taken shelter. They seemed to be concentrating on the dock area although one or two did drop pretty close but by the time Gerry had finished it was time for me and my mate to return to our base which was almost alongside the docks.

Liverpool is a great place for a run ashore, there is so much to see and plenty of places to have a good time, being so close to the docks it is great to walk down to the front and watch the big ships coming in and see all the action that goes on in these big ports, now and again a warship would arrive and to us land lubbers it was really something, never having been so close to ships before we spend hours down there when we are off duty, watching the Merchant Ships unloading their Cargo's and the movement of the different ships coming and going. Once we decided that we would take a ride on the New Brighton Ferry so I actually set foot on my first ship, it was also the first time that I had ever been on the water, yet here I was 'Me' a sailor in the Royal Navy, yet I couldn't swim a stroke 'I must be mad!' Just the thought of being on a warship in mid ocean is exciting enough and both of us talked about what it would be like when in action.

The training at Liverpool is a lot more interesting for us too, the atmosphere is entirely different than Skeggy and even the instructors are more friendly, and of course being among all the sea faring people around the docks, they are always very helpful if you wanted to know anything. My mate and I learned quite a lot just watching the people at work on the docks, I will be sorry for both of us when our training is over here at Liverpool despite all the air raids.

That day was to come sooner than we expected when the senior officer called us together one morning to tell us that our course would be finishing at the weekend and we would all be drafted to our respective naval Barracks. A lot of the lads are also very sorry to be leaving but some are glad to be on the move, but the most exciting thing is that we are being sent on leave first, the first seven days leave since joining up, I am really looking forward to this and can't wait to get on that train at Lyme St Station and how nice it will be to get home again if only to stay in bed an extra hour or two, but my girlfriend is the real reason that I needed to be on leave, I had missed her so much, I know the writing of letters to one another is alright but it only makes me realize just how much more I love her, then again seeing her only a few times in those seven days is going to make it very hard, I just wanted to be with her every day for there is no telling how long it will be before I see her again, but as expected this was not to be, I had to make do with what I had been accustomed to before the war started, but I loved those short times that we spent together anyway, and in no time at all found myself on a train speeding back to Liverpool and back off leave. Everything had been arranged and we are all mustered on the parade square the very next day in the early morning, each rating is issued with a draft chit, a railway warrant and told that we would now be going to our respective bases, of course mine and my mates is Portsmouth, this is what my mate and I had been waiting for. Our kit Bags and Hammocks would be following on by road and we will be arriving at each of our destinations the next day. When we arrived at Lyme St Station we are all split up into different groups, my group are for the Royal Naval Barracks at Portsmouth (Pompy). So it is cheerio Liverpool and the long journey down the country before arriving at our destination and being met by a Chief P.O. There we piled into trucks and are transported the short journey by road to the Barracks known to all as H.M.S. Victory. I am really surprised at the size of the place, it is a massive building enclosed by walls with iron railings with spikes on the top and a great big parade ground in the middle of it all, one entrance gate which is being guarded by a naval rating is opened and closed by a leading hand or a P.O. Through the gates we pulled up in front of what we now know as the drafting office, "everyone out" was ordered and to report to the drafting officer by another P.O. (for the benefit of you land lubbers I will define what some of these new words mean. For a start P.O. is short for a Petty Officer).

After the visit to the Drafting Office and answering to our names, the P.O. then gave us all the number of the mess that us ratings (That is what we are called in the navy) will be allocated to then we are given a card and on that card is what is termed your part of ship. Now, any ship in the Navy has to have a routine for the running of the ship and so the word "Watches" comes in and be it establishment or Ship the entire navy is run on port or starboard watches, the new card said that I was in the port watch and luckily so is my mate, this meant that at all times while we are at Pompy whenever the port watch is called for, that meant us. (Get It?) Further more when shore leave is given in our watch you have to hand in that little card at the gate and on returning at or before the time the shore leave expires you are given the card back, woe betide if you are late.

Now, some of the lads who had been with us at Liverpool have been drafted to Devonport or Chatham bases, but now we are Pompy ratings and this sticks with us for the rest of our time in the service. Once again we found that this is a very different place to all the other places we have been, the food, the routines, the real strictness that must be observed at all times, the saluting of all officers and run don't walk across the parade ground at all times. We have divisions every morning, this means that we have to fall in on the parade ground early morning in the rig of the day, that means uniforms. After divisions the work parties of ratings are detailed off to do different jobs and these could be things like sweeping out the mess decks or the parade ground, going down to the dock yard (A job I really liked) doing guard duty, which is another job I like, and fire watch, this was at night, it's a job that excused you duty during the day time as this entailed being on duty when the air raids are on.

Portsmouth is really in the front line of this war and the air raids are happening every night, so most nights are spent in the air raid shelters which just happens to be under the parade ground, now, remember I said that it is a huge parade ground and it is honey combed with shelters, so I can tell you it is pretty nervy hearing the bombs dropping all over the place while you are stuck under there, the ground really shook yet the barracks has only been hit once while I've been here, although hundreds of incendiaries have been dropped.

Working part ship was mentioned before when I spoke of going down to the docks, when I say 'part ship' it means just that, because as I pointed out the Barracks here are aptly named H.M.S. Victory so just like when we are aboard any ship we are detailed off to work part of a ship, you could be washing down some paint work or polishing brass work, scrubbing out the mess decks or even splicing ropes with the sail maker, on board a ship afloat I am told that they do all of these things plus a heck of a lot more, like cleaning down the guns and there are an amazing amount of brasses on a ship, there is scrubbing down the main decks, going over the side painting, washing down paint work on the upper decks and of all things, when it's your turn there is also being Cook of the mess, now this is something I really want to see I just couldn't believe this but it came from a leading hand and I don't think that he was joking either. There are umpteen jobs to do on a ship afloat and these are decided by the leading hand or the

Petty Officer of your watch, a leading hand by the way is a navy word for a leading seaman or "Killick," he may also be in charge of the mess that you are on if you are a seaman, don't forget that there are quite a few different branches in the Royal Navy just like any of the other services, Stokers being one of them. Although no ships in today's Navy are run on coal they still have jobs has Stokers down in the engine room of a ship. Then there are the signal men "Bunting Tossers" is the nick name for them, torpedo men, stewards, stores ratings and lots more that I was yet to learn about.

There was one thing that I pointed out before that I liked very much and that was going down to the docks, this is where we began part of our training which I have not touched on before and that is Boat Drill, again this is something entirely new to me as I have never been in a boat before in my life so the dockyard at Portsmouth is the ideal place to start off., for this drill we are put through our paces by a leading Seaman, the boat that we are going to be training on is a 32 foot cutter, the learning points are how to handle a boat, the names of boat parts, and "Learning the Ropes," you have to learn the different types of ropes that are in use and how to work with ropes, there is splicing (joining two lengths of ropes), knots, bends and hitches and to add to these there are the wire ropes, these too have to be spliced just the same as the ropes and that is extremely hard work, all of these things have to be perfect when doing your exams for the Able Seaman group and that is your first step up from the class of Ordinary Seaman rating that we are at this moment, I must add that the passing of the exam means a little bit more money so like all the lads in the group we are dead keen to learn and being down at the docks is a lot more interesting than being stuck in the barracks, also a part of our learning while we are at Pompy is a short spell at the H.M.S. Vernon barracks which is a mine and torpedo training school, which is also right down on the docks.

But I did like my time at the Vernon barracks be it very short, It was entirely different to the Victory, there was no strict routine for a start, everything was done at a normal pace, and to add further to my reason is that we could get ashore every night also the training there was not so much knowing about the working of mines and torpedoes but what a heck of a lot of damage they could do and how the different mines are laid, to this end the men who actually do the work there are very skilled and also very brave I might add, they have to be as the work they do is extremely dangerous as well as vital.

A part of the work that they do here at H.M.S. Vernon is the examination of mines which are brought in from the sea and some that they get are perhaps a new type of German mine so they have to be stripped down to find out how they work and this is what the Germans expect so they set booby traps inside them and this leads to some dire consequences sometimes like the one that occurred one bright sunny morning, we had just had stand easy (this is a break that is taken during the morning or afternoon work period) and had just moved off in a lorry to pick up some ratings from Pompy station, we were going along the road in Vernon when there was a terrific explosion on our right, the air filled with a terrible amount of flying debris, when it had all cleared it was easy to see the extent of the damage, the workshops where the men had been working on this new mine and a few of the adjacent buildings was no longer there, what had happened was that the mine had been dragged up by a trawler and brought into the base for the usual examination and during the examination the mine exploded killing everyone in the buildings.

This had never happened before at Vernon I was told, and was a big shock to everyone on the base but as I have already said they were very brave men they knew the terrible danger that they were working under but still got on with it. Even though this terrible thing had happened the work of H.M.S. Vernon still went on as it was very important work right here on the docks, very handy for any handling of mines dragged up by the different ships, this way there was no danger of having to transport them long distances putting even more lives at risk by doing so.

The air raid sirens are constantly going in Pompy, so many nights are spent underground and although bombs are dropped the damage has been very slight until the night that I will never forget, the sirens went off early and we had taken to the shelters and was expecting the usual few bombs but this night was to be a very long one, It turned out to be a terrible night and it seemed as though they were flattening Portsmouth to us, but when we came out of that shelter in the morning even with fires still burning fortunately the damage was not as bad as feared.

Well, it wasn't long after this that I sadly left H.M.S. Vernon, with loss of a few more good mates that I had made and a lot of very fond memories I was returned to Pompy Barracks and the same old routine here. The first thing that I found out was that my old mates from the Wellesley are still here and nothing had changed except that the air raids now had begun to get more regular and we are kept very busy apart from the boring job of working part ship, and as I have said before we do get shore leave pretty regular while we were in Portsmouth but as usual there is not a lot to do, of course being wartime there is nothing going on apart from going into the pubs with one or two of the lads, I am eighteen now and pubs are the only place to find some sort of life, that is Portsmouth and how it is in war time.

The Girls! now that is a subject and a half, well they are spoiled for choice and playing hard to get, you can see why when there are so many sailors about here, some of these girls come down from London at weekends solely to have a good time, but you couldn't have the sort of good time these girls wanted on the kind of money that we as ordinary sailors pick up, you can on an Officers money, that's why you never see many girls on the arm of a rookie and it was pitiful to watch some of these lads trying it on with them, but they just didn't want to know. We do find some enjoyment in the pubs though, we have a sing song, play darts and getting drunk is a regular thing, all this we do to break the monotony up until we get some leave, that only amounts to a week end now and again as you can't have these regular because we are only allowed so many railway warrants and every time you did get one it is stamped on your pay card, you can still take weekends off when it is your turn even if you had run out of your quota of warrants, but unless you have the cash you have to spend it ashore here or in the Barracks, because if you live close it is fairly easy to hitch a lift, but to get one to as far away as Derby is just a bit too much to expect.

I don't really have a lot of time at home with my girl while I am down here in Pompy and of course when I do they are very short due to her Father only allowing her out on those few days of the week even though he must have known that I was on leave, the rest of the time at home was very boring, even more so now because most of my old mates had been called up and were now in the forces themselves, only on the odd occasion would one of them be on leave at the same time otherwise there really was nothing to do, so on the nights that she was not allowed out my time was spent across the road from my home in the pub, what a rotten situation you might say but that was my lot and because I loved her so very much I was prepared to put up with it until I could see her.

My days at H.M.S. Victory ended one bright morning in August 1940 when on rolling down to breakfast just like any other morning, Walt my mate and I were handed a note to say that we are to report to the drafting office at 09.30, so when breakfast was over we went along and were given draft chit's, It is a Foreign one so we had to report to the 'Pussers' store and draw out a complete tropical kit.

The Pussers Store is where you can get anything that is required for use of the navy and this consisted of anything that we would be needing in a very warm country, that turned out to be two tropical helmets, two white shorts, two shirts, shoes and stockings, and to hold this lot another small kit bag.

Well after that bag of surprises we went back to the drafting office to collect our leave passes, now when l looked at the dates I could hardly believe it and as I turned to look at Walt he had a great big grin all over his Yorkshire face has he shouted "Eleven Bloody Days" we were then both handed our railway warrants to our destinations, we went to get them stamped as we needed these just in case we got stopped on the railway stations by the military or the civilian police, very often when you ware traveling between stations you can be stopped by one or the other and asked for your passes to make sure that you weren't AWOL (absent without leave,) anyway I am really looking forward to this long leave at home all dressed up in sailors uniform and looking very smart in 32" Bell Bottom trousers, as I lived in a very small village in the Midlands and I was one of only two sailors in the village the other was one of the lads who volunteered with me at Derby, most of the other lads out of the village had joined either the Army or the R.A.F.

I can only say now that I had a fantastic eleven days leave and there was plenty of free beer if I wanted it from most of my local pubs though I wasn't a big drinker It was very hard to refuse people who offered the free beer especially for a lad of 18 at any time, I visited the works were my Father worked and also the factory that I had left on joining the Navy and was very surprised how well my old friends and work mates received me, the girls really went for this sailors uniform, it was great being back home again and I spent every moment that I could possibly have with my girl friend, we would stroll down by the river to a favourite place of ours and spend some wonderful moments together mostly talking and holding hands. I know that I keep on saying it but I really love her so very much and, I don't think that she realizes just how much, I really cherish every moment that I can spend with her. And how long was it going to be before I was going to be coming back to England something that I just daren't even think about now.

Going back to Portsmouth on the train my thoughts are as before, just how long it is going to be before I saw my girlfriend again, you see she is never very far from my thoughts and the future for us, well I could only hope now that we are at war that things would turn out right for us in the end, when that was going to be and how long this war is going to last, also what would it be like the next time I go home are going through my mind, things that I shouldn't be thinking about at all, daft enough as it sounds but who is to know what the real outcome of this war is going to be, anyway, we could even lose, that didn't bare thinking about did it! then a more scary thought what if my girl friend got tired of waiting for me and found someone else! It could happen, any of these foreign drafts are known to last two or three years and that is a long time for a girl to have to wait for her boyfriend.

So that is something else now I had on my mind apart from those other things, because when we were at Skegness I had already heard of girls even married women packing there husband or boy friend's up because they had fallen for someone else while they were away from home, I had seen at first hand the real heartache it brings to the lads who are trying to fight this war, to some it turns out to be just too much and they desert or even worse, now here I am with all these thoughts while traveling back to Pompy after a great leave at home and it really begins to make me feel as though I have made a big mistake in joining the navy too soon but I guess that these thoughts are only natural for someone returning back from leave, now let's forget all this silly thinking! no I trust my girlfriend, I knew what I was doing when I signed on for this war and I am just going to keep the hope in my heart that this business will not last too long and that all my dreams will come true. So as our train pulled into St Pancras station I put the silly thoughts out of my head as I dashed down to the underground platforms to get my connection for Waterloo station and eventually to Portsmouth.

Back from leave and passing through these gates at Victory into the Royal navy barracks. Two days have passed and both Walt and I get the call to muster outside the drafting office with our kit bags and hammocks, after a short wait transported by lorry down to Pompy station with our travel warrants we are on our way to that great port of Liverpool once more.

The ship that we are going to join is H.M.S. Mooltan. What a coincidence to be back where we had spent so much time watching the big ships come and go, now here we are about to join one of them, on entering the dock yard we showed our passes to the policeman on the gate and asked him if he could point out where this ship is berthed, Just imagine our surprise when he pointed out this great big liner well you could hardly miss her she is massive, for war purposes she had evidently been converted to what is termed as an Armed Merchant Cruiser in the navy, just what sort of arms she carries we have yet to find out, but for now our first job is to report on board and on going up the gangway she really did look huge and we found out later that her tonnage is a massive 21.000 tonnes.

We are met by an officer on arriving, then a leading hand who took us down to the mess deck and showed us where to stow our hammocks and kit bags, then we are escorted below decks to an office to receive the news that we will be taking passage on board the Mooltan and given our boat stations (this is in case of emergency) also our action stations, then down below again to be shown our mess and onwards to a further office where a Sub Lieutenant gave us the news that our destination is the port of Freetown in West Africa. The ship stayed at her berth for the next three days taking on supplies and other equipment then we sailed early morning on the fourth day. The Captain spoke over the tannoy as we cleared the harbour explaining the danger that we are now in and the necessity for vigilance at all times.

And so here I am, first time on a ship unless you can count the Gosport and the New Brighton Ferries, I have certainly never been on the sea, further more I still can't swim a stroke! There is no doubt about it that is dear old England receding in the far distance and just then lots of things started going through my mind, such as when am I going to see that scene again and hopefully with the ship then approaching England, at that moment Walt came up behind me and jokingly said "when are we going home?"

We sailed on all that day and night without any problems, the sea being fairly calm, but then the next morning just as we are eating breakfast and without warning the alarm bells begin ringing throughout the ship, what a noise that made so off we dashed to our stations which as passengers is one deck below only to find that it is an exercise, what a relief that was. We sailed on through the night and through the next day it is into the afternoon watch when the alarm bells started ringing again but this time it is for real, I was below decks on a cleaning job at the time when I heard a loud explosion and the rattle of gun fire, it sounded very much to me like we are being attacked by air as I could hear the roar of aircraft engine, I poked my head above the hatch and had a quick look, sure enough the ships guns were banging away at what appeared to be fighter bombers diving in so I quickly headed for my quarters thinking well this is my first taste of enemy action out in the open sea! As I got into a position I could plainly see one enemy aircraft diving in low, firing at the ship with machine guns and I thought 'hell' here we are only just over two and a half days out of Liverpool and this is happening already.

It was a very short piece of enemy action due to the fact that the planes had probably used up all their ammunition or fuel in just over half an hour at a guess, well, they had evidently done some considerable damage to the ship, damage that meant that we couldn't carry on to Freetown. Walt and I had a tour of the upper deck later that day we could see there are holes in the Superstructure, apparently there is some damage to the sides of the ship as well although we are not told anything other than that we could not carry on and that we are returning to the port of Liverpool. So we turned round and started our journey back, day and night steaming for Liverpool fortunately not seeing any more enemy aircraft, we arrived late at night on the third day and went straight alongside the jetty. A good night's sleep was had by all that night.

There is quite a bit of damage on the upper deck, bullets had splattered all over the place and there is what seemed to be holes in the side plates, after looking at all the damage it is amazing that there were no casualties. Quite a few ranking "Bods" came aboard during the morning, also a lot of white coats which I reckon must be Engineers of some sort, they are making inspections down below decks and other parts of the ship, going up and down that gangway all that first day, finally the outcome is that the ship will have to go into dry dock for repairs, this resulted in the Captain making an announcement to the effect that all the ships company will be sent on indefinite leave, In other words sent on leave until you get a recall back to the ship, usually by telegram "Great" eh! And of course that also means us. So with best uniforms on Walt and I set off on leave once again, now this is too good to be true! Going on leave so soon after the last one and thinking that it is going to be such a long time before I have any leave again, yet here we were heading once again for Lime St. Station and the train journey back to Derby Station and home to see my girl, so very soon.

I just couldn't get it out of my mind it is wonderful, the war could be a million miles away now for all that I cared, nothing mattered except the feeling when that train pulled into Derby station, it is really something. I had been at sea and into my first action with the Germans, now here I am safe and sound heading for home so I was going to forget the war for a while.

To say that I surprised everybody turning up like I did is putting it mildly they all thought that by now I would be somewhere on the high seas, but it is a pleasant one for my family of course. I just couldn't wait to let my girlfriend know that I am home on leave again, I think that she will be very surprised because the last thing that I remember is telling her that I couldn't say when I would be seeing her again, I know that it is something that I can't really explain in writing, the few times that we can spend together seemed to us more precious than ever. The recall as I stated before could come at any time so we just had to make the most of every moment that we could spend together short though they are, we are two people very much in love, the days that I spend on my own as I have said before are very tedious so I sit and think how stupid this situation is, here I am sitting here with nothing to do my girl friend sitting there at home doing likewise and my time on leave could run out at any moment, also I would perhaps not see her again for a very long time with the war at sea being nothing at all like the one on land. we are in danger every time the ship leaves the safety of the harbour, the danger coming from three different directions and you never know from which one it is going to be, so every minute could be your last.

That 'Telegram' duly arrived all too soon for me to return to the ship immediately, my leave is over so with a heavy heart I begin my journey back to Liverpool and the ship, I just couldn't help but think of the good times that I had just had on leave and was very thankful that I had been given the chance of seeing my girl friend once more, short though they are, but all the thoughts soon passed from my mind when we arrived back in Liverpool. I headed for the docks then boarded the Mooltan again apparently the repairs had been completed and the ship is ready for sea again, so I dumped my gear on the mess and went in search of Walt my mate to find out how he had gone on at home. I found him up on deck leaning on the guard rail staring out over Liverpool, the answer too my question is 'Bloody awful.' I didn't push him anymore but we stayed on the upper deck watching the crew preparing H.M.S. Mooltan for sea there is no sign of any damage to be seen now, It had all had been newly painted over.

It is bright and early the next morning that we sailed out of Liverpool Docks once more into the open sea, bound for Freetown. While walking on the upper deck later the conversation soon turned to what an easy target this ship made for any enemy ships or Submarines and what a field day the dive bombers would have with a large ship like this, although we didn't know much about dive bombers we had heard quite a bit from the other members of the crew, our opinion is that she wouldn't stand a cat in hells chance as it is not at all speedy, we reckon about seventeen knots flat out.

But for all our guessing it turned out to be a very smooth passage and the port of Freetown was duly reached without any mishap. Our first thoughts are that what a barren place it looks, what is very surprising is the amount of ships there are lying at anchor, these are mostly war ships, one that caught my eye is tied up to a buoy close in to the shore, it looks more like a small Cruiser and it is the only one here that's got awnings over what appeared to be the quarter deck, little did we know at that time that this is the ship that is going to be our new base for some time to come. There's also a cruiser here at anchor and she is carrying a small aircraft this is the first ship carrying an aircraft that we have seen.

As we dropped anchor, Walt standing alongside me said "which one do you reckon is for us?" as I have already stated we had no idea but we didn't have too long to find out as all the ratings taking passage were piped to fall in with their kit bags and hammocks at the after gangway at 0945hrs, ready for transfer to their respective ships, so down below we went with very little time to lash our hammocks up properly and get everything stowed away neatly in our kit bags, then back up on deck to await whatever is next to come, as we stood here looking out over the water at Freetown I don't really like what I see, my first impressions are that it looks a dump, from here we can see a few buildings of a sort and what looks like a heck of a lot of mud huts surrounded by nothing but jungle. The real noticeable thing about Freetown is the heat, It is only early morning and the sun is only just on the horizon yet it is very warm, we are also in for another surprise as we are preparing to go down the gangway into the waiting boat alongside the ship, there are scores of canoes around the ship in no time at all, most are piled high with all sorts of different fruit's, but we didn't have much chance to carry on viewing the sight or to do any trading with the natives before we are ordered to take up our gear and get into the large boat that was waiting to transport us to our new base. Then off we went across the Harbour to find out that the ship with the awning on, lying close in to the shore is the one that is going to be our next base, only this time it is the real thing 'a warship'. We closed in to her gangway and then saw the name of the ship, which stood out in big letters on her bow "H.M.S. Edinburgh Castle" she is being used as a depot ship.

We were met at the top of the gangway by a Officer and Petty Officer with a leading seaman hanging around in the background who is then called forward and told to take us down to the mess decks, he showed us where to stow our hammocks and kit bags then we had to report to the office of the Chief P.O. who gave us all the details of the routine on this ship, what would be expected of us, gave us our mess number, the part of watch that we would be in then finally he told us that we will be working with the ships company as spare ratings, this meant that at any time a ship could come along that is short of crew members and we can be drafted onto that ship straightaway, then he then told us that at all times the rig of the day on board is tropical kit so we went to change, what a relief that was for us.

Oh what a god forsaken place this is, it looks even worse now that we are closer to the shore, the next day or I should say the day after we arrived aboard we fell in with the rest of the crew, surprisingly there was no part working, our first piece of duty was a chat with the Petty Officer in charge and he gave us the usual stuff on joining a ship and a small lecture about our duties which are quite surprising, these are mostly the cleaning of the ship, also we only worked here in Freetown until midday as the heat got so severe that it is thought unfit to work afternoons, the rest of the time is your own until the liberty men fall in later in the day, but the biggest surprise of all came on our first night aboard. It was in the middle of the night when I was awakened by a terrific noise, it was thunder and lightning, it was storming like nothing that I have ever heard or seen before in my life! But apparently this is a regular thing here and occurs almost every night, so it's just a matter of us getting used to it.

Getting used to it was really hard for us especially the terrific heat in the day time, the lads that have been here the longest say that at times it gets so hot that you can easily fry an egg on the steel deck plates, so you can see the reason for not working after midday, now, you may ask how did we spend our leisure hours if we didn't work after midday, well most of the time is either spent writing letters home or sleeping, but as I said before I think Freetown is a dump in fact for our first run ashore (to me) proved my words correct, it is nothing more than a large native village, as we walked around I was really amazed at the primitive way that these people live or I should say how they exist. We walked around the native quarters of what is Freetown, I am really amazed to see people living in these mud huts, the women walking about with only bit's of cloth tied around their middle, well, that is really something 'as a village lad' I had never seen in my life before, talk about primitive, no shops, if there were any I can honestly say that we didn't see them, but what we see are natives trying to sell Bananas and Coconuts everywhere, In my opinion there is not a lot to come ashore for here except the beer. The forces have a small place ashore where you can buy things, but the beer is sold in tins and it is terrible stuff, most of the time it is warm and very gassy, but I suppose that if you want a beer then you just drink it, even Walt who is a regular beer drinker had to admit that it is terrible stuff, so if you think that there is something to do when you get ashore here then you would be sucked in.

But the days rolled on and my mate and I are now getting used to the working aboard a real ship, we are beginning to pick up quite a lot of the good things about the real navy, all the naval terms had by now become a lot easier to use for us, we didn't have to ask too often what they meant when they used some word that we couldn't understand before and we were now thinking more like sailors so everything was ship shape, we also knew what most parts of the ship are and lots of the terms that a sailor uses in his every day work.

My mate and I only went ashore occasionally it is something to do and stretching our legs, a bit of exercise, it was just anything to break the monotony of ship life, when we are not working a lot of the leisure time was spent aboard watching the young natives diving into the sea out of their canoes for pennies thrown into the water, or plying their trade of coconuts and banana's from boats piled so high it made you wonder how they could manage to keep the boats upright as passing motor boats caused waves that made them bob up and down something terrible, yet I never saw any of them overturn.

Quite a lot of our leisure time is spent trying to catch fish over the side of the ship, apparently this is a very popular pastime in the navy back home in England, out here it is quite a regular thing, It was nothing out of the ordinary to see an officer playing a line over the side of the ship trying his luck. 'Monotony' that's the word I keep thinking, I wondered if the duty of these officers is such that even they had to resort to the quiet and peaceful art of fishing to break the monotony of this god forsaken place? I know that's how Walt and I feel about it, but to these people who are based here regular how do they manage the day to day same old routine, day in and day out, but I suppose that to most of them being here so far away from the danger of the war it is a cushy number.

Some of our duties might seem a bit odd to say the least but there is one that I particularly like very much and this is doing guard duty on a Sunderland flying boat which is doing a lot of patrol work here, I think it's job includes being the lookout for enemy submarines around these waters as this is a very busy port, the plane is used during the daylight hours so an armed guard is required during the hours of darkness while it lay at it's berth, another job that I like to volunteer for regularly is the working party that is sent up to what is called 'The Officers Rest House' (no joking) It is a place that's been built right up in the hills of the jungle for Officers only, this place has to be seen to be believed for it is built on a lovely spot overlooking the bay of Freetown and in a clearing, which I reckon must have been made by sailors. A few times a week seven or eight of us from the ship are detailed off with a leading hand or a Petty Officer, we trek up a ready made path through the jungle and on arriving at the rest house the first thing is to take a break first as it is very warm work getting to this place, then start clearing scrub and generally tidying the place up all around, now this is what I call a cushy number, we always take a packed lunch with us to eat while we sit in the shade watching the antics of the monkeys in the trees, the place is alive with them, but can you imagine it as a rest house of all things? My mate summed it all up when he remarked to the leading hand, "It must be damned hard work giving orders and such."

Letter writing is a subject that I have not said much about yet but I love writing them, but there is not much pleasure in writing to loved ones or friends when you can't tell them where you are writing from, this is the general thing I believe throughout the forces it's all down to censorship, so this meant that every letter I write is carefully censored by an officer on board ship before it is sent on it's journey in case you might be accidentally telling the enemy where your ship is. Whilst on the subject of mail, since I have been here I have received both air and sea mail that have surely been damaged by enemy action which amounted to some of the sea mail being in such a poor state that it is a job to read some of the pages, some had evidently been in the water and got soaked then dried out again so you had a heck of a job trying to make out some of the writing.

The mail by air is of course a lot quicker but at times the air mail letters would be quite burnt at some stage making it impossible to read them at all and some of them even have pages missing, so it is pure guess work as to what was in them at times, but most of the lads preferred the air post although we had to pay for these but it did get them home and the reply quicker, the sea mail is free but in a place like Freetown there is nothing of interest to write home about any way. Apart from my girlfriend and my sister I didn't get a lot of mail from home, it is hard enough to find a subject that will be of any interest to them so it is just a matter of the answering of their mail.

Anyway things carried on with the same old boring routine, the only bit's of excitement that we ever get is when warships of any description entered the harbour even that is not very often, there are times when warships arrive that are bringing in others that have been in convoy from different countries, some are troop ships which always started the guessing game on where they would be going next. Then early one morning Walt and I were just coiling up some boat ropes on the upper deck when in through the boom, (this is a steel Wire netting that is stretched across the entrance of the harbour and is open and closed by a small boat to let in friendly ships and keep out enemy submarines) came a big three funnel Cruiser looking majestic to say the least. The sight of this big Cruiser aroused a lot of interest on the upper deck, within minutes the guard rails around us became crowded with onlookers just admiring this ship as she came to her anchorage, she is without a doubt a real beauty and is looking very smart in her battleship grey paint with those big guns ready for action, everyone is asking what can she be doing here? Well, she hadn't been at anchor long before a small tanker went alongside her so she was evidently taking on fuel, then a Petty Officer who is in charge of Walt and I remarked that "those were 8" guns that she is carrying and can really do some damage," we also noticed that she is carrying a sea plane high up on what appeared to be a catapult, on questioning the P.O. we found out that this plane is actually catapulted off the ship then lands back in the sea to be picked up later, that is a bit risky when it's rough sea I would think, this is something that very soon we were to find out for ourselves after trying for a time to figure out just how they did retrieve that plane from a sea that is never dead calm. The shock came on the third morning after the ship had arrived here in Freetown, my mate Walt and I got a call over the tannoy system to muster outside the Master at Arms office immediately, so down we went to receive the brilliant news that we had got a draft chit to H.M.S. Dorsetshire, that same big three funnel Cruiser that was at anchor just across the harbour, go get your kit bags and your hammocks to the after gangway ready for transport 'Hey this is it,' we had a ship at last after we had spent over three months in this dump. Well, Walt and I just couldn't contain our joy and were doing a bit of a dance till a Petty Officer came along and told us to get on with it as the boat from the Dorsetshire would be here any time now.

H.M.S. Dorsetshire

And so the cutter arrived alongside and off we went across the harbour, as we got closer to this ship she looked even more massive, we duly arrived alongside and up the gangway we went, hammock over one shoulder kit bag under the other arm. the date I had noted is the 29th of October 1940. Straight away we had to report to the Master at Arms office and after having a bit of a chat with us he issued us with our watch cards then detailed us off for our mess, once again Walt and I were to be on the same mess although this time we were in different parts of the watch, Walt is in the starboard watch and I am in the port watch, this meant that we would no longer be going ashore together but we are on the same mess so it isn't too bad.

A leading hand escorted us down to the mess decks and a good job that he did, for I am sure that if we had got to find these mess decks by ourselves we would have been wandering round for some time lost! anyway he took us in charge, on arriving he showed us our lockers then sat us down and gave us a run down on the routine of this ship—what would be our duties as new ratings, now on this big ship he advised us to take it easy the first few days and if we wanted to know anything at all to ask the leading hand or any of the lads on the mess who would soon put us in the picture, we are not to forget that now we are ships company aboard a sea going ship that things would be different to what we are used to aboard the Edinburgh Castle, but I think that Walt and I realize that we might have to change our ways a lot once we found a ship as we would have a heck of a lot to learn. After our chat with the leading hand he then took us along to yet another office, the 'Gunnery' where we met the chief G.I. who had a chat with us, then gave us our Action Stations, Defence and cruising stations, then as we already had our watches—mine port and Walt starboard, he told us that I will be in the first part of the port watch and Walt would be in the second part of the starboard, he then explained to us that watches are all split in two which we already knew.

For the special duty routine I was given when we are in harbour, (this is a real cushy number for me) "Telephone switch board operator" I was shown where the switch board is and given a rough idea on how to operate it, now this is a real good start to my first day aboard my new ship, then we went down to the mess for our first meal with our new mess mates they all said that I couldn't have picked a better special duty job if I had tried, so I considered myself very lucky that I am not working part ship washing down paint work or other boring jobs but this didn't mean that I wouldn't be doing these jobs later when we were at sea, only when the ship is in harbour will I be what is called a Watch Keeper.

After my first meal and introduction to my new mess mates by the killick of the mess I thought what a great bunch of lads they are, the surprising thing is that a few of them are South Africans, I took to them straight away they are so friendly, but none of the lads come from my part of the country, though one or two do come from Walt's Yorkshire, they are all quite a friendly lot but this is something that you met with in the navy when you joined any of the establishments, they always try to make you one of them, so it is fairly easy to settle down and not have any worries at all, when I first joined up I was a bit worried and a leading hand sat me down and made me realize that everybody gets that feeling at first until they settle in.

What a big difference Walt and I found on the Dorsetshire from the other ships that we had been on up to now, everything done aboard here is done in true navy fashion, this is the real Navy. The bugle is here for everything . . . waking you, calling the hands to fall in, action stations, oh, almost everything, then there is the Bosun's pipe or Bosun's whistle as it is also called, this calls you for so many different things, in naval terms Hands to dinner, Up Spirit's, were the ones that most sailors wanted to hear, a very nice one that I like to hear most is when leave is piped to the watch, there is also other pipes for different orders of course the best one of all is up spirit's, this is for when you are of the age that allowed you to draw your rum ration, that is at the age of eighteen not before as the rum that is issued is almost neat.

About the rum ration, now the general routine I found out is that at the pipe of "Up Spirit's" the rum bosun on each mess takes up his 'Fanny' a receptacle with a handle attached and proceed to where the rum is being issued (always in the same place) and queue up, there he would find the issuing officer and a supply rating, when his turn came he sings out his mess number to which the supply rating then checks his list then shouts out the number of tots that mess is entitled to, then he will measure out exactly that number of tots and empty them into the Fanny, on returning to the mess each rating entitled to the rum would hand over his cup to the bosun who measures out the tot to receive in return what is termed in the navy as 'Sippers' (when you have had your tot you always leave some in the bottom of the cup) who would sometimes drink this up there and then, or pour it back in the fanny, then after issuing to all those entitled he will have a fair drop of the Bubbly leftover and this would then go into his bottle for a rainy day "Oh to be a rum bosun."

And so back to reality of real life aboard our first sea going warship. The next day on the 21st October 1940 during what is known as the forenoon watch we weighed anchor and slipped silently away from Freetown out into the open sea, now if I never see that place again it wouldn't bother me one little bit, so now out of sight of land and closed up at cruising stations, (I will explain these terms later) the ship is really moving through the water at some speed not the 17 knot crawl of the Mooltan, as we sat at the mess one of the lads started to tell me just what our real job is out here and that is to seek out any enemy raiders or blockade runner carrying supplies to enemy territories right down into the South Atlantic ocean, he added that they had already had some success.

Working part of ship while at sea is a bit surprising to me when falling in for duty after breakfast, our first job is being detailed of as either forecastle or quarter deck, or as waist port or waist starboard, the first thing that we did was to scrub down wooden decks in our bare feet, for this we line up and the order is given by the P.O. to scrub forward then after this was done a few times I was told by one of the lads that this is a regular thing in the peacetime navy and that amazed me no end, then there is the usual job of polishing brasses and washing down the paintwork, then during the morning there is what is term as 'Stand Easy,' this is a break for just a few minutes to get a drink then back to work until the pipe for Hands to dinner is sounded, after dinner the pipe goes for the first part of the port watch to close up at cruising stations, that is me.

The port watch closes up to do the afternoon watch, that runs from 12 midday until 4pm, on my first watch I am lookout on the Bridge, there are four of us, two on the port side and two on the starboard side, we each take it in turn to do the masthead lookout one hour at a time, being masthead lookout means that you can pick up things in the water ahead of the ship and on the far horizon much quicker than any other lookout down below, Immediately that you do pick out anything be it an object in or on the water you report it straightaway to the bridge by phone and repeat the message, "ship or object bearing so many degrees port or starboard or dead ahead," if you are on the Bridge a similar message depending on what side of the Bridge you are sitting, this job is OK but gets a bit tiring staring at the water all of the time, especially when there is brilliant sunshine reflecting off the water.

My first watch ends with nothing to report so I go off watch and the second part of the starboard watch take over to do what is known as the first Dog Watch, this is from 4pm until 6pm. these dog watches are used for the purpose of changing over and making sure that everyone on watch is able to stay alert, any longer than this could mean missing objects or ships until it's almost too late.

I am now making friends with quite a few of the lads on the mess 'this is comradeship in the navy,' some of them are on the same watch as me so you can't help but swop yarns and chat to one another, the South Afrikaans are great lads always ready for a bit of fun and plenty of laughter, like the lad said if you wanted to know anything at all these are the ones to ask as they would go out of their way to help and think nothing of it.

So sailing on into the Indian Ocean on our way to what the lads tell me is the ships main base, Cape Town in South Africa, long before we arrive we can see far out on the horizon a glow in the sky, that was the first sighting and as we came closer it became even more brilliant, what a fantastic sight it is, the lights are everywhere, the night sky is ablaze, this is really something to see from our point of view, don't forget that we are used to blackouts at home and hadn't seen anything like this for some time, it is such a sight, Charlie Johnson, one of the South African lads on our mess came up behind me as I was taking all this in and said "What about that then Nick?" It is a truly amazing sight, it just showed that there is no war here and that made you think more of home, it got us to wondering how they are doing at that moment, I can honestly say that there were a few tears in my eyes then.

As we arrived late there is to be no shore leave for our first night here, but there is one thing that we could look forward to and that would be a good sound night's sleep, without the fear of enemy submarines or the like, so it is up with the hammock and turn in.

The next morning after breakfast it is my first watch as telephone switch board operator, but before I take over I was genned up on the thing by the leading hand in charge. It became very easy for a while though much busier once the ship to shore line had been connected, I didn't get much rest at all then and somebody had said that this is a cushy job? I am amazed at the amount of calls from people on shore wanting to speak to different officers or ratings, so I can tell you I was very glad when my relief took over although as he did explain that it gets so much easier after a while.

There is one good thing about being a watch keeper and that is when the ship is in harbour you are either on watch or excused duty, so you could be writing letters or doing your dhobing, a naval slang word for washing your clothes, while the rest of the ships company are working part ship. It is the second day of our arrival here in Cape Town and it is my watch that is going to be the first to get shore leave, I am going ashore with a mate from the mess, but first we have to fall in the port waist with the rest of the liberty men of the port watch, after an inspection by the officer of the watch we are all given a lecture on the strict ruling that the South Africans do not look kindly on, any talking to or mixing with the local people at all, fraternization is the term used, so in plain English don't have anything to do with them at all or you are in trouble.

Now, that is a big shock to me for a start and I wondered why, the lad who I am going ashore with told me that I would have some more shocks after we had been ashore a while, It was soon very plain to see that they certainly didn't mix here as there are places for whites in toilets, bus stops, signs over doorways and in waiting areas, also the areas for the black people are plainly sign posted all over the place, well this really made me think because on walking amongst them they seemed to be really quite decent people, but orders are orders. The shore leave here turned out to be fantastic and the locals, well they couldn't do enough for us. The first noticeable thing when we stepped ashore is all of the cars that are lined up outside the harbour gates, all waiting to take us to their homes or to ask us what we would like to do while you are on leave, the beauty of it is that you don't have to spend a penny.

My mate said he wants to Show me what Cape Town is like so we had to politely refuse the kind offers, my first thoughts are what a beautiful place this is, It had just about everything you could want for, and the food! Well, now if only the people back home could see some of this food in the shop windows, the cafe's and restaurants they would be drooling. But of course the main problem for us poorly paid sailors here is the money, we could see all these lovely things in the shops here that we are unable to buy so it is heartbreaking, what little money we get is very soon spent as it certainly doesn't go very far in a place like this. The night life is like something that you only read about in books or see the films or papers but never expect to see in real life, but then again as just a country lad what do I know about city or town night life.

The other big surprise for me is the girls and what their wearing, the fact that it is quite fashionable to see them walking down the main street in Cape Town in bathing costumes, now I couldn't imagine that happening back home in a place like Derby for instance, they would soon have the police on to them, but here it is a recognized thing, of course what with the weather being so entirely different here to what it is back home I don't blame them at all. The people the weather and everything about Cape Town is fantastic, so I hoped that I will have plenty more time here in the coming months to see lots more of this place and enjoy the company and hospitality of the South African people, most of all I would like to accept some of their kind offers to go and visit their homes, go on picnics and of course some of them had lovely daughters so if you don't have a girl friend well here is your chance.

And so we spent three lovely days here in Cape Town having a great time before we got our sailing orders, though it turned out to be a very short trip just down the coast to Simons Town, this is the South African Naval base where they had Dry Docks, so this is where all the major repairs are carried out on all our Royal Navy ships, here I got the surprise of my life, it happened when we were pulling in alongside the jetty where all at once I spotted a great big dog, a Great Dane bounding along the wall and as soon as the gangway went down he came running up onto the deck, I was simply amazed and said to Walt who was standing next to me as we were fell in for entering harbour "now somebody is going to koppit" (Get into trouble), Later on I found out that this Great Dane was Simons Town's now famous Able Seaman 'Nuisance' and that he had been given that name by the navy, the reason for this is that he greeted most new ships when they entered the harbour and was allowed on board, hence his name, they also called him the sailors friend according to the lads on the mess, and that there isn't many sailors that don't know him, also it is really uncanny how he latches himself on to any drunken sailors so all they have to do is to hang onto his collar and he takes them back down to the dock yard, they also told me that this dog has saved many a sailor from being adrift when they have been really drunk, that he also knows when you want to go to the train station and not the docks, they said that they are not kidding either.

Simons Town is not a very long stopping place for us, for after just a few minor repairs we sailed out again and were soon heading back to Cape Town, there after only one day in harbour we are back at sea, I am on watch and we are back to our usual job of searching the seas for enemy shipping. We covered hundreds of miles of ocean while on these patrols and visited places like Aden, this place I will never forget, for it is a terrible place. On my first day ashore with a couple of lads and killick, we were walking just on the outskirts of Aden, on approaching what appeared to be a road into the Town and I saw the most heart breaking thing that anyone would wish to see, for there on the side of this so called road sat three old people all huddled up and covered in flies some young children playing nearby them, as we approached, one of these children ran up to these figures sitting at the side and struck one of them on the side of the face with what appeared to be a small branch from a tree, the figure almost fell over and even though there were adults walking about in the area it seemed as though not one was bothered by it, I wasn't having any of that so I quickly ran up and stopped him from hitting anyone else and shouted at him, but just as quickly following up behind me was the Killick, he pulled me over to one side and said pack it in, then explained why, "these are mostly old people sitting out here who are dying, or not far off, no one wants them, nor does anyone care and we will see this quite often," well to say that I was amazed was putting it mildly indeed.

Some of the islands that we visit in the South Atlantic Ocean are really beautiful, we call there mostly for fresh provisions and only on the odd occasion are we allowed ashore. Another of my favourite places right dawn here is the port of Bombay which is a very exciting place for a run ashore. So my mate and I when we are on off duty watch together and go down into the markets and the Bazaars, oh the things that you could buy here, It really is a dream place with such beautiful things to buy but again at a price and I'm afraid that lots of items are well out of our price pocket. But just to be able to roam around and see so much of this great city of Bombay of which we wrote about when we were at school, wondering what it must be like to see all these wonderful buildings, well here we are now actually seeing it for ourselves.

There is one thing that I will always remember about Bombay though, and it happened when my mate and I went ashore on our second visit, we were strolling down a street, stepping over sleeping bodies wrapped in their Saris and coming to a bit of what we would call a park where we noticed these Fakirs with their mongoose and snake charmers performing, we strolled up just to watch how these chaps worked with these things and found it quite fascinating as this was the first time that I had ever seen snakes close up, fascinating yes! But I don't really like the things, but the small monkey's were different and on display, It was great fun watching these lovely little animals and the things they get up to, but the thing that I always remember was when a Fakir came up to us and offered to tell us our fortune's, we tried putting him off by telling him that we thought it was all a load of rubbish but he was very persistent and said OK but if I can tell you your names will you believe me then and give me five rupees each, if I can't then I will give you the rupees, so we thought well he has got to be good if he can tell us our names and so we agreed, after standing there looking at us he closed his eyes for a second and then on opening them he just rattled off both of our names without any hesitation so we parted with ten rupees on keeping to our promise, just to show us what a good Fakir he is he proceeded to tell us what is supposed to be our fortunes, he should have said at the finish you two are the biggest pair of mugs that I have ever come across.

Well, all the way back to the ship and right up to lights out on board ship Walt and I were still trying to fathom out just how the heck did that Fakir do it because that fortune telling of his was a load of rubbish. So at breakfast the next morning we brought the subject up to the lads on the mess and was amazed when they all started roaring with laughter, this went on for most of the morning, every time we passed one of the lads we got the same treatment, then at dinner time the Killick decided to put us out of our misery explaining how the Fakir does it, he simply looks at the names on the white belt that you are wearing holding up your shorts, he knows that every sailor has to have their names on all of their kit, so he gets his money every time.

But there you go, you live and learn, as the South African lads said to us "have your wits about you when you are ashore in these foreign ports." Columbo was another one of those great runs ashore but as I have already stated we needed the money to buy the exotic things on show and the food here, well, just like Bombay it was very good with plenty to choose from, although there was some that I wouldn't fancy eating at all but everyone to his taste I suppose.

Sailing further into the Indian Ocean we arrived at another port that I didn't really go a bundle on and that is Trincomalee in Ceylon, we found that there is absolutely nothing at all here to make a run ashore worth bothering with and even the beer here is terrible just like Freetown and the place was very primitive, nothing but natives and jungle, thankfully we didn't stay here very long just a few hours and sailed out again.

So on with our patrols calling in at some of the most Beautiful Islands that anyone could wish to see like the

Seychelles, Mauritious, the Azores, the Ascension Islands and St Helena, so many more beautiful little islands in the South Atlantic and we were allowed shore leave on some of these but not all, just to write about these really exotic islands, it would take a few pages to write about each one as there is so much of interest about their different ways of life their style of living. The reason that we are not allowed ashore on some of them is that when a big ship arrives with a few hundred sailors on board and the Island in question has half that number of females, well, can you blame the Governor for not wanting to let a horde of young men ashore.

The port of Durban is our next calling stop which is not a great distance from Cape Town and like the Cape the lads say it is always a blaze of lights, after a long spell at sea they say a run ashore here is just what's needed to recharge your batteries, it's more like a seaside place than Cape Town. The thing that makes Durban stand out above all the other places, and the thing that will always be remembered by me and every sailor that enters this harbour is "The Lady In White" and why? has Dorsetshire sailed into the harbour for the first time through the entrance I could see people standing on the jetty, but what stood out from all these people is a figure standing on something higher than the rest and dressed all in white. As we closed into our berth on the jetty I could see distinctly that the figure is that of a women and she could be plainly heard singing through a microphone loud and clear "Land Of Hope And Glory" I can tell you that there wasn't many sailors who didn't have a tear in their eye's or a lump in the throat, I know that I did, to me it is so unexpected, such a wonderful thing, most of the lads on the ship had heard her singing before, this Lady is famously known by all sailors as "Durban's Lady In White" the South African lads told me that she greets all our Royal Navy ships entering the harbor with a song and apparently her favourite British one's say the lads are "There will always be an England, White Cliffs of Dover" and her most favourite of all "Land Of Hope And Glory," her voice is so lovely to hear I asked the lads on the mess "does this lady do this for British Ships only," no one could give me an answer.

But I know one thing she certainly gave my moral a boost and I only hope that I hear her a lot more times. On my first run ashore in Durban, now, what can I say of my first impressions, as have already stated previously it is more like a great big seaside place and so clean with lovely beaches golden sands and "Wow" some beautiful girls, not only on the beaches but also like at the Cape, walking along the main front in bathing costumes, what more could you want? you may ask.

Now, you might think that this is just what Jack wants but no, the first thing that a sailor wants to know on stepping ashore is where can I find the nearest pub or Bar, but unfortunately not out here, they don't have any and you have to search around some before you find a place that sells beer, but then again there are plenty of lads like me who being on the young side don't indulge too much and are looking for a good time other than beer drinking.

The people of Durban are very friendly just like those at Cape Town but they don't queue outside the dock gates like the Cape, and the weather here is nice and warm not hot like the Seychelles or Freetown, of course the shops here are full of every kind of goods and the food well there is no war on here so you are spoilt for choice, plenty of everything, but there again you still have to watch your spending, Durban is home to a few of the lads off the Dorsetshire, English lads who in their time on the ship had met girls ashore out here before the war and had got married, with homes and perhaps families here, a fantastic place to live, no war or rationing to bother about just go into any shop or restaurants and buy whatever you want how nice eh? But there is also another thing noticeable here in Durban there is no Apartheid, we could talk to the black people just the same as the Whites.

As I have stated before I really liked some of these black people they are quite sociable and easy to talk to, I still can't see what the problem is in Cape Town, there are Military police on patrol as well as the civilian police keeping an eye on things there, as we had already had our orders from the skipper so it was best to keep to the rules. The black convicts working on the docks here are quite willing to chat to us all the time and the warders in charge of them didn't seem to mind at all and there are also a few white prisoners among them working side by side without any trouble of any sort, the lads on passing them by sneak them cigarettes, that happened quite a lot, I say sneak but the warders often saw this and turned a blind eye as they also got their share, the prisoners will barter these cigarettes for different things when inside so I reckon it helped out a bit.

On this particular day we sailed out of Durban during the afternoon watch after three enjoyable days leave and also provisioning the ship. Out on patrol we go after sailing along in fairly calm weather and a flat sea for two days, covering once again hundreds of miles of ocean, when during the first dog watch on the second day, our aircraft out on patrol reported the sighting of a ship some way off flying a French Flag, which when signaled by the plane for identification purposes had ignored the request and was fired on, so speed is increased to intercept this ship, after a short time we arrived at the scene and by signal she is ordered to 'heave too' but she now ignored our signal as well and carried on, from where I am on the bridge she looked as though she is increasing speed so our Skipper ordered a shot to be fired across her bows and she soon heaved too, a boat with a crew of Royal Marines is sent across, they boarded her and signalled back to state that the ship is carrying ammunition and other war material, her destination is the port of Madagascar in the Indian Ocean which so happened a Petty Officer told me after wards is controlled by the Vichy French who are now allied to the Germans, so 'one prize to us', then the skipper ordered our Officer aboard the blockade runner to take charge of the ship and sail her into the nearest allied port where the crew would be taken prisoner I reckon. So on we sailed, we are now searching for another ship that has been reported by the Sunderland Flying Boat not far out of the port of Freetown. This is possibly one of the Flying Boats that I used to do guard duty on, apparently she is doing a routine patrol and sighted a ship which is a fair size, but on approaching was immediately fired on at some force but managed to get close enough to establish that she s flying a Liberian Flag, and so here we are doing a search for yet another blockade runner or a suspected one, that search has lasted a day and a half, searching miles of ocean once again it was our plane that first sighted her during the afternoon watch and as we closed at speed with our 8" guns trained on her she stopped immediately and gave her name as "The Mendoza" she is a fairly large merchant ship but yet again a Vichy Ship running supplies to the West African ports this time and she is fully loaded, another prize crew is needed to take this one into Freetown.

But up to now having seen no real action I am very pleased that we didn't have to escort the Mendoza back into Freetown anything but that, so we sailed on deep down into the Indian Ocean again in glorious sunny weather. Our pilot while on patrol reported that he had sighted an enemy submarine on the surface and that he Is going in to attack it, well, this is great news, some real action for our Plane and Dorsetshire but also for the pilot because his job of flying must be terribly boring, covering miles of ocean only occasionally like today sighting any enemy. It was some time before he radioed back to the ship and everyone had been keeping their fingers crossed for him, but it was good news, he had attacked the U-Boat and sank it with no damage to the plane "Splice the Mainbrace one of the lads shouted but no such luck."

And so with some success this time on our patrols we sailed on back to Cape Town, straight away we had to refuel and we are our way again, out of the harbour in a very short time so no shore leave this time, here we are at sea once more and for once there is a bit of a gale blowing but it doesn't really bother me now as I have got used to the rolling and pitching of the ship 'I have not been sea sick yet,' anyway it wasn't long before we sighted land, sailing into Columbo once again we went straight alongside the jetty this time and shore leave is granted to the port watch, So my mate and I decided to take a run, a matelot likes to get ashore to break the monotony of ships routine even if he hasn't got much cash, I'm afraid that we had got very little and in any case we had decided some time ago to save most of our cash for Cape Town and Durban, but as I said it's just nice to get ashore even if it is Columbo.

Well on this occasion we have only stayed one night before sailing out again into what is still a very rough sea, our destination is Cape Town once more (I forgot to mention this before that the Dorsetshire has been adopted by the people of Cape Town) this is a recognized thing as most of the Towns and some Cities back home in England have ships named after them so are adopted by them, but some ships are adopted by any town and in doing so the people of these places write to members of the crew sending them parcels and such like, it acts as a good moral booster to the crew, some of the lads do write back to them.

We arrive back in Cape Town again, it's my turn for duty watch and as usual I had not been on duty one hour before the outside line was very busy with people ringing in with all sorts of requests, this spell of duty can't go quick enough for me. We stayed here in harbour for another two days before sailing out again into much calmer weather, now, we have been out on patrol for over a week with nothing much happening then one night we go in towards some coastline, it is a very dark night with not a star in sight which is very unusual and the word was past around the Ship that we are going to bombard the town of Dante's on the Italian Somali-land so we sailed in very close to the shore then opened up with our eight 8" guns and we really plastered the place setting fire to big oil storage tanks warehouses and harbour installations, also setting fire to some small ships at anchor in the harbour, but not to fire on any civilian properties of any kind is the order so we avoided the Town of Dante's, but just after the bombardment finished the torpedo men had their chance and fired tin fish (Torpedo's) into the jetty leaving it a complete wreck, So it wasn't long before the big shore batteries opened up, 'lighting up the sky' we got out of there pretty fast with shells falling all around us.

Back out in mid ocean there are long days and weeks of seeing nothing but Flying fishes and the occasional Albatross, we did have one piece of really bad luck when we called at the Ascension Islands to refuel our aircraft who is doing a routine flight around the Island when it got into trouble and crashed killing the pilot, it was just rotten luck and no one could understand why this happened, all we know is that it was a terribly hot day when this happened, I was lying in the shade of "A" Turret when this accident happened, I was saying to my mate how very peaceful it is here, but you get that same feeling whenever you visited any of these exotic islands it didn't seem as if there is a war on at all, also you can really understand why they don't want a horde of Matelots to descend on these places. But I don't think that we can grumble because we do get plenty of leave at most of the ports as it is certainly good for the trade.

As the weeks rolled by into months of just doing our regular patrols and nothing spectacular happened to write about, the war seems a long way off to us, but by now my mate and I are hardened sailors, we have learned such a lot, also getting our rum ration every day now and this is the real stuff not the watered down rum that we got at first. Shore leave begins to get a lot more interesting our runs ashore in places like Cape Town also Durban get even better and we meet people regularly each time, some that we know and some complete strangers but they are all so friendly and can't do enough for us, don't forget I told you how the cars are always lined up outside the dock yard gates, well, I can give you an idea how some of this came about, on duty at the telephone switch board I would get all kinds of messages not only asking for certain officers or ratings but things like "I am giving a party at 7.30 pm tonight and I would like to invite about a dozen crew members" and another "It's my Daughters Birthday on Thursday how would you and a couple of your friends like to come along" then how about this one "I am a young Widow who owns a few horses, are there six or seven sailors aboard who would like a day out riding in the country" and the picnic party one "A group of us are driving out into the country and would like to invite a party of sailors" but there are also lots of invites just for the Officers only, lots of these are similar to the ones that I have already said.

But I can assure you once the ship to shoreline phone is connected up it never stops ringing and all the invites are the genuine thing, that is just how friendly the South African people are, they really want to make us feel at home, nothing is too much trouble for them so it always turns out to be a good run ashore.

Back out on patrol and the weather is now turning rough again, if you have never been in the crows nest on a big ship when it's blowing up a bit then you have never really had the full experience of the sea, the ship pitches and rolls but of the two the roll is the worst, she leans right over to port or starboard and your high up looking down into the sea but after a few times you get used to it, but the hardest part is when it's really rough, you have to climb up the masthead to reach that crows nest, the ladder is a rope one and it swings about a bit, but it's all in a sailors daily routine.

Patrol finished after being at sea for a few weeks, so we sail back into Cape Town and alongside the jetty. After tying up my mate Walt and I are leaning over the guard rail when he suddenly remarked on the large number of Merchant ships that are lying in the harbour, there's quite a lot more than there was when we departed some weeks back, more than we have seen since we have been based in Cape Town, we didn't think any more about it but In the next couple of days we noticed that there have been an even bigger increase of ships, both large and small Merchant ships, to top it all a big Armed Merchant Cruiser entered the harbour one morning she started to signal Dorsetshire before she dropped her anchor and our flags began to reply. Unfortunately all shore leave has been stopped and we are at one hour's notice for sea.

This really set the buzzes going round the ship and I don't think any of us got it right, but then sure enough the following morning came and during the forenoon watch "Hands to stations for leaving harbor" was piped all the starboard watch closed up and out of Cape Town we sail, but there's nothing unusual about that we thought but we stopped just outside the harbour and watched aghast as the harbour started to empty of Merchant ships one after the other they came out passing us, out into the open sea, last of all out came the Armed Merchant Cruiser, after some time the convoy (that is what it appeared to be) got into some sort of order and appearing as if from nowhere came quite a few Destroyers, evidently from Simons Town, all the ships begin to take up positions and we sail off with Dorsetshire in the lead, the destroyers are doing the screening with the Armed Merchant Cruiser bringing up the stern.

The name of the A.M.C. is H.M.S. Bulola we have been told, now, on looking round this lot I can see that we may be in for a lot of trouble, if the submarines find us they will have a field day as some of these old tubs look as though they were around during the last war and worst of all a lot of these are coal fired and will be lucky to make twelve knots flat out, we have to slow down the whole way to the speed of the slowest ships so has to try to keep this lot together. It's reckoned by some of the old hands on the Dorsetshire that this must be the biggest convoy out of South Africa, so what and where are we going with this big convoy? Everyone wants to know as we don't usually do any convoy work, But nobody could come up with any ideas and it isn't until we are well into the first watch that the Skipper spoke over the tannoy to say that we are escorting this convoy home to England. Everybody was really excited about that news I know that me and Walt are over the moon as this lot had come straight out of the blue, I was also a bit worried what it would be like back home, I wouldn't think that my home out in the country is much of a risk, after all it is only a small village, so I can't see the Germans wasting bombs on villages. What I am really looking forward to more than anything is seeing my girl friend again, talking about girl friends mine gave me a lovely photo of herself before we left England and I had it enlarged at a photographers in Skegness so that it is now a very large one and up to this day I have kept the big photo of her on the door of my locker, in all the actions on the ships that I have been on to date, I also keep the small one of her on my person at all times so if I have to go over the side I will at least have her with me (balmy isn't it) but that's love, I am not the only one because lots of the lads have their girl friends photo on their locker lids or carry snaps. It seems so long ago now since I last saw my girl and the letters have been few and far between from her but I know that this could be put down to the fact that the mail follows us around all over the place and can take weeks to catch up with us, also sometimes the sea mail doesn't reaches us at all.

We sailed on into what is a fair sea by that I mean that it isn't rough then again it isn't calm, at the moment I am on watch on the bridge acting as a look out on the starboard side of the ship and my girl friend came into my thoughts once again, as the waves went crashing down the side of the ship I thought of all the thousands of miles of ocean that I have traveled since that day that we parted and all the wonderful countries that I have seen, here we are now sailing back home once more I just can't wait to get my feet back under a table that doesn't have things moving about all the time. But our waiting has not been half as long as some of our mess mates who have been aboard this ship far longer than me and my mate, how about the South African lads, I wonder how they feel as we are going home and they are sailing a long way from theirs, I feel sorry for them but at least they have had the chance to see their friends and families while we have been stationed at Cape Town.

Once again we are having problems with at least two of the smaller ships not being able to maintain the speed set for the convoy now the weather begins to worsen and I reckon that some of them must be taking in a lot of sea water as I can see clearly through my binoculars that one in particular is having a bad time of it but that is the sea and just what sailors have to put up with, but there you go and the old salts say "you should have joined the Army, they don't get their feet wet." I must say the sea is getting worse 'heavy they call it' and even the Dorsetshire is doing her share of pitching and rolling so just imagine what it must be like on board these old merchant ships, I reckon that it must be a case of battening down the hatches and one hand for yourself and one for the navy. But despite all this very rough weather these little Destroyers are still ploughing along and pushing their bows into those big waves and at times it does look as though they are being completely engulfed when the sea goes over them, now I've been going on about all this bad weather when some very bad news has just been passed around the ship to all positions, the Skipper on the Tannoy announced "H.M.S. Hood has been sunk in an action with a German Battle Ship" now, if this is true it would be devastating news, one of the old signalmen on the bridge has just said "how the hell could this have happened I would think that there isn't a ship in any man's navy that could sink the Hood," she is the greatest battle ship that we have got, I just can't believe this could have happened what a 'Bloody Terrible Loss.'

After the news had been passed around the ship the Skipper spoke over the tannoy to state that he had received a signal from the Admiralty announcing the loss of the Hood in an action with the German Battleship Bismark and that we had now received further orders to leave the convoy and prepare to make all speed to intercept and engage the enemy "Prepare the ship for action" as at this moment we are now increasing speed and intend to leave the convoy in the sole charge of the Armed Merchant Cruiser H.M.S. Bulola. "Well how about that then, a big Battle Wagon against a light Cruiser" said my mate standing at the side of me, I was like rest of the lads 'in shock' we had certainly put on some speed now and after that grand old tradition of the Royal Navy we bid the convoy safe passage, the Bulola replied "And Good Luck To You."

That afternoon and all night we plough on, through very heavy sea's with the decks awash at times and just before day break prayers are said below decks, I can tell you something, I think that we are going to need them very much so, one of our mates passing by on his way to his action station said "this would have to happen just when we were on our way home" he couldn't have said truer words just our rotten luck rounded it off, during a very quick early breakfast I don't think anyone spoke a word.

All the hands are ordered to close up to action stations immediately, it is just about 9am the date is May 27th 1941, I am lookout on the bridge when all at once the lookout on the opposite side to me reported gun flashes on the horizon and as we closed in to our firing range I heard the fire bell go in the director over our heads and all our 8" Guns opened fire at once, as we did, a shell or shells from the Bismark went screaming over the Dorsetshire just like a jet plane, we also saw one of her shells appear to hit H.M.S. Rodney one of our very oldest Battle ships lying just over on our starboard bow, but the Rodney was finding the target, the Dorsetshire was also contributing now that she had got the range, I could see close up that the Rodney's shells alongside ours were smashing into the Bismark's superstructure sending debris flying into the air, I have never seen such a sight it was really devastating. I did see through my binoculars another big ship on the horizon and while watching her she only fired her guns once, but could also see that she was in some sort of trouble as there was a lot of smoke coming from her stern, but both Rodney, ourselves and another Cruiser of the same class who I could also see firing at the Bismark, to actually see the Bridge metal flying through the air was really something. Well she was really on fire now 'this was an awesome sight too' her guns no longer firing I noticed, but an amazing thing happened our 'X' Turret jumped her mounting so was now out of action, now this surely couldn't go on much longer and we moved in even closer to see that she was starting to list very badly because of the horrific state that she was in. The Rodney had stopped firing some time ago as they could also see that the pride of the German Navy was finished, she was on fire from stem to stern and what a pounding she had taken.

Looking at her from high up on the bridge made it even more horrible, I really hated to think what it must be like to be aboard that ship "Sheer Hell" I would imagine but this is the biggest Battle Ship in the world and Adolf Hitler's number one, she had sunk one of ours "H.M.S. Hood," so now it was our turn and it was the Navy's job to sink her and that is just what we intend to do at all costs. But let's not forget we are all sailors and we have a lot of respect for one another. I could see from my high position that the Bismark was now stopped in the water, which I must say was fairly rough and god help those poor souls who are going to have to swim in this lot. The flames and the smoke was now pouring out of her from all different parts of the decks and superstructure, that is what is left of it and as we stood off just watching this victory you might think that this is great, but not to my way of thinking this is horrible, I can't get it out of my mind the terrible things that they must be going through in this action. After some time of just laying off here, watching this massive ship burning from stem to stern I begin to realize that this is my first piece of real action up to now, we had come through it and this is a real 'big one'. The Rodney was seen to turn away now, making steam for home I reckon, so we were on our own except for a Destroyer that had suddenly appeared. We then received a signal from the ship over on the horizon which must be the Admirals Battle ship the 'King George V' "Dorsetshire go in and 'Finish Her Off' with torpedoes," and as we moved in closer I could see some of the Bismark crew jumping over the side into the very rough sea, dozens of them in fact, on looking around I couldn't see any life boats being launched or in the water but I suppose that most of the boats have been smashed or burnt in the fire. <u>This really is an astonishing sight</u>.

The Dorsetshire moved in close up on Bismark's starboard side making ready to fire our torpedoes when the order was given from the bridge behind me, I looked on as two 'Tin Fish' (torpedoes) left the tubes and headed straight for Bismark's starboard side, then a huge flash and explosion as we started to move in a big circle around her bows, we then fired a third one into her port side and after that explosion we lay off and prepared to pick up any survivors, then watched as she slowly turned onto her side and finally rolled right over bottom up, then we were met with the most terrible sight that I never wish to see again, there scrambling on to her red painted bottom (so clean and clear as if it was a brand new ship just come out of the dock), was scores of men, some of them started to slide off into the sea and there was a hell of a lot of men still hanging on, when right before my eye's she slowly started to slip below the waves taking those poor souls still hanging on to a 'terrible end.'

After that amazing scene I looked down onto the water which was full of men swimming around or just trying to keep afloat in the rough sea, there must be hundreds of them, among them you could see bodies everywhere lots of them still with their life jackets on, now the order we had received by the Admiral to finish the Bismark off was also to pick up any survivors, so on the orders passed down from the bridge some of the after gun crews and other ratings are told to start lowering boats falls over the ships side,(these are the ropes used to lower and raise the boats from the upper deck over the side down to the sea level) and to rescue as many as possible. So the rescue mission started, the Dorsetshire being stopped in the water for this job has now become an easy target for any U-boats in the area.

This was a very difficult task as these County Class Cruisers have very high sides, But over the side the ropes went and our lads were shouting to the lads in the water encouraging them to swim to the side of the ship urging them on as the waves kept on taking them away from the ship, it was really heart breaking to watch them struggling to get back to the side again but some were too weak, that is another big fault in this rescue mission, these type of ships are known to be very unstable in heavy seas and when they are stationary as we were at that moment it's very noticeable, this was making it a lot more difficult, one minute the side would be near the water and the next high out of the water, but the lads were very slowly pulling these men up the ropes onto the deck, as I pointed out some of them were too weak they just couldn't hold on to the ropes, the lads made loops in them so all the men in the sea have to do is put an arm or a leg in the loop and then just hang on, but it isn't that easy, one poor soul pulled up in this way had lost an arm and was in a very bad way, 'what that poor lad must have suffered,' quite a few of them that came aboard were wounded and most of them covered in oil. This was another factor that was making it very difficult for them to hang onto the ropes which had by now become very Slippery, but all is going reasonably well because our lads had pulled inboard a total of eighty seven men in what is a heart breaking task, after all they are human beings just like us and some are so very young, it is only later that we found out that some of the survivors are 'Boy Seamen.'

Despite the heavy rolling of the ship the rescue is going along very well, that is until someone on the bridge made a report of a sighting what is described as a "Wake" (now this could mean lots of things like a U-boat Periscope moving through the water, or a freak wave).

One of the lads on our mess who was helping to rescue these lads still in the water said afterwards "how can anyone possibly sight anything that looks like a periscope in this very rough sea?" Well, how? we will never know because it was terrible weather, the spray flying about everywhere but all I can say is that if by any chance it is a U-boat periscope which does show when they are moving, then we are sitting ducks and a very easy target 'being stopped', even more so as the admiralty had already sent us a signal that there are submarines in the area and that enemy aircraft are on the way to intercept us, well, I for one thought that we had been very lucky not to have met up with one of them before now.

Anyway the skipper is not taking any risks and decided to get under way very quickly, the order from the bridge is to move at full speed ahead, so now just imagine what was happening in the sea, the survivors who are almost on the deck are being pulled inboard but those poor souls hanging onto the ropes are being banged about as we picked up speed, it is an impossibility for them to keep hanging on to those ropes and I could see them dropping off into the ocean again as our lads began hauling in the ropes, even from my position I could hear the cries and screams of the German sailors, we were leaving them to a terrible death just when they would be thinking that they are going to be saved, their only chance now of being picked up would be the small Destroyer which is the only other ship in this area but she is a fair way off and wouldn't know what is going on here.

The last signal that we received from the Admiral had been to get the hell out of there as soon as we had picked up these survivors, as the Germans would do everything in their power to seek revenge on the ships that took part in this action. Those poor souls that we had left in the water certainly can't last very long in these conditions, I can honestly say that I will never forget that moment for as long as I live <u>It Was Horrible</u>.

The Dorsetshire is steaming for home waters and safety now after having covered over 600 miles since leaving the convoy steaming at speed through heavy sea's to take part in this action, which actually lasted just over two hours.

Christ! I can still hear those lads back there screaming, what the hell must they have thought of us leaving them like that, perhaps believing tales that they had heard about the British not caring much about survivors, which of course is completely untrue, we could have saved god knows how many if that sighting of the U boat had not happened, but then again what if it had been a U-boat, would the German Skipper let us carry on picking up those survivors from the sea? I think not, so myself and everyone on board say that our Skipper Captain Martin had no alternative but to push off at full speed. So May 27th will be a day long remembered in WW2, when in just two hours over two thousand German sailors lost their lives in action and in terrible conditions to the Royal Navy, it was a great victory and revenge for the Hood.

And so speeding away from what was my first real big action and I don't suppose that they could come much bigger I thought that I would be delighted but not so, in fact I think that most of the lads were if anything a bit subdued, and even more so when they heard that the survivor who had lost his arm in the action had died, we were informed that there would be a burial service for him. Shortly after the ceremony was carried out with the Dorsetshire slowing down almost to a stop, the lad was buried wrapped in a German ensign with military honours and with most of the survivors in attendance, we sailed on making speed and headed for England. Over the radio some of the lads said that "Lord Haw-Haw" gave the news on the radio about the loss of the Bismark but stressed that to revenge her Captain and crew the perpetrators namely H.M.S. Rodney and the Dorsetshire would not reach the safety of the English coast and that German bombers are already on their way.

And so the Admiral had ordered us to push off and at high speed so we headed for England and safety with only slight damage, as the light began to fail we sailed up the Irish sea in gale force winds and around the coast of Scotland during the night then sailed safely into the port of Newcastle On Tyne on the morning of the 28th of May. The news must have already reached here because we saw people waving and shouting as we sailed up the Tyne, when we finally docked the welcome that we received 'well, it was a great feeling I can tell you' the dockyard matey's where shaking our hands and patting us on the back but I summed it up for one chap when he put his arm around my shoulders and said "well done lad, what was it like?" I replied "Hell," now in dock all the survivors were lining up ready to go ashore, the first group to go down the gangway were the injured and a few of these had to be carried down on stretchers, they were evidently heading for some hospital but it was a pitiful sight, there were so many on lockers or standing around just watching as the remaining survivors walked down that gangway, the transport that would take them away as far as I could see was Army. Just at that moment I was very glad to be home that is all I cared about although I couldn't help but think about those poor souls left out there in that awful weather, there was a lot of activity going on as some high ranking officers arrived and came aboard, the jetty was now getting a bit crowded as newspaper men turned up in fair numbers and one of the lads leaning on the guard rail remarked "It didn't take them long to get here did it."

I could see the photographers on the jetty taking photo's but despite their pleas none were allowed on board, my Hoppo (slang word for mate) Walt has just come up on deck and he told me some interesting facts, he told me that Dorsetshire ended up firing Two Hundred and Forty Eight rounds of 8" shells in the action against the ill fated Bismark. With all the activity going on here I don't think that there will be much work done on board today, the only thing that I and I suppose all the other crew members wanted to know is when are we going to hear something about shore leave, now while we were at dinner my mate asked the killick what was the normal procedure when ships arrived in harbour after serving time abroad, he said that leave was nearly always announced to either watch very shortly after the ship had secured, so it looks as though we shall have to be a little patient.

But we didn't have to wait too long before the announcement was made over the Tannoy that there is leave being granted to the port watch from tomorrow which was the 29th May for fourteen days, 'Wow' leave at last and I thought well this is it home at last, I was really looking forward to seeing my family again but more than anything my girl friend, she wouldn't know that I was back in old England, my wouldn't she be surprised it has been so long and I have missed her so very much! oh I know that I've had that lovely big photo of her in my locker but it wasn't enough for me, anyway it's not the same absence does make the heart grow fonder doesn't it or so the saying goes, well mine had gone way beyond that another thing I was no longer a seventeen year old youth I was a man now, I had seen things which would make men's hair turn grey I had also seen a heck of a lot of the world since last leaving the shores of dear old England. All the port watch are piped to muster before tea and were issued their railway warrants leave passes.

It was a very busy morning for me and the rest of the lads going on leave tomorrow, some sorting out of the best collar for a quick wash and iron then out comes the No1 Uniform with a brush over then pressing of all those creases into the 32inch bell bottom trousers so that Jack looks a real 'tiddly' sailor (In this man's navy if a thing looks smart and tidy, it's termed as tiddly), now for that very small suitcase the packing of anything that will be needed back home possibly anything that was brought for presents believe me there are some queer things going into that case. I had promised one of my Fathers work mates that I would get him a souvenir if I could, so he was going to get a Leading Stokers Badge off the Bismark and a 'Prick of Tobacco' made by yours truly well what's that you may say, I think that it may sound a bit rude, but not at all, this is another term used by the old sailors of yesteryears and still used in the Royal Navy today, it's made with a small sheet of canvas tarred hemp tobacco leaves soaked in rum is termed as a prick of tobacco.

This is a tobacco specially for the pipe smoker and is made by laying the moist leaves of the tobacco plant which is bought on the ship, you lay the leaves onto a light thin piece of canvas which is soaked in rum and is then rolled tightly into a thin rope of Tarred Hemp and left in this state until wanted for use after some considerable time, then on starting to use' it will be found by undoing the end of the rope that the whole thing has set solid and formed very strong thick pipe tobacco which is similar to thick twist tobacco but is they say far stronger, anyway into the case that goes, along with other presents for family and old friends, now the hammock gets slung early for a good night and a well earned sleep.

At last the train pulls out of Newcastle station, we are on the way to Derby and it can't go fast enough. I am once again beginning to wonder how my village (Tutbury) has fared in the time that I have been away and as I am not expected on leave some people are going to get a big surprise. I suppose that most of the people living in my village would know that I have been involved in the action against the Bismark because news of the Dorsetshire is in all the daily newspapers so my sister and all of my relatives would have spread the word but obviously there would be no reception waiting for me when I get home because my two sisters and my younger Brother would be at work, and to top it all on thinking about meeting my girl friend it just happens to be the day that her Father doesn't allow her out even though she is now turned nineteen and working 'What a Father' yet he was in the last war himself. I have never met him face to face but I think he knows that his eldest Daughter has a sailor boy friend and probably knows when I am on leave, but that is how our love life seems fated to be.

Where ever I went in the village during leave I was being greeted with handshakes and being patted on the back by countless people, I was asked for the whole story over and over again and to top it all I found out from my sister that they had even started a collection for me around the village, then the young members of the British Legion stopped it, now I would just like to say that at no time did I know that this collection was being made on my behalf as this collection was started by two old WW1 sailors before I went on leave and before anyone knew that I was coming home, but further to this I wonder by what authority these young British Legion members had, as almost all of them were in excused call up jobs and didn't know the first thing about the war, what an insult to the Legion was my thoughts but apart from all this I really didn't want any fuss as it wouldn't have been fair on the rest of the lads from the village who were all doing there bit towards this war all in the forces, not like the young British Legion members hiding behind their cushy jobs

My leave was all that I had expected that it would be, I loved my girlfriend more than ever now, every night that I wasn't with her I went into my local pub as there was nothing else to do also the drinks were all free every time they wouldn't let me pay at all, then there was the chap who I had promised a souvenir, well I went to his place of work which was the Glass works where my Father and a few of my relatives worked the place that I got the sack from on my first job after leaving school, I gave him his surprise of the Tobacco and the Leading Stokers Badge off the Bismark which he couldn't thank me enough for, everyone on the shop floor crowded around to have a look, and the Tobacco caused quite a stir as no one had ever seen anything like it before so I had some explaining to do.

I heard a long time after the visit to the Glass Works that the person who has the Stokers badge takes it out to the local pubs, showing it to everyone, it used to get him lots of free drinks 'and why not' the Tobacco I was told went down very well with the old pipe smokers and had asked for more saying It was far stronger than any that could be bought, the leave went all too quickly for me and I'd had a really smashing time although there was one funny incident that happened on my second night at home I was asleep in my bed when I was aroused by my younger Brother who was an ARP Warden shaking me a bit strong and saying "Come on the sirens have just gone there's an air raid on" my reply was get back into bed what the hell would Gerry want to bomb Tutbury for, he dashed off while I lay there listening to the German planes with their familiar engine sounds receding in the distance I dropped off to sleep again.

Well before I knew it I was walking back up the gangway onto the quarter deck of the Dorsetshire who was now in the dry dock and the very next day I watched my mate Walt go on his fourteen days leave with the rest of the Starboard watch, now the everyday routine of a ship in Dock was being carried out except that now we had a lot of the dock yard workers on board doing repairs and checking on the Boilers, in fact all sorts of jobs, the noise is terrible it's going on all of the time, although we had sustained only minor damage that was caused by ploughing through heavy sea's at speed. But it does look as though we will be here for a few weeks the way things are going. Back home in an English harbour my job as telephone watch keeper is entirely different now, nothing like it was when we were abroad it's not half as busy for a start and certainly not as interesting as most of the calls are for officers.

There is none of the invitations to functions of any kind so it gets rather boring, so my job has become the cushy number that the lads said it would be and with having so much time to myself with long duty hours off watch I elected to be the 'Mess Man' for our mess, the job entailed making sure that the mess drew all the food that it was entitled too from the stores extra stuff like Tea, Sugar, Butter, Cheese and all tinned food this issue is made according to the number of men on your mess, so that meant that if you had sixteen men on your mess then you as mess man drew the rations for that number every day but the breakfast and the dinner meals were drawn from the Galley, but when we were in harbour there was always so much surplus food due to the lads going ashore.

So the food locker on the mess was always full and when the lads who were aboard on watch sat down for their evening meal it was mostly eat what you want, now one or two would fancy tinned fish where a few of the others would go for cheese or corned dog (Beef) or even Jam, anything that was on offer, so I was very often left with half a tin of fish or corned beef and left over cheese, not forgetting that these were big tins so what was left over usually gets thrown overboard and you might say what a terrible waste of good food but Jack didn't see it like that as any scraps left over was Seagull food, but there is not the same waste when a ship is at sea because every sailor likes to tuck in to whatever is going, appetites seem to be a lot stronger when at sea.

Well it came about that on my off duty time I would wander around the upper decks just having a look at what was going on and watching the dock yard workmen, slang word in the navy 'Matey's' at work, and one morning I was watching a particular chap who had been working on the aircraft contraption that sends the plane off the ship so I stopped to have a word with him and I found him to be quite a nice chap so it turned out that for a couple of mornings I stopped to have a chat with him, on this one particular morning I just happened to catch him preparing to have his breakfast and on taking out his lunch box I said cheekily to him have you got something nice? And he opened his tin to show me a sandwich which he opened, it appeared to me to be scraggy bit's of what looked like bacon,

To say that I was shocked is putting it mildly to think that a grown man has to do a full day's work on food like that, I knew that there was rationing but this was ridiculous' you hold on a few minutes I said and off I went at the double dashing down to the mess decks and in a few moments I was back again and I said to him put some of this between your bread handing him what appeared to be a bulky folded newspaper and in between I had slipped a big piece of cheese and two flat tins of fish 'Pilchards' I also produced a tin of corned beef from my overall pocket, well we certainly did get really fed up with fish for a start and we had tins of it in the food locker as well as corned beef, as the chap started to thank me I just said jokingly I hope you find some good news in the paper as I walked off.

I didn't see him again until just before I went on watch, the poor chap didn't know what to say so I asked him how it was, he then said that the cheese was lovely and that his wife would be a bit worried when he handed the stuff to her because she would think that he had stolen it, I told him "Tell her it was a gift from a sailor," he told me that it was some time since they had cheese because his Wife always used the coupons for other things, now before I go any further there may be some people who might say that this wasn't right to give this food away like that, well all I can say to these people is 'Tough' I can tell you that the cheese would have been left in the food locker until it went mouldy and would then have been ditched over the side of the ship, as for the pilchards we accumulate so many tins of the stuff that I have to stop drawing our normal issue which I may say that we are entitled to, so in actual fact I am really giving away what is mine.

Now a bit more on the subject of food I was telling you what happens to some of it, well there's something I would like to add, for example the pilchards, now just imagine that you are at sea for weeks at a time these tins of fish stay in the food locker until they are well out of date and then the lads just sling them over the side and imagine again being in the tropics, places like Freetown where you could fry an egg on the upper deck plates and you have food in the locker (we didn't have freezers on the mess decks to put food in) but don't get me wrong we were well fed, but stuff that was spare in the way of food when we were in harbour we would ask the workmen if they could use it sooner than throw it over the side.

And so my friend is in luck and at every opportunity if there was anything going spare on the mess I made sure that the men had first choice before it was thrown away, I happened to be talking to him on the upper deck a few days before the men of the starboard watch came back off leave and he invited me to his home to meet his wife and family and have a home cooked meal and a night out afterwards as they were so pleased at what I had given him, but I had to turn him down for I was on duty that day so couldn't make it, but Sunday would be fine as I would be on seven bell leave that day if that was OK with his family, so he arranged to pick me up outside the dock yard gates on Sunday morning.

When Sunday came and the Starboard watch were back off leave I found my friend waiting for me, and was transported by car to his home where I met his Wife and family and received a lot of thanks for the food I had given them, After chatting to his family about the action against the Bismark some of the miles and the different parts of the world that I had visited we sat down to what was a very nice meal 'Home Cooked' I can't tell you how good it was so vastly different to some of the meals that we get, I wondered how long it had taken his wife to save the coupons for the dinner that we had just eaten, not forgetting that everything is rationed so I thanked her for the invitation and the grand dinner that I had just enjoyed, then we sat down to a nice coffee then a night out, quite a few more of the family turned up and it was decided that we would go to their club in South Shields. In the party there was his younger Brother and Sister who were about nineteen and very nice, we all set off for the club and on our arrival we settled in at a couple of tables then I noticed straight away that this was something entirely new to me, that they were all joining in with the women that was singing then the drinks started to come my way and they wouldn't let me pay for anything, I was still having a great time having so much to drink I'm afraid I can't remember much about the latter part of the evening at all, but it must have been late when they finished my first recollection of the events was when waking up in the morning after finding myself lying on a double mattress on the floor in just vest and pants with the young sister lying beside me. Well, I can honestly say I felt terrible.

Now, at first I didn't even know where I was and just at that moment someone brought me a cup of tea which after sitting up I did manage to drink, then I began trying to remember what went off last night and it suddenly hit me I had to get back on board ship for eleven o clock as that was when my leave expired, Just then I was asked if I wanted breakfast but I had to decline not that I could have eaten any as there was no time, it was a quick wash and dressed then I just had time to say goodbye to his Wife and thank her for the dinner and the lovely time last night, we left in his Brothers car for the dock yard where they dropped me off at the main gate, now how I found my way to the Dorsetshire I will never know for I couldn't remember anything in fact I didn't even know where I was and must have been going round and round in circles in a daze, later I was told that I was staggering around when some of the lads off the Dorsetshire spotted me took me on board and down to the sick bay.

Somehow I must have collapsed and cannot remember anything more until a marine came to get his hammock from the rack on which I was lying, I was in such a state that two of them had to carry me into the sick bay by which time this had closed as it was after dinner I only vaguely remember the remainder of the proceedings a bright light appeared over my head and someone was leaning over me then in the distance a voice repeating over and over something about getting this man off the ship immediately because he has scarlet fever and pneumonia, in no time at all I went from lying in the sick bay to lying on the upper deck to being lifted high into the air and deposited on to the jetty, I only found out after a long time that I had to be lifted off the ship with the aircraft crane onto the jetty because the dock was being filled with water ready for the ship leaving.

The Ambulance arrived after a short wait and I was then journeyed across to the other side of the dock yard to a jetty where I was then transferred to a boat then a journey down the river Tyne to the dock yard at North Shields then into another ambulance with screaming sirens which took me to North Shields Isolation Hospital where I ended up in a little side ward for two weeks, I was so weak that my voice had gone and I couldn't speak a word, day in and day out I lay in that hospital bed not knowing who I was or why I couldn't speak, I was just lying there staring at some big bay windows which opened onto a field or a grass lawn, there was hardly any sound at all it was very quiet. So, week after week the same thing at first I was being spoon fed by a nurse every day it was the same nurse every time she used to talk to me quite a bit but then it changed to another nurse who was not so patient with me and hardly spoke at all, but then one night I woke up to find my first nurse sitting on the bed apparently I was sweating buckets and she was wiping my brow, she was talking to me but the thing was I recognized her but I still couldn't understand what she was saying, the doctor used to visit me every morning and I began to recognize the Matron or Sister.

It took about ten weeks before I really started to make some form of recovery and my voice came back one night during an air raid, Gerry was trying to find the docks at Newcastle, I could hear the explosions as I lay there, but at that time I always stayed in the ward and the night nurse used to come and sit with me, sometimes I used to sleep through these air raids but this one must have been a bit more severe and I was awake when the nurse came in and I think that she was a bit afraid on this night as the noise was fairly loud and it sounded as though the docks were getting some hammer, then I noticed that she seemed very nervous, it was then that I just came out with it and said in a whispering sort of voice "It's OK don't worry they wouldn't be dropping their bombs up here we are a long way from the docks." I was amazed I'd actually spoken for the first time in weeks I can tell you it came as a bit of a shock as well but I think it calmed the nurse down as we carried on trying to make conversation, although she did warn me to take it easy but I was so delighted that at last I could speak again, I did know my favourite nurses name 'Florence,' she was the one that always talked to me when I couldn't understand what she was saying, the sirens went some time after and I was rather pleased that at last things seemed to be getting better, this was reiterated by the doctor the next morning when he came through the door and I surprisingly answered his greeting "we will soon have you back on that ship again young man" was his answer.

Now, I began to wonder what my girl friend would think had happened because I hadn't written to her in all the time that I was in this Hospital, but how could I? Even in the condition that I was in now, I doubted that I could hold a pen steady enough to be able to write a letter but I must at the first opportunity. I began to notice that a part of this hospital was for children as full awareness came back to me and I realize that I could often hear the sound of kids running about in the passageway outside my door but they had not been allowed down my end of the Hospital while I was ill, now, once those kids found out that I was OK my little side ward became a noisy place, they all wanted to see mister Matelot, I was even introduced to their mothers when they came on occasions and a lot of the children used to tell them that I had been on the ship which as they told their mums "had sunk the Bismark."

The way that I will always remember these kids was when the air raid sirens went they never panicked at all, the nurses used to waken them all up and in two's they would file past my door on their way down to the shelter, one or two would pop in the door and shout "Come on mister Matelot the Germans are bombing us again" and when the all clear had sounded they would come back and pop in again shouting "It's OK mister Matelot they've gone now you can come out" well I couldn't help but laugh, they were always coming into my ward and climbing onto my bed offering me sweets and asking all sorts of questions, when I started to get better I told them that I was unable to speak or answer for a long time. Yes they were a great bunch of kids and I loved having them around as I got better.

Well, my time here at North Shields is beginning to draw to a close as I begin to get my strength back and take more walks round this lovely hospital which I enjoyed so much and I have made some great friends in the time that I have been here "not forgetting my favourite nurse," I know that she fancied me very much. I was not surprised one morning when the doctor came round and gave me what turned out to be my final examination, he told me I was fit enough now to leave the hospital but not 'in his opinion' fit enough to return to active duty just yet, and so he was transferring me to a convalescent home in Northumberland where I would stay until the medics there confirmed that I was fit enough to report back for duty, so after just over thirteen weeks I said goodbye to most of the staff and in particular one nurse who I had seen so much of during my stay there and I left her in tears.

The name of the Convalescent home is Howick Hall, I was conveyed from the hospital to the home which was a fair journey in a large car and duly arrived at this very large beautiful country house standing in it's own private grounds, it was surrounded by lovely gardens and lawns which is quite secluded, in what is a very beautiful country side and a bus ride from the nearest small town of Alnwick. On my arrival I was introduced to the person in charge, he was an Army man that is all that I knew about him at first, he explained the system of the home re-meal times lights out and shore leave, my bed by the way is right up on the top floor against one of the windows that overlooks the spacious gardens and beyond, it is a really beautiful place.

We didn't have any duties to perform, when meals were over we were allowed to find our own pleasures there are games rooms indoors and outdoors including Croquet which I found fun although I had never played that game before, but the thing that interested me the most was the miles of woodlands to stroll through, in the evenings we could go ashore by catching a bus that stopped right outside the gates and have a night in Alnwick which I found a very nice pub there where the lads from the home were always made very welcome that is why most of them ended up in there, the nights were long so it was great company.

But we were very often warned that we are here at Howick Hall to recuperate and to get our strength back so drunkenness would not be tolerated at any time and any trouble makers would be immediately reported to their respective services, also a further rule that had to be adhered to was that all inmates had to be back in the grounds by a certain hour as the last bus to run to the hall was 22.30hrs, there was to be no excuses taken, well as the days went by I began to get into the run of things although every time I looked in the mirror I realize that I was still very pale and still felt a bit weak I was determined to get out into the fresh air and try to get back to my normal self I was pretty sure that a few weeks of rest and this bracing country air would do the job.

My thoughts turned to my girl friend once again, I love her so very much and I at twenty years of age I knew in my mind that I would never love anyone else in the same way, with being invalided all this time I had managed to save a little money so what about a real decent present "An engagement rin" it would mean so much and I couldn't get it out of my head, but what about the size and what sort? well I hadn't a clue so in conversation with one of the new nurses I happened to mention my predicament and straight away she said that she would help me, so it went on from there and I gave her all the money that I had saved including my Navy pay from the Dorsetshire, after explaining that she was about the same build as my girl friend I just crossed my fingers and hoped that it would be OK although as she said it can always be altered to suit the finger size.

And sure enough after a couple of days wait I ended up with a beautiful ring in a blue box which she told me it had cost a little more than what I had given her, but she had explained the situation that I was in to the jeweler so I got it for a good price thanks to that nurse, I was made now and the very first time that I go on leave I'm going to pluck up the courage to ask Joyce! That is my girl friend's name if she will except my ring and I sincerely hope that she does because I know that there is no one else for me, who knows I may still get another draft on foreign service and be away for a lot longer next time I really don't want to lose her, if she does except I know that we will have to keep it a secret for some time.

I was finding the lads at Howick a great bunch but I hadn't made any real mates yet as there was no Navy lads here, they were all mostly Army or R.A.F. and even one or two Merchant Navy seaman so it was a bit difficult at the start, but it is my usual practice first thing in a morning after breakfast to go for a walk in the fields right down to the sea and one morning I came across a field that had quite a lot of mushrooms in it so in no time I picked a large handkerchief full, I was just about to leave the field when I spotted someone watching me, at first I thought that I had been caught by the farmer and I was a bit worried but I thought oh well I suppose I shall have to give them up again (Just like I used to do when I was caught as a kid), but no not this time as the figure started to walk towards me I could see that he was wearing the blue uniform like me, and that is how I met my great mate Jim Thurston a Canadian Army man, now I showed him the mushrooms and said that I loved these when they are fried with a bit of bacon, well I was very surprised when he told me that he had never tried eating them things, but walking with him for a while he told me that he was fed up with hanging round the hall just watching people playing games walking round the gardens, he loved to get out into the wilds as he put it and so I just said 'Snap' I then said that I was doing this every day now being a country lad I loved getting out into the fields early in the morning when everything was so fresh. On arriving back at the Hall I took the mushrooms down to the cook house and asked if they would do me a favor and make up two plates of the Mushrooms with the tomorrows breakfast and that they could have the rest and they obliged, sure enough the next morning I went down to the galley and there for me was two plates nice and hot with two sausages a fair few of my mushrooms nicely fried, so I put that lot in front of Jim at the breakfast table everyone looking on a bit surprised as it was different to their meal but I told Jim just tuck in and you will not find anything nicer, so after being bit slow with them at the start he said afterwards that he had really enjoyed them so it becomes a regular thing for Jim and I to go gathering those mush rooms almost every morning always sharing our finds with the staff.

I think that one of the reasons that Jim and I stuck together was because we both loved the outdoors where most of the other lads liked to stay in and play games of different sorts, now Jim didn't like to talk about why he is in this convalescent home but I finally got it out of him one day and this is what he told me. He was with the Canadian commando's that landed at Dieppe on the French coast and it turned out to be a disaster as they were driven back by the Germans in what he described as "Bloody fierce fighting" and they sustained a lot of casualties, Jim was wounded very badly in the escape back to the coast and had since spent a lot of time in Hospital. He told me that he is married with two children and that at the outbreak of war he was living in Manchester, he has now been in this home for a few weeks and due to the extent of his injuries the doctors have told him that there is no chance of him going back to his unit so when he leaves here he is expecting to be discharged from the Army, he has told me that he doesn't want to leave because he has a lot of good mates back in his mob, well as I said before Jim and I like to spend most of our time outdoors doing things that we liked best which is the very long walks that takes us right down to the coast then stand on the cliffs and look out to sea, they are wonderful times for us and one morning Jim said "I don't think that I will ever forget these days," nor I Jim.

I know that I shall never forget my Canadian pal he was a grand chap now medically unfit for active duty, but he has done more than his bit for this country and knowing what he had gone through in that landing on the French coast I think it would be a crime to ask him to go back for some more, days rolled by and the time comes for me to leave Howick Hall, I am very sorry to leave I can tell you I am certainly going to miss Jim and those daily walks down through the fields, but he will stay here until after the war then he will be going back to Canada.

And so the morning arrived when I was called for the last time with no kit except a carrier bag containing a few odds and ends which I had managed to save while at the Isolation Hospital here at Howick and I was handed a sealed envelope which was addressed to the Naval Officer in charge 'North Shields' and after shaking hands with many of the Lads I found myself on the way down to the Navy office at Shields which I may say took a lot of finding, but eventually it was found by way of a naval rating on the docks, to my surprise the officer in charge was a three ringer in other words a Commander and on reporting to him I handed over the sealed envelope, which he explained was from the medical officer at Howick Hall "So they are yours are they" was his actual words after reading the note, I just stood there thinking what the heck is he talking about but I had to say "Beg Pardon Sir" and he promptly replied "That Kit Bag and Hammock that's been cluttering up my back room these last few months." Sorry Sir was my reply but I thought that they would still be on board the Dorsetshire, then the questions started and he said sit down lad you look all in, "so you were on the Cruiser Dorsetshire in that Bismark action was you well what was it like? Did your ship have any casualties? Did any other ships sustain any damage at all?" So it went on and after a very lengthy discussion on how she went down all about the survivors that we picked up I think that he could see that I was tired and offered me a cup of tea he then said I wouldn't have thought that you would want to go back to sea again so soon and just looking at you at this moment and reading this report I don't think that you are in any fit state yet to travel all the way up to Scapa to rejoin Dorsetshire again but I will get the M.O. to give you a check up just to make sure.

So, a further wait for the Medical officer who then gave me a thorough going over I was then told to wait outside his office while he had a conversation with the Commander the result was I was not passed fit enough to rejoin the Dorsetshire, now what to do with you said C.O. back into his office he went and after a short time of speaking to someone on the phone back he came and said I'm sending you home on sick leave for seven days you are to take it easy, your kit bag and hammock will be sent on to the Portsmouth Barracks where you are to report back to when your leave is over, and then he asked me my station for my railway Warrant, after a few moments he handed this to me with a further one for Portsmouth also my pass for seven days leave with parting words of "Now don't forget these words Take It Easy," don't forget when you get to Pompy report to the Medical officer straight away.

And so with thanks I left North Shields heading for home again and so soon, I never really expected this but it was very nice after being so ill and this time I was looking forward to it even more as I was planning a big surprise for my girl I just couldn't wait to ask her if we could become engaged and to slip that lovely ring on to her finger, it was something that I had thought long and hard about while I was at Howick, I know that it must be our secret on account of her Father being so strict, but I am determined this time, just the thought of being away from her again for such a long time without her knowing just how much I love her, well this ring will really show her just that.

I was really getting excited at the thought of what I was going to do as the train arrived at my destination 'Derby station' only a few more miles and I would be home, a very short journey where on my arrival I as usual surprised everyone again, and dropping my things asked my sister the time of the next bus to Derby in reply I found that I had only a short wait, so between having a cup of tea and catching that bus I explained to my sister what I was planning, showing her the ring she said how pleased she was for me, and so the moment duly arrived I caught the bus which dropped me off at the stop near to my girl Friends home, the walk from the bus stop up to where she lived was slightly up hill and I went straight to the house, something that I had never done before. "I <u>am</u> scared of her Father see."

With my heart in my mouth I knocked on the door and was met by her Mother who told me that she would be home at any moment, so I set off to meet and surprise her, after walking for a short while I met her coming along the road on her cycle, she got off when she saw me and we started talking as we walked back towards her home and that is where my whole world fell apart so quickly, firstly I explained to her the reason for my being on leave and that I had been told by the M.O. to take things easy, now all that I wanted was a nice quiet evening just to be with her so that I could ask her that very important so vital question and to slip that lovely ring onto her finger but the answer that I got from my first question deeply shocked me at that very moment I felt so very weak, she said that she was going dancing with her sister and a friend and it had all been arranged, but what really hurt me so deeply was that she wouldn't change her mind when I asked her, she just carried on walking to her home.

Well, it was really heart breaking for me so I immediately turned and walked away from her without speaking another word and set off back down the lane of which I had traveled up only a short time before to meet her so full of love and joy now here I was thinking what girl would dump her sailor boy friend who comes home on sick leave after being seriously ill just so that she could go dancing, when she could go dancing every night when he was away at sea, I could be away for another long time that must surely be an answer but the only answer that came back at me was your girl friend couldn't care all that much for you. Well now I had a bus to catch that would get me back home as soon as possible and after checking my watch I remembered that one was due very shortly then I made the stupid mistake of starting to run 'the warning that the M.O. gave me completely forgotten' and as I reached the bottom of the lane I must have passed out a few yards from where the bus stops across the road, then I found myself already on board the bus on my way home but I was very dazed luckily there were people on the bus who recognized me and some had actually seen me collapse as the bus stopped and had carried me over to the bus, on my arrival home I explained to my sister what had happened, she could see that I was in a rough state, but I was really very angry to think that I had been such a fool all this time I wanted to go to the pub across the road and get drunk but I was told to take it easy, well I did have a rest for a while then I did go to the pub.

But to top it all my rotten luck continued, in the morning I was putting my uniform on after breakfast when I suddenly remembered the little blue box in my inside jumper pocket but it was no longer there so I searched around thinking that it must have fallen out when I undressed last night then I asked my sister if she had picked it up or taken it out of my pocket for safe keeping, "No" was her reply "you could have lost it at the bus stop," now thinking back I realize that I wasn't in much of a state to move about when I was on the bus coming home, then it came to me all at once, the inside pocket of my navy uniform is very shallow that little box could have easily fallen out onto the road when I passed out at the bottom of the lane where those people picked me up.

So, off I went to catch the next bus back to where I had passed out, on arriving I searched every inch of that road over and over again but to no avail, I was as sure as I could be that it would have been here where the little box could have shot out of my pocket but who could have picked it up although I don't think the people who helped me on to the bus would have kept it knowing that it was mine they all new me well enough, so feeling very down I set off on the long walk back home, all my dreams of something special had gone, I thought it was going to be very easy, as I took that walk I couldn't help thinking of the way that things had turned out, I just couldn't feel any lower than I did at that moment, but luckily for me my thoughts were broken by a perfect stranger in a car stopping at my side and offering me a lift which I accepted with a great deal of thanks, although it was only part way home.

My sister was not surprised on learning that I had not found the box but had a surprise for me, she had received a visitor while I had been out, it was my girl friend wanting to see me but it was far too late for any talking now I had been hurt badly as I said to my sister before I set off on my journey to where I was picked up off the road "If she comes round you can tell her that I don't want to see her" as there was no going back now and no excuses were needed for what she had said last night, as far I was concerned it was all over between us and back off leave I went feeling like not caring what happens now.

Why all the panic? was the question on everyone's lips, Why? Out of the blue you might say! Well it just so happens that the King is paying the people of Portsmouth and the Barracks a visit so everything must be spick and span, so if it's got paint on it then you must paint it that was the order. when the great day came we all fell in on the parade ground, ready for inspection in our best number 1's and when the great man came onto the parade ground and walked along the rows of sailors quickly when he passed me I thought he looked as though he was ill, very gaunt and ashen faced, that was King George and it was the first time that I had been inspected by royalty that is if you call it an inspection. But that was the navy all over.

Only a few days after the inspection I received a draft chit to Whale Island gunnery school in Portsmouth on a training course, I was told by one of the lads that it's a real tough place where all the sailors in the Pompy area are sent to learn about all types of gunnery, they are renowned for really putting you through it and yet here I am still not fully recovered from my illness, anyway with kit bag and hammock I was driven through to the outskirts of Pompy and dropped off at what appeared to be a bridge I came face to face with a sentry who I had to show my draft papers to before he would allow me to cross over the bridge to a small building at the other end were I had to report, I was then directed to a large block of buildings which I found out was the Barracks where I handed the draft chit to a Petty Officer who then gave me all the usual gaff when joining a new ship or establishment. But the instructions that I received were entirely different to anything that I have ever had before when joining any other ship, first I was given my mess number where I was to stow my hammock and kit bag, then I had to report to the gunnery store there was issued with my class number also told to draw a rifle and gaiters from the armoury I would be starting my first gunnery course in the Morning, so my first days training and oh no! not the rifle drill stuff again, but yes it was only they were more severe here it was real classy stuff, everything pertaining to drill was carried out with precision you had to handle that rifle as though it was just a piece of light wood believe me when you have been handling a '303' rifle for a length of time they get really heavy.

The gunnery course was a little complicated, but training on those big guns was the undoing of my course, as I said at the beginning I am still getting over my serious illness having lost quite a bit of weight too, and the handling of those heavy shells in the training program really let me down so I didn't do so well, the weight of the shells slowed me down and in a guns crew things are done pretty quick, but I did pass in the Quarters and that meant that I was competent in knowing all about the ammunitions that most guns fire and about the workings of most guns, also how to strip down small arms then be able to put them back together again, it was all very hard work but as the instructor told us when you are manning these guns in action you will find that the training and the sweat of your brow would mean saving your ship and your mates lives one day.

But there is one thing about Whale Island, when you have finished here you would be perfect, you can do guard duty outside Buckingham Palace and you wouldn't be out of place, It sounds so easy but I was very apprehensive when I first tried this but I was now beginning to take a liking to it and was very surprised when on finishing the course I was made ship's company to my great delight, a real cushy number if you get the chance to stay here, now as I pointed out Whale Island is only accessible by a bridge and various jobs are allocated to the ships company, one that I liked very much was guard duty mostly on the bridge entrance and in the guard house at the opposite end of the bridge, but there were also guard duties on other parts of the Island especially at nights, this was to make sure that no one could make a landing of sorts. Every guard was armed and issued with live ammunition and knew how to use it after having a lot of practice on the rifle range, but the guard on the bridge was my second best job night or day, your duty was to stop everyone entering the Island ask for a pass and search all vehicles, when satisfied ring the guard house by phone to let them know that you had passed someone so that they would be ready to receive them, then the P.O. on duty would ask them their business and either let them through or send them back and then it was the guards duty to see that they cleared the area. But the number one guard duty that I really liked best of all was the one that meant traveling to different parts of the country to pick up prisoners, the men who had probably over stayed their leave, deserted or perhaps got in to some trouble with the local police and had been arrested for some reason or other, And so that is where we 'the guards from Whale Island' come in and there would be two of us detailed off for special duty, we would be given railway warrants and the Naval Authorization certificate to pick up the prisoners and escort them back to their respective ships from which they were adrift from, or in the more serious cases back to Portsmouth were they would be installed in the cells until such times they would be tried.

On one occasion we had to pick up a prisoner in London and when we arrived we were told by the police that the man in question was now in Hospital so we had to get new orders, they were to remain there and wait if his stay in Hospital was for less than 48hrs, we were given an address to stay at for this time, And so both my mate and I booked in at this small Hotel if you could call it a that, the first night was one that we will not forget in a hurry, we found out what the local people had to put up with, I might add that all the time we were there was spent in a public air raid shelter the bombs rained down, some landing very close, the ground shaking every time when the all clear went in the morning and we walked out "What a shock" we had the whole area had been flattened except for the odd buildings here and there.

But these journey's were not all bad like the London one in fact some were just the job, one day we had to pick up a prisoner from Derby Police Station which is only a few miles from where I live, on arriving there they seemed a bit surprised that we had traveled all the way from Portsmouth to pick up this chap, but what they didn't know was that he was a deserter from his ship at Greenock in Scotland and was a week over due then I surprised them when I said that I was no stranger to Derby as I lived only a short bus ride away, but it was too late for me to make a quick trip home and so my mate and I both spent the night sleeping in the cells which I might say was quite comfortable even more so with the breakfast that we got before we set off in the morning back to Pompy.

This was a great job and one that I liked very much, apart from one bit of trouble one day when we were escorting a lad from Plymouth back to the Barracks, he gave us the slip right at the Station in Portsmouth by climbing through the toilet window at the back, but luckily for us he had to come round onto the platform to get out of the station so we spotted him and despite him getting out into the streets of Portsmouth we gave chase and finally caught up with him then marched him back to the barracks, this was the only time anything like this happened while I was on this duty, I found that most of these lads had some good excuses for being adrift and it was mostly to do with family problems. I would have given anything to have stayed here on Whale Island but it wasn't to be for after a few more weeks the inevitable happened and I got another draft chit but this was entirely my own fault, something that I regretted very much and this time it was to a ship that was in dock at Davenport, and so with the old hammock and kit hag I set forth with another rating a Steward who was going to another ship and the date was the 24th December 1941. I travelled down to Devonport by train finally arriving at the dock yard gates I asked a policeman if he could tell me where the Destroyer H.M.S. Javelin was berthed but he could only point me in the direction that she would be, as it was over on the other side to which we were so I set off and was beginning to wonder what this ship was going to be like as I had only been on big ships before I had never been in Devonport either and I was really dreading it, then a policeman patrolling the docks came to my rescue and asked me if I needed any help at the same time he asked me for my papers and before I could say anything he pointed to three ships and said the Javelin is the first one.

And so humping my kit bag and hammock I headed for these three small Ships berthed together alongside the jetty and was surprised on going up the gangway that there didn't seem to be anyone about and as I dumped my kit bag onto the deck an Officer appeared, he was a young 'Subby' who I assumed was the duty officer so I reported to him and was told to leave my kit and go find the Chief Buffer and report to him, so I was in a predicament right from the start, where was I going to find this chief, so as I strolled off thinking this routine is different to a big ship without a clue I began my search and was saved by a Petty Officer who dropped down off a gun platform asking if I needed any help when I gave him the message that I had received from the Sub Lieutenant he just shook his head, "what was your last ship" asked the P.O. as we started to look for the Chief of the Dorsetshire I replied that answer really got him talking about the action against the Bismark until we finally caught up with the Chief down below decks, I was taken to a very small cabin where I reckon that the Chief did his duties and in a matter of minutes I was a member of H.M.S. Javelin, after going through the old routine thing my part ship number, action stations and other bits and pieces that go into forming the ships company, I was then told to report for duty in the morning with the rest of the crew (by the way a Buffer is Navy slang for a Chief Bosun's Mate, and Subby is a Sub Lieutenant).

Now, moving forward (said differently in the navy) with my kit I was surprised to find when I got onto the mess deck how very small and confined it was, there I met the leading hand of the number I mess that I had been assigned to, he told me that at the moment there was only four of us on our mess and also found that there was only a few men aboard also very few Officers, in our conversation I told him that my last ship was a cruiser and he said that I will find a vast difference aboard a Destroyer as we take things a lot easier there is also a lot more comradeship being so close together all the time, also the Petty Officers are more pally with the lads, everyone pulls together.

I took a great liking to our killick, his words soon rang true as it turned out to be pretty easy going right from the start, with shore leave every day for the few crew members that are aboard at the time. although I had a couple of runs ashore with the Killick I didn't reckon all that much to Devonport apart from the pubs, but it was better than sitting on the mess when the other lads had gone ashore and I did get a lot more of the 'Gen' from the killick (all the routine of a Destroyer at sea) I was now looking forward to that day. I found out how working on board these little ships was so easy there not being a full ships company yet made it all the more easier to find my way around, but it was so vastly different to the Dorsetshire hardly room to sling your hammock also when they are up it is very cramped, but there is one thing that I liked about these Destroyers they are very well armed with the torpedo tubes and six 4.7" guns as well as a pom-pom which is a fast firing gun, made up of either four or eight Barrels and some smaller fast firing ack-ack guns (Oerlicons) mainly used when being attacked by enemy aircraft but like the pom-pom is just as useful when firing at surface craft as the Killick says these ships are not called the greyhounds of the navy for nothing as they can move through the water very fast, so it will be very interesting to see her first performance when we go to sea and I can't wait, but I'm also wondering if it will have any effect on me even though I have been out at sea in some very rough weather (I know these destroyers pitch and roll quite a lot in bad weather), so we will just have to wait and see. I haven't given a lot of thought to what all these work men are doing on board until I got into a conversation with one of the Petty Officers and was quite surprised to learn that this ship had been in action in the English channel against some German Destroyers, she had her bows and stern blown off with torpedoes, also a great number of her crew killed, then only just managed to make land after being towed by another Destroyer, the Captain of the Javelin in that action with the Germans is very well known for his daring, although I've heard from plenty of the lads and some members of his crew that he is a bit of a 'Glory Boy.'

I hadn't been in the navy very long when I heard about Louis Mountbatten, the word used to describe him is not very nice and not many sailors fancied being in his crew, how true this is I wouldn't know, but I am very pleased because the Killick said he is not the Captain now, as this Skipper is a big tall bearded man by the name of Simms and you certainly can't mistake him. Things began to pick up a bit as more as more Officers and ratings started to come on board, the mess decks started to get a bit more crowded and noisy, a few squabbles began over the lockers and hammock spaces, being on board early I've already had the pick of the lockers and the hammock spaces so I have no worries at all.

The thing that I noticed most as the crew gradually begin to get to a full compliment is that they are a mixed crowd and some are brand new recruit's straight from the barracks, anyway our mess soon begins to fill up and after a few days of getting to know these lads I began to like most of them, I already know that we have the best leading seaman on the ship, now, I haven't said too much about him, I know that if he is aware of me singing his praises, he would knock my block off, he is an active service sailor who is serving his time in the Navy and it showed, if you want to know, or were in doubt about anything you only have to ask 'Robbo' (short for Robinson) and he will put you straight.

I picked out one lad among the new recruits who was probably among the last to join our mess and I found out he is from Derby, also straight out of the Barracks, so we soon got to be friends, being almost neighbours you might say, I know that he is a bit nervous with this being his first ship, I am going to put him right and show him the ropes to make it a bit easier for him. It is very noticeable to see that some of these new ratings are a bit slow to start with, fresh ship and fresh faces, I know how hard it is to get into the swing of things when you join a ship for the first time it seems so hard, it takes time to settle in with the rest of the crew but you do make friends quite soon, on a small ship like a Destroyer you just can't help but have mates, as Robbo says "your life depends on one another."

The captain has come aboard again now and we now have a full crew (ships company is the correct word), the repairs have all been completed and after quite a lot of exercises at all the main stations like gunnery, signals, communications, and others like closing up at action stations, now, I forgot to say about the watches on board a ship, they are of course entirely different to those that are carried out ashore, every rating is given his watch when he arrives on a ship, that can be either port or Starboard watch as I think I have said before, so you have a cruising, action and defence station, these three stations are the degree of readiness at which the Captain requires the ship to be in at any given time, according to each situation as it comes up, that is if the ship is in a convoy, he would usually want second degree of readiness, which would be the defence stations also the same for dangerous waters, so this would mean that half of the ships company would be in the navel term 'closed up' ready for action, the rest would be off watch, an explanation of all this watch routine I will explain more clearly later.

We are now at short notice for sea 'not surprisingly.' After moving to the oil terminal for refueling purposes the Javelin sails out of Devonport on the 29th January 1942, heading for her trials on a fairly rough sea, we are here to test the engines. I soon find out what it's like to be on a Destroyer after only half an hours sailing as the safety lines have to be rigged, these are steel wire ropes that are strung from forward to aft in each waste of the ship (port or starboard), waste's are the walkways on each side of the ship. I noticed the speed of the ship increasing as the spray began to fly inboard, with waves breaking over the bow, now, this is really something I have never experienced before, the Captain is really put her through her paces but unfortunately while these speed trials are being carried out two ratings are washed overboard, as I said there is a hell of a lot of water when these greyhounds of the navy are flat out, you really have to have your wits about you. We made a big search covering miles of ocean with everyone scanning the water for any signs of the unfortunate ratings 'but to no avail,' I wouldn't think that they would stand much chance in this very rough sea. So we are sailing back to port, that little run out made quite a lot of the lads sea sick and were very pleased when the ship stopped bouncing about.

Devonport and back to the old routine of cleaning ship and training at closing up actions at speed every day for a week, I forgot to say that there is also a big job of cleaning up on the mess decks now we are back from the trials, there is all sorts of food down on the deck, pots and pans mixed up with sugar and other foods, also a fair amount of sea water running about, the hammocks are also wet so the air is a bit blue for a while. I am breaking off here to give you the rundown of how a ships company works at sea. I mentioned earlier that every man on joining the ship is given a watch which are port or starboard, these two watches are split so that you could be in the first part or the second part of the port watch the same goes for the starboard watch, so you get on occasions a pipe of "all the port watch close up" at let's say defence stations, it could be on a gun be it 4.7" ante-aircraft gun, transmitting station lookout on the bridge or down the magazine, but each rating according to whatever branch of the navy they are in would close up to their respective duties (Signal men obviously on the bridge) torpedo men would be manning the tubes, the Stokers down in the engine room, now, this is classed as second degree of readiness. But if the action station alarm went while you were at defence stations then you would leave that station and go immediately to your action station which is probably at a different part of the ship, also a different one than your defence station, in other words down a magazine instead of a lookout up on the crows nest if you were on a big ship (Get what I mean?) of course action stations is classed as the first degree of readiness, so we go into the cruising stations, now this is the third degree of readiness and might only need just a part of the watch to man the ship but once again you could still be at any station on the ship while the rest of the crew both Starboard or Port would be working what is termed as part ship, this could mean washing down paint work or any job that the Petty Officer of your watch wants doing.

And so it works out that if a ship is in dangerous waters the Skipper would most likely want the ship to be at defence stations, the same would apply if you were on convoy duty, but if you were on convoy duty in dangerous waters then the ship would most likely be at action stations, so it's prepared for any enemy attacks, that is a rough idea on how a ships routine is worked when you're at sea, although some of the routines of working part ship may depend on the type as some of the big ships have wooden decks and the morning duties start by scrubbing the deck, then there is all the brass bit's that have to be polished my stations on the Javelin Cruising stations are S1 Oerlicon just a baft the bridge on the Starboard side right facing forward, my defence station is P1 Oerlicon on the port side left, this is a small fast firing single barrel anti-aircraft gun manned by two men, one does the firing and his mate is the ammunition supply in this case my mate Tom is the gunner and I am the supply man, this is also our action station.

As for the crew well, the young sailors are settling down OK but some of them are having a bit of a problem with their hammocks and are still falling out of them, they do take a bit of getting used to at first, but to most sailors they are a great comfort especially when you are on a Destroyer, they can actually save your life if they are lashed up properly because when a ship sinks, those made of canvas will float, other good uses of the Hammock is when a ship is holed or suffers damage to her sides they can be used to plug the hole (from here onwards I have decided to keep my diary up to date). The 7th February dawns with that old familiar sound of the Bosuns whistle piping hands to stations for leaving harbour, all the port watch close up that's me and my mate Tom.

Now where are we off to? Out of the harbor we go, it's pouring down with rain and still a bit on the rough side, you know I really pity these young lads who have never done any sea time before it must be terrible for them when they are sea sick, and I've seen plenty that are I can tell you, it's "B" awful, they say that they think they are dying, yet for most when they get over it they never suffer from it again, although even the most hardiest of sailors get sea sick at times it's just one of those things, that is why I am still keeping my fingers crossed, it can happen for some even when the sea is very calm.

Well here we are at this moment sailing up the Irish sea with Ireland on our port beam, the coast of England is on our starboard side and the Skipper is speaking over the tannoy saying that we are heading for Scapa Flow which is in the far north of Scotland and from there we are going to do our remaining trials. So after a few hours of ploughing through some heavy sea around the coast of Scotland we arrive here at last, having just dropped anchor we find out what a desolate place it is, there is just nothing here at all, it's a great big bay surrounded by hills and fields with no sign of life except for cattle and it's miles from anywhere, now I wonder how long we are going to be stuck here for. The days passed by and the lads on the mess are simply bored stiff spending most of their time writing letters home or to their girl friends.

So after what seemed a heck of a long time but in actual fact is only a few days 18th February to be exact, we sail out of Scapa, heading into the north sea for more trials as a new ship and crew, everything has to be tested so as to bring the ship up to fighting force standards, gunnery target practice for the big guns and for the anti-aircraft guns firing at a target that's being towed behind an aircraft called a drogue, then there is the depth charge throwers which also have to be tested. After the exercise permission is granted to pick up all the dead fish as there is quite a lot floating on the surface, this would mean more work for the lad who's turn it is to be the next mess man on all the messes, after this operation we returned to Scapa Flow.

Just a few words on the subject of food, some ships have different ways of distributing the cooked food, one is called general messing and the other is canteen messing, which ever ship you are on you certainly get plenty of good cooked food, I have mentioned the way that things are done on the big ships before but the only thing that makes the food business awkward is the times you get your meals. I will write down how the watches work then you will see just how we fit our meals in

Port Watch doing the Forenoon Watch		— 0800hrs until 1200hrs-Midday
Starboard Watch the	Afternoon Watch	— 1200hrs until 1600hrs
Port Watch	First Dog Watch	— 1600hrs until 1800hrs
Starboard Watch	Second Dog Watch	— 1800hrs until 2000hrs
Port Watch	First Watch	— 2000hrs until 1200hrs-Midnight
Starboard Watch	Middle Watch	— 1200hrs until 0400hrs
Port Watch	Morning Watch	— 0400hrs until 0800hrs

And there you have the entire watches exactly as they are worked on board every warship in the Royal Navy, these watches are worked on what would be defence stations, which in war time is possibly the only watches that are worked, due to the ship having to be on alert at all times. Cruising stations are very rarely worked as the ship would only have part of a watch on duty that is unless they were in waters where it was considered the ship is in no danger at all, and in my opinion every time a ship goes to sea, now then, they are in danger.

Back to the subject of food! I forgot to mention that every day each mess is detailed off a cook by the leading hand of the mess, his duties are to see that the mess table is prepared ready to receive each ratings meals (breakfast and dinners), collect cooked food from the galley and serve a fair meal to each rating on the mess under the supervision of the leading hand, when meals are finished he washes all the dishes, utensils and cutlery then cleans the mess table down ready for the next time, all the utensils and the containers used to carry the food are inspected by the Officer of the watch on occasions which are called 'rounds' so everything has to be perfect, 'now, don't you think that we would make good husbands.'

But not to worry there is always the leading hand to help you out if you make any mistakes, old Robbo is always doing that.

All thoughts of a break are soon gone because after refueling at a Tanker the very next day, we then sail out with some other Destroyers who have arrived at Scapa Flow doing escort duty for the Battle Ship 'Duke of York,' she is also coming with us to do some gunnery exercises, so this looks like being our first piece of duty back out into the North sea and it turns out that the Battle Ship was only testing her small stuff not the main armament, we had sailed a long way out before she started to fire those guns and it turned out to be quite a sight.

Our main job out here seemed to be looking out for mines which appeared floating on the surface of the water, these had evidently been dropped last night as there is so many bobbing about, the lookouts are reporting them every few minutes, well, they provided some good target practice for the small guns mostly the rifle which in a way is a good idea as blasting away at the mines with the pom-pom or the Oerlicon would surely be a waste of ammunition, there is quite a lot of explosions now with more ships firing at them, although some of them did manage to get past which was bound to happen, I can only say that if one of these had hit the Javelin, well I wouldn't be sitting here now on one mess writing up this incident "no way" for a mine doesn't leave much left of a small ship.

We sail on at a steady speed, the pipe has just gone for the "port watch to close up at defence stations" that means me (I must break off now as I am due on watch in a few minutes).

So after four hours of being closed up on P1 Oerlicon in a very blustery windswept sea and not sighting anything except the odd sea bird I am now back off afternoon watch, I will not be having much rest as I am back on watch again in two hours to do the second dog watch at 1600hrs until 1800hrs, then on again for four hours on the middle watch—Midnight until 0400hrs, that is 'life at sea.'

So sailing on. After a short time land is sighted on our Starboard bow and very soon we are off Iceland, we slowly enter the port of Seydis Fiord going alongside the jetty, not long after supplies arrive for loading on board, we are not getting any shore leave here 'all night' is the saying, that means no middle watch for me. Come the morning we start to prepare for sea and sail from Iceland during the morning watch, the Battle ship and the entire escort are doing the same up to now, no one knows where we are off to or what we are supposed to be doing with this Battle Ship right up here in these waters.

As we sailed from Iceland out into the North sea we meet up with another group of ships, quite a few Destroyers and what looks like three Cruisers all join up together to make what appears to be a striking force. So buzzes start to come thick and fast as to what we are about to do with a Battleship and Cruisers, the betting is a bombardment somewhere, that is unless one of the German big ships is out this way, but they were all wrong, for after a couple of hours we approach the coastline of Norway and move in close doing a big sweep for any enemy shipping, the weather has now changed and it is blowing up quite a bit, but despite covering a lot of water we didn't see a thing, eventually this lot turned around and sailed into a gale (big sea's) with the Destroyers shipping a lot of water.

And so at a steady speed this large number of warships ploughed on passing Iceland in the mist on our port bow, eventually arriving back in desolate Scapa Flow, most of the Cruisers, the Duke Of York and it's escort including the Javelin went into the bay, we stay here for the next few days. Now, you can imagine what it has been like in this god forsaken place, we couldn't get much further away from the war up here if we had tried, apart from writing letters, reading and boring part ship work there is not much else to do except for those lads who have a hobby of some sort and some do have one.

At sea thank goodness, if I never see Scapa Flow again well, it will certainly not be missed, the weather has eased up a little and I am on watch closed up at defence stations as usual, it appears that we are heading down the west coast of Scotland, sure enough, after a short trip we arrive at the port of Greenock and on entering the harbour we immediately go into the dry dock, after securing the buzz goes around that we have some sort of engine trouble so there is going to be some inspection work done, and what do you know after only being here a few hours we realize that we must have a big problem because it's just been piped around the ship that leave has been given to both watches for 72hrs.

Now, that is something to look forward to, then it came to me that I had not really got much to go on leave for, after all

I can get as much beer as I want ashore at Greenock, there's bound to be plenty of girls about as well, it is a very busy port and I no longer have a girlfriend waiting for me back home, why not stay here? it might turn out to be more exciting, I would still get my meals on board ship, but it was my mate Tom who finally persuaded me to go on leave because it wouldn't be very good on the ship with most people away on leave, so my mind had been made up for me and off we went.

My leave is mostly the usual thing, loafing around really with nothing much to do, it's not much fun sitting on your own drinking beer as this time none of my mates were home on leave. My walks down by the riverside which I used to love so much tended to make me feel worse as the peace and quiet brought back all the lovely times that I used to spend there with Joyce my ex girl friend, now it seemed as though it was only yesterday, I can tell you in all honesty I had a job to stop the tears from rolling down my face, but that is all in the past now.

And so with nothing to do, the very next day on Saturday morning I decided to pay a visit to my old works which is Nestles Milk Factory, where I was working before I joined the Navy as my Sister, two Aunts, mates and female friends work there. Seeing my old work mates when I walked into the place bucked me up quite a lot, but what really caught my eye while I was talking to my Aunt was a new face that of a young girl and I could see that she was dying to meet "this sailor," I went over to where she was working which was next to an old mate of mine, very soon we were in conversation her name is Betty and in no time at all we had arranged to meet that afternoon after work also in the evening to (it was all so easy). I spent the rest of leave seeing her, but don't get me wrong it was only something to pass the time away "well you know what sailors are," well I no longer had a girlfriend so I thought I was doing nothing wrong and I had nothing to lose. The one thing that really made my leave was on the Sunday I was due to go off leave, I was walking with Betty down the lane where she lived and coming towards us was my ex girlfriend Joyce, well, I couldn't wait to rub it in, so I put my arm around Betty's waist and pulled her close I wanted to show her that I no longer cared. The leave was soon over and I wasn't sorry to be going back this time, not like the other times of which I never wanted to end, there is no heavy heart now 'nothing.'

Here I am back off leave after a long and tiring journey. I can honestly say that I did not really enjoy leave even though I found another girlfriend, who I know thinks a lot of me already, but my heart wasn't really in it, I was only trying to make my ex girl friend jealous when she passed us in the lane that day, now, you tell me why? I have obviously been kidding myself. Back here on board I have no more time to think as we start to ammunition ship, we take on a lot of supplies and stores, anyone who has not been issued with tropical gear is ordered to draw what they required from the "pussers" store on shore, I have already got my complete kit to the surprise of some of the lads. The buzz soon starts to go around the ship that we will be going somewhere warm (although it was obvious to those who had already done Foreign Service. The pipe has just gone to fall in so this is it, "no rest for the wicked." It's after the first dog watch now and it's been rather a busy day, sitting here on the mess deck thinking that I have just done one stint of Foreign and now I am all set to do yet another so soon after the last one but I didn't care this time, last time I was leaving behind someone I loved very much it was heart breaking, but this time apart from my family I left no one.

On the 22nd of March 1942 we are given orders to prepare for sea, I am not on watch for a change it's the starboard watch taking us out, I am very surprised at the size of the convoy as we form up outside of Greenock very early in the morning, there are quite a few big Merchant ships, one Aircraft Carrier, some Cruisers, supply ships, a fleet of Destroyers also quite a few troop ships, now, that is a surprise and they are full of soldiers, the question on everyone's lips is where the hell is this lot going? And so the guessing game begins, the top of the list is relieving or reinforcing the Eighth Army in the Western Desert, that would mean we are going to the Mediterranean, I wouldn't mind if it was the Med. as I didn't go there on my last service and it would be a change, maybe it's Burma? someone said or Bombay? It is all guess work though.

We take up our stations and slowly the whole convoy moved out into the open calm sea away from the coast of Scotland, (those soldiers on the troop ships wouldn't think it is very calm), the usual sea duties are being carried out by everyone on board ship, but it so happens that it's my turn as mess man so I had better tell you what I will be doing very shortly, the first job is to lay the cloth on the mess table and put all the cutlery in order of each rating seated, when cooks to the galley is piped, go there and call out the number of my mess, in return the cook will hand me the receptacles with the Dinners or Breakfasts for each number of ratings on our mess, on returning to the mess Robbo and myself will measure out each meal then hand them out, when finished I will wash all the pots, pans, Cutlery and mess table then sweep up, I can honestly say that there is not much left for the fish.

Sailing along on the fourth day out, we get a contact on a U-boat (submarine), so straight away we go into the attack with depth charges while the rest of the convoy carried on. We are left to carry on with the attack for a considerable time, and each time those depth charges go up all eyes on board are on the watch for any tell tale signs of a submarine coming to the surface or any bits and pieces of debris floating, well it seemed like hours that this went on and at last oil, clothing and paper appeared on the water covering a large area, this being greeted with loud cheers from the lads watching over the sides yours truly included, but the contact was lost and even though we made a big search all around the area it proved negative.

So, we have to push off leaving the area at high speed to chase after the convoy before it got too dark, so we don't know now if we sank that submarine or not, most skippers know that these submarine captains try all sorts of dodges when they are being hard pressed by a Destroyer, the biggest one of all is the oil, paper, articles of clothing and all sorts of rubbish which they send to the surface through the torpedo tubes to try and make it look as though they have suffered some serious damage or it's sinking, I suppose it works sometimes but not very often as these old Destroyer skippers know all the dodges they try to pull and are not easily fooled, so are not caught out very often, but it does happen sometimes.

Well, night was not very far off when we eventually caught up with the convoy, I was on duty doing the first watch. Sailing along without any more alarms we eventually arrive at the port of Ponte Del Garda which is a small Island in the Azores during the early morning on the 28th of March, some of the ships have gone straight into the harbour to load up with fresh provisions, being on watch I could see that it was mostly fruit. I have been here a few times before when I was on the Dorsetshire but we were never allowed on shore owing to fact that the population is so small, I understand from one of the Bunting tossers that this order still stands today 'to the annoyance of the lads' so we have to stay outside with most of the convoy (near and yet so far).

The business of hanging around with the convoy means that us escorts have to keep on the move all the time, sweeping for any enemy submarines that might be waiting to attack, so it must be a bit nerve racking for the lads on those Troop ships waiting around for the other ships to come out of the harbour, it did take up most of the morning but finally we're on our way again, after all getting in some sort of order takes time and is a bit worrying as these big ships are a bit slow in getting into proper formation (they make easy targets for enemy U-boats).

Sailing on at last after almost a week of seeing nothing but flying fishes and a few porpoises trying to race us, we finally sight land again on the 4th of April.

On entering the port of Bathurst in West Africa where refuelling is the main priority for a few ships.

This is a place that I have been ashore in once before and is not too bad a place for shore leave, it would have been a change for the lads, but no luck, shore is not being given this time, and further more we have been told once again that Tropical gear is now the rig of the day, not before time I may say as it has been getting a bit warm wearing these blue's in the day time, so it's white shorts, shirts and white hats now. Sailing on from here, I can only guess where our next port of call will be.

Five days now we have been pushing on and the heat is beginning to tell, when land is sighted at last. We enter the port of Freetown on the west African coast on the 9th of April, looking through my binoculars I must say that it hasn't altered much from the time I spent here on the old Edinburgh castle in 1940 and I see that she is still here, what a life the ships company must have aboard her, I pointed her out to old Robbo and one or two of the lads, explaining that I used to be aboard her while I was waiting for a draft chit to another ship, what was it I used to say "the only interesting thing about Freetown is the monkeys," now, would you believe it, the bosuns mate is going around the ship piping "leave is granted to the port Watch," but no! Sorry, not for me thank you I have seen quite enough of this place, some of the lads might like the place though, my mate Tom asked me what it is like? And I told him to go as it was something that he might want to remember when this war is over.

I don't suppose that you can blame the young lads for wanting to see the place, but if they had been in this dump for as long as I was they wouldn't be in too much of a hurry to get ashore, I suppose to the first timer it's a fascinating place, surrounded by Jungle, but I would never want to stay here again for any length of time because there is nothing of any interest for me, but I suppose the beer would suit some of the beer drinkers, personally I wouldn't give you the time of day for the stuff, it is always warm and fizzy, horrible stuff in my opinion, there is one place ashore that is especially for the forces, where they sell this stuff and it is served in tins, I should think that It is still be there.

There is one person that interested me when I first came here, an old native who is stuck with the nick name by the Navy of "Liverpool Joe," he used to paddle his canoe alongside the ship and ask you to throw pennies into his canoe, you could recognize him because he always wore a Bowler Hat, now, if the coin didn't land in his canoe he would use some terrible language, the young natives would give a display of diving when you threw pennies into the sea, they dived overboard and kept the money they retrieved. While the lads are ashore I am going to write a couple of letters back home, then sling my hammock and have a nice quiet night in before all the noise starts.

I am trying to guess where we are heading with this convoy as nothing has come up yet even from the 'Bunting Tossers' (Flags or Signal ratings,) they usually get to know all the Gen before anyone else. Letter writing finished I am going to climb into my hammock with the knowledge that come the morning we will be out of here again.

I can honestly say that I didn't have the peaceful night that I wanted due to the usual nightly display of lightning, we are almost at the end of the morning watch and sailing out of Freetown harbour, we are joined by some other warships including the Battle ship H.M.S. Malaya also the Cruiser H.M.S. Devonshire (she is the sister ship to my old ship Dorsetshire) there is another Troop ship coming out, this one is loaded with soldiers.

I pointed out the Cruiser to my mate Tom explaining that she is exactly the same as my last ship and showed him where my action station was, I also told him what it is like up in the crows nest in bad weather. After the problem of getting this lot back into some formation, making a very large convoy we set off at some speed into a fairly rough sea. The conversation at dinner really gets going again, Battle Wagons, Aircraft Carrier, Cruisers and Troop ships well this has got to be an attack of some sort and the only place it could possibly be is the Mediterranean because that is where all the real fighting is at the moment, that is the conclusion of most of the lads on the mess.

After five days of pushing through some rough weather we arrive at the beautiful port of Jamestown St Helena on the 14th of April.

This is another place that I have had the privilege of visiting a few times before, it is a very beautiful place but only a small island and it gets very warm.

If you have never been on a Tropical island well, this is surely the one for you, I have had the pleasure of going ashore here once or twice but I doubt very much if they will allow this lot that privilege as I reckon that there are more people on these ships than there are on the Island, so apart from a boat off the Battleship going ashore, for some reason we didn't stay here very long before sailing out straight into a gale and it is rough going, force eight they reckon.

"Wow" don't these Destroyers do some strange things when they are in rough weather I am sure that this is without doubt the roughest weather that I have been in since joining the Navy but it still doesn't seem to bother me a bit, I do feel sorry for those poor squaddies aboard the Troop ships as they are doing some pitching and rolling, 'they must be suffering some in this lot.'

I have just come off afternoon watch after doing four hours, luckily we have had the shelter of the bridge to help keep the bad weather off us, but watching the water coming inboard down aft as it sweeps down the sides of the ship, I reckon it is really scary for these young lads.

We have been at sea five days now, I am pleased to say that the weather has eased a bit over the last couple of days and things are definitely getting better, being well into our fifth day I decided to take a stroll after tea on the upper deck with a couple of the lads off my watch, when we clearly heard the bridge lookout shout "land in sight dead ahead" now although for a time we can't see anything it is only a matter of a few minutes before, on the horizon land can be seen, of course as soon as the mess deck hears that land has been sighted they are all up here, but we are too far away to have the remotest idea what the place is, my mate who has now come on deck alongside me remarked "I hope that it's not another Island where we can't get ashore."

Yet as we slowly close in on that far distant land a very familiar land mark begins to appear to me, one that I have seen so many times from a distance, I can't sustain my joy and yelled "Cape Town," all the lads look at me in surprise, then I tell them that big thing that is sticking high up on the horizon is Table Mountain, from this distance it's only just discernible "dear old Cape Town, fantastic," so on we go and I said to my mate I have seen this same sight scores of times, a sight that you never forget, I just can't believe this was happening as I never thought that I would ever see this place again.

As we slowly approach the harbour, lights begin to come on and by the time we enter, the whole city is ablaze with lights, the date is the19th of April 1942. So here we are again, now all I want to do is get ashore here, as I said to Tom "I will show you this place, it is one of the greatest runs ashore that you will ever likely have, anywhere." What a fantastic sight it must be for a lot of the lads on board, unlike England there is no blackout here, I just can't wait to get ashore and meet some of my old friends again, don't forget what I said early on in my diary about this place, when I was on the Dorsetshire "the people here just can't do enough for the British Sailors."

I should be doing the first dog watch now, but for some reason we have been stood down as we entered harbour, "special sea duty men to their stations" is piped and we are now at anchor like the rest of this lot that came in, so it doesn't look as though we are going to get any shore leave tonight, there has certainly not been any mention of it. It looks as though some of the ships are taking on fuel and there is Cape Town ablaze with lights, I can only feel sorry for those who have never been here before, but I'm afraid that it's a night in again although there is always tomorrow, well, we can but hope.

Morning comes bright and early with brilliant sunshine, our hopes are soon shattered as a little later (one hour into the forenoon watch to be exact), "hands to stations for leaving harbor" is being piped, in no time at all up comes the anchor and we are on our way out of Cape Town, 'what a shame,' I was really looking forward to seeing some of the old faces again.

The 20th of April, we are once again on the high seas and the Captain is about to speak over the tannoy, this is probably what we have been waiting for ever since we set sail from England, sure enough after listening to his message we know were we are bound for now, with this very large company of ships we know that it is not the Mediterranean after all, but a very large island in the Indian ocean called Madagascar, as he explained "this place is being run by the Vichy French who are now collaborating with the Germans and are allies to the Japanese, they are using this place as a submarine base to supply their U-boats with fuel so that they can attack enemy shipping in the Indian ocean."

Our job is to attack the place, first to bombard the landing sight from the sea then land the troops who will have aircraft cover from the carrier, their job is to take over the Island then the supply ships will enter one of the ports. The date now is the 21st of April. There is one thing that the Skipper didn't tell us and that is when this battle is going to be, so we are still in the dark but we do know that it is not going to be yet. The lads have just come in off the upper deck to say that they have seen the Queen Mary who Robbo says "is evidently on her way to America."

The 22nd comes and goes and the weather has turned very bad, we are now in sight of a favourite place of mine, arriving at Durban Natal on the 23rd of April, this is where everyone in the convoy gets the most welcome sight you could ever wish for, we are greeted by a Lady dressed all in white.

Yes she is still here and gives her usual greeting on entering the harbour, now this Lady greets most ships on entering Durban by standing on a platform and singing 'Land of hope and glory' also 'there will always be an England' in a very loud voice as I mentioned early on in the Diary, she has now become "Durbans Lady In White" to every sailor and you don't ever forget her. I know that I have said it before but she deserves a medal. We sailed straight into the dry dock to check on some damage that we sustained to the bows during the gale after we left the harbour at St Helena, I believe that there are quite a few plates buckled, now, how about that for rough weather, anyway this must mean some shore leave, there are plenty of girls here but the main thing is the food, all kinds of it and plenty too, the beer here is not bad either. Now that I have no girl friend back home waiting for me I'm free and I am going to make the most of it, I know from the past that the girls here really go for English sailors.

So let's get ashore and have some fun, and that is what is being piped at this moment that shore leave will be granted to the port watch from 16.30hrs until 22.30hrs, that means us, but being just after the dinner hour we still have to work part ship during the afternoon watch, it will give us plenty of time to get our kit ready for tonight, I have told my mate that first thing I do when step ashore is have a slap up meal. I can tell you that unless it's changed they have everything here, no rationing like back home and the food is not unlike what we are used to but more plentiful, you know the old saying "eat drink and be merry for tomorrow you may die" and nothing can be more truthful than that in the Navy.

And so come the hour and ashore we go, so it's "Look out misses here we come, so lock up your daughters because Bobs on the run," off we went, then something happened that you would think was almost impossible, we had not gone far and are on the lookout for a place that I used to know which served up some real good food, when we saw two soldiers coming towards us, I just couldn't believe my eyes when they got closer because one of them I recognized immediately as a chap from my own village of Tutbury, it's amazing to meet him right out here thousands of miles from home it's a blinking marvel. I know him very well, his name is Arthur Yates, well as he got near to us I stopped him as I don't think he recognized me, what are you doing so far from home I asked? As he just looked at me puzzled I said three words that I knew he would remember "Tutbury Glass Works," then he grabbed my hand and started to shake my arm off "Eh, now I recognize you it's that uniform."

He told me that that they had only just arrived here in Durban after sailing from England, I asked him "do you know where you are bound for after you have enjoyed yourself ashore here?" he already knew and said they have known since they left England, he was a bit surprised when I told him that we had been part of the escort that had brought him all the way here. Tom joined in the conversation and asked Arthur how he felt about the landing at Madagascar? He replied "all his mob is up for it and very confident," he wanted to know if we new Durban at all as they had been looking around for some where to get some decent food and a drink of good beer, also one question that a lot of the forces want to know and that is are there any Brothels here? Now although I know this place very well I could put him right for the first two but with regards the last one well, I hadn't a clue and that is the gospel truth, we said goodbye wishing them the best of luck.

It wasn't very long before we caught the eye of two very nice girls, and we spent the whole evening with them having a smashing time they also made it very clear that they want to see us again . . . I should think so too. We also had big eats and beer as there is no rationing here, so for our first night ashore I think we did very well.

We are back on board again now also had a very restful night in the hammock which is some relief after nights and days of watches hurried meals and the crashing of the sea down the sides of the ship when you are trying to get a quiet rest on the lockers, it's the morning after the night before and I have the head that I wish would give me some peace and quiet for a while, I do feel rough so thankfully I am on watch.

I certainly don't remember falling out of my hammock last night though Robbo said I did and he had to help me get in again, now, I wonder how he managed that, come to think of it I haven't seen my Hoppo (mate) yet this morning so I don't know how he feels, but it wasn't long before he put in appearance coming from the direction of the heads (Toilets), he looks terrible I must say, according to Robbo he had been in and out of his hammock all night so evidently the Durban beer and wine doesn't suit him, but he should be OK after he has had his tot of rum, it will probably make him think about that little number he was with last night, my, he really had his hands full with her! I am not going to say any more about that, the one that I was with is a bit on the quiet side and I am hoping to see her again.

'I thought that I said that I was going to take it easy today,' some hope of that, instead of my usual job as ship side working party I have been detailed off as loading party, that is because we have come out of the dry dock moving alongside the jetty, It is now late in the afternoon and I have been helping to load supplies which is a bit of a back breaking job, the repairs to the Bows is not such a big job as first thought, so the day has ended on a quiet note, I am writing a letter home to my sister then slinging my hammock and turning in, there's nothing like the old Bubbly (Rum) to buck you up.

Early morning on the 25th April, after breakfast I should be working part ship because my job in harbour is still ship side working party, I am reckoning that my first job will be over the side painting the repair work on the bows in a Bosuns chair. Well, I wasn't wrong for after the routine of the ships company of falling in for their duties that is my first job, now a Bosuns chair is a gadget made by two pieces of rope secured to a board on both sides like a swing and believe me working on one of these trying to paint is a bit dicey at times, but there again you do get used to it, just imagine being over the side on one these when stand easy is piped, well now, unless your mate who is up top looking out for you is very quick then most of stand easy could be over as it only lasts a few minutes, now, just for you land lubbers 'stand easy' is the break that we get while working part of ship.

So after a long day the repaired work on the bows can no longer be seen and I am very pleased that there is no more paint work needs doing over the side for a while. The Starboard watch are ashore today so we can have a nice quiet evening in, let's hope that we are still here tomorrow as we still don't know when this attack on Madagascar is going to be, I suppose that information is top secret so that no one ashore gets to know, anyway it will come soon enough I reckon then it will be time to forget all about leave, I am now slinging my hammock, then a game of cards with the lads before I turn in.

Another day has dawned so what job will be waiting for me I wonder, but what the heck it's our turn for a run ashore and this time we are going to take it a bit easier on the drink so as to keep some of that hard earned cash in our pockets, not to throw it about as if there is no tomorrow like we did the last time, that is sailors all over, it's live today for tomorrow may never come of course, that is certainly true every time we put to sea, there is no hiding place out there as you have more than one enemy to contend with. It's washing down paint work for today so after dinner I must do some 'Dhobying' I hope that I have spelt that right as that is the sailors word for washing his clothes (laundering of course,) after that comes the ironing bit, with having to wear all this tropical gear which is all white it's a regular job to keep things clean.

I have just had a dinner that was rotten so let's get ashore and get some real Scran (food) into us, I must say that it's not very often that you get a bad meal although if you don't like what is dished out then it's just your hard luck, but never mind off we go ashore. The girls are outside the dock yard gates in charge of a car this time, they take us out into the country, you wouldn't believe what an amazing time that we had, now this is what sailors desert their ships for, it would be so easy to take to this sort of life instead of putting your life on the line, you know that when you find a nice girl it makes you think quite a lot, well you may never see them again, Eh' I'm really getting morbid aren't I, well, Matelots are renouned for loving them and leaving them.

Back on board again after a night that we will not forget in a hurry, it was just what the doctor ordered, the girls wouldn't let us pay for anything, how about that then? It just goes to show that the girls are genuine and fun loving (and they want to see us again). Back into the old routine, it's the morning after and I feel great, the date is the 26th of April, of cause we are on watch aboard working part ship, my thoughts are still with those two girls, what a fantastic time we had my mate Tom is still full of it, he just can't get that girl out of his head, he has been up to me twice during the morning watch talking about her. It's night time already and the starboard watch have gone ashore again, it's very noticeable as the mess decks have gone very quiet, I am sitting here on the mess bringing my Diary up to date, later there is Housey-Housey aboard the Kelvin who is lying next to us on the Jetty so I will be off to try my luck, I must sling my hammock first.

The morning of the 27th. It should be watch ashore for us tonight if we get the chance, after a lot of scares and buzzes that we might be sailing today, but nothing happens and the Pipe at dinner time clears all that talk, the port watch have been granted leave at the usual times so we get another run ashore, I tell my mate that I think that we better make the most of it this time because we surely will not get the chance again. The girls are there outside waiting for us in the car again and off we went. By the time our leave is up my mate and I are almost broke, what a night we had but we were determined that we would pay our way that time as we guessed it would no doubt be the last time we would see these girls again, although we couldn't tell them that, I am very sorry because I was beginning to take a liking to the girl that I was with (love them and leave them).

It is now the following morning and already the buzzes are going around the mess deck that we are sailing tomorrow, but that's all it is as we never know when we are going to sea until we are told, so if you have told your girlfriend you will be seeing her the next day, well, you could be somewhere on the high seas, and believe me this has happened to me on many occasion, this is to prevent information being passed on ashore (careless talk they call it back home,) well as long as my mate and I get one more run ashore I don't mind, you know it could be that the buzz might be correct because it is now dinnertime and I was to have gone over the side this morning to paint the pennant number G61, I had all the paint and brushes ready, when up came the P.O. to tell me that job is canceled for today, there must be a good reason behind this order (the paint would not be dry if we sailed).

I was correct there is no shore leave for the starboard watch tonight, that can only mean one thing, this ship is sailing tomorrow. I wasn't wrong for early in the morning on the 29th April the starboard watch are already closed up at defence stations and we are preparing to sail, some of the destroyers are already outside the harbour and have been joined by some supply ships also another Cruiser, so we sailed from Durban. My mate sitting here on the mess has just said "hey, there will be two very disappointed girls waiting for a couple of sailors tonight," but as I have said before that is how it goes sometimes, it just can't be helped.

Here we are at last heading for Madagascar and probably some more action. On looking at this convoy I reckon we have twice as many ships now than when we left England, it's a bit choppy at the moment and we have a fair way to go so I hope for the sake of the army lads that the weather doesn't get any worse than it is. I have been thinking that this will probably be the first real action that most of the Javelin crew will have experienced, so let's hope it will be a success. I have just had dinner and I am going on watch this afternoon, so for a few days I reckon it will be back to the old routine of watch keeping.

After sailing for three days we have now closed up at action stations, without any problems we arrive off the coast of Madagascar on the morning of the 5th of May 1942 and hoping to make some history as old Robbo says, that if this is a success, it will be the first made by our lot in this war. It's a fine morning but the sea is still a bit choppy but not enough to worry our lot going ashore. The first thing I saw was the aircraft starting to take off the carrier and heading inshore, we were told their first mission was to drop leaflets warning the Islanders what we were about to do, the idea was to get them to surrender before we started any action so as to save the loss of civilian lives, but apparently it was of no use they didn't want to know. After waiting for some time to pass more of our aircraft went in and this time they were loaded with bombs, very soon explosions could be heard coming from inland.

The troops started to land at different points along the shore, I didn't think they met up with much opposition, but according to reports coming in there was some fierce resistance at some points, an enemy plane came over the convoy but when we opened fire they soon pushed off, unfortunately one of our planes was shot down but the crew managed to parachute safely into the sea very close to the Javelin and was picked up by us. As far as I found out most of our troops were landed at a place called Currier Bay, the Javelin and other Destroyers escorted the troop ships in and screened the Carrier, but a torpedo was fired at her from a submarine which only just missed her, "a very near thing" they said, I wondered why they only fired one 'tin fish,' we were under very little fire but I didn't see any of our ships get hit, I would say that there wasn't much enemy opposition for us, not from the land anyway.

Closed up at action stations but the fighting is still going on ashore, this is the second day of action now and we hear that things are going very well, but the weather out here is getting very rough with the wind getting stronger so we can no longer hear any gun fire coming from ashore and our aircraft seem to have the sky to themselves, they keep on landing on the carrier only to take off again almost immediately so there must still be some action going on inland, funny though we have only seen a few enemy planes, when we all opened up they soon vanished. We are into the first dog watch now and it's <u>all</u> <u>over</u>, the word is that the "Enemy have Surrendered" so all the ships will be going into Curryer Bay.

The storm out here is getting worse, we have been getting buffeted about from these big waves so it was great that the Javelin turned and went into the bay, being the last ones to enter, what a relief it is as this bay is well sheltered land, so we can now take it easy! but I think I spoke too soon because although we anchored we did so for only a short time as we have to move alongside a Tanker we are very low on fuel. A brief respite then back to anchor and all night in for a change, but even though we are not out in the open sea we must stay at a second degree of readiness, we remain at defence stations so we don't have a lot of rest. Sure enough during the morning watch we sail out of the bay and around the coast entering the harbour at Diego Suarez which is the Capital of Madagascar.

I hope that I have spelt the capital right only that is what I have been told, I must say this place is not showing very much damage that I can see from where we are, the good thing is that we are well sheltered in here alongside the jetty, I wonder how long we are going to stay here?

We didn't stay very long that is for sure as at this moment we are now back out at sea again, doing sweeps for enemy submarines and Blockade runners, so it looks like being an all night job for two of us out here, we will certainly not get any rest in this sort of weather, lord help any other ships that are out in this lot. Sure enough comes the morning, it turned out to be just a normal night at sea without a single sight of a ship or pick up of a submarine, it's not surprising that at this moment we are heading back into the harbour. We go alongside one of the supply ships loading up a few provisions, 'I cannot believe it' we are sailing straight out again after we finished loading the few supplies, once more back on patrol, reason being according to Sparks, a signal has been received from a patrolling aircraft that they have sighted a Submarine on the surface, but despite searching all morning, part of the noon watch and covering miles of ocean, all for nothing, so we finally returned to harbour to hear the news that we are going to get some shore leave, well I am amazed! After all that lot we have been put through in the last 24hrs.

Being the watch that's off duty my mate wanted to have a look at the damage on shore, so we changed out of our working rig that we usually wear when we are working part ship or closed up on the guns, into our number one's and fell in on the quarter deck, this is lining up Aft which I think that I have mentioned before in columns of two's, anyway off we went expecting to see all this damage but on walking around the outskirts we were quite surprised as there didn't seem to be much damage at all, what was very surprising was the attitude of the people, they just completely ignored us even though some sort of conversation was attempted, in fact some of them looked as though they could make some trouble, but it was nice to get our feet on solid ground once more, my thoughts are what a beautiful place this must be in peace time.

So strolling along with my mate we didn't bother any more we just carried on and found a couple of the leaflets that had been dropped by our planes, we also happened to find some post cards that had been blown out of a shop window that had come off the worse against the bombs (no looting was the last order), well although it was what I would call a poor run ashore also the first place that we couldn't get a drink of any kind, but as we had only a few hours to see the sights we couldn't go too far away from the dock yard, after all this had been enemy territory only a few days ago.

Back on board again now, while we have been ashore the mail had arrived from home, it's the 14th of May and this is the first lot of mail that we have received since we left England, I have two letters to answer when I get the chance, the other watch have gone ashore for their short time of viewing the place, I hope they have some better luck in communicating with the people of this Island than we did, but we know that they are not going to find anything exciting. Here on the mess deck the lads are wondering how long we are going to stay in this place, while thinking about that we have just been piped to fall in to prepare the ship for sea, that is even before the Starboard watch have returned back on board. But they did just manage it.

Here we are once again out at sea having sailed out of Diego Suarez harbour into gale force winds, on patrol duties we are doing sweeps for any enemy submarines or shipping that maybe heading into Madagascar not knowing that the Island has been taken over by the allies, but the only thing that we did pick a up after almost running them down is a small fishing boat from the Island out doing a spot of fishing, but no harm done, so we sailed back into the harbour during the morning watch going straight alongside one of the supply ships taking on more provisions, then sailing straight out again as usual but this time we are in the company of another Destroyer.

On patrol once more. This weather has turned really atrocious now, it was bad when we went in but it has turned even worse now, I wouldn't think that any one in their right minds would be out in this lot as the sea has now turned mountainous, we rolled, pitched you name it we did everything except sink, it is that bad no one is allowed up on deck and everything had to be battened down, we stuck it out there for so long but it began to be difficult to make way so slowly we made it into Currier Bay again for shelter and safety, It is certainly not fit for any ships to be at sea, I was thankful that we were out of it. The gales carried on for a further two days so we enjoyed the rest although it can also be a very boring time for us sailors as we can't go ashore, Robbo has just summed it up "very easy, it reminds me of Scapa Flow" he couldn't have put it any better.

The gales are beginning to ease up a little now, the Starboard Watch are on duty at defence stations and we have just got under way again, sitting here on the mess I can hear the waves beginning to bang on the side of the ship, on checking the time I find that I am on watch in the next hour. So, here I am now closed up at defence stations and it was a short run back into Diego Suarez Harbour where things seemed to have quietened down considerably, I noticed that a lot of the ships have now gone but the Battleship Ramilies is still here, there doesn't seem to be much left for us to do either except the boring patrols, I don't think the enemy will be trying to take this place back again, but then you never know as Madagascar could be a very big loss to them.

We have been in harbour for a couple of days now doing nothing, but I am pleased to say that we are at one hours notice for sea, (This means that the ship must be ready to sail within one hour) I can't say that I am sorry although it has been a very successful operation, we attained what we set out to do but for us I would say that it's been a bit of a bore with plenty of sea time for the Javelin, but can't wait to get out of this place.

The 19th of May and it's "hands to stations for leaving harbor" has just been piped around the ship so that's the port watch, off I go closing up at my defence station to sail out of Madagascar for the last time I reckon, the aircraft carrier H.M.S. Illustrious followed by a few Destroyers came out and formed up ready for the off, everyone on board giving a sigh of relief I guess as we begin escorting this Carrier to where ever she is going.

No problems while sailing on when we sighted something in the distance, as we approached it we found it to be a craft with five men on board so we lowered a boat to pick them up, we could see they are in a rum state and it turns out that they are four Lascars and a Russian officer, they informed us they had been adrift 32 days.

Watching from the Javelin as a boat is
sent to rescue five Men on a craft

We have now been at sea for three days when land is sighted and we sail into the port of Mombasa on the 22nd of May, we went straight alongside the jetty, after securing I was very surprised that shore leave was piped straight away to the port watch, now having been here lots of times before I know what to expect and I must say that this is not a very exciting place for a run ashore, although there is some places of entertainment where you can get some beer of a sorts and plenty of girls if you wanted one of course, well they did used to have two Brothels here according to one of the lads off the ship that I used to be on, they are of mixed nationalities 'that is all I can tell you.'

Well, as my mate Tom had never been here before as I expect neither have many of the Javelins crew, it will be a big change to Madagascar so I am going ashore with my mate, but the first thing that I noticed on entering the harbour is the amount of shipping that is anchored here, they are mostly merchant ships, this struck me as unusual for this is not a port were you see so many ships, I mentioned it to Robbo and he said it looks like another big convoy because most of them are already Loaded, you can tell by how low they are lying in the water. Anyway off we went ashore straight into one of the dens there which is pretty crowded all ready with Matelots also some civilians, while we were having our first drink of beer I couldn't help but overhear talking on the next seat to us and the lingo is definitely "Midlands," so I said Hey up! what part of the Midlands do you come from, I wasn't surprised when he answered Staffordshire, so I got talking to him only to find out that he comes from the potteries and has a lot of relatives living in Burton-On-Trent, he is off one of the merchant ships, he told me that they are going into the Mediterranean but he didn't know the destination, well we wished him luck which I think that he will really need according to how things are going in the desert, the news is that Rommel's troops are pushing our lads back in the desert right up to the outskirts of Tobruck.

While here in Mombasa I received some very sad news which upset me quite a lot, when Tom and I was ashore we went into a place that is frequented by most of the forces especially the English Matelot's, anyway who should we see in here but Robbo, he called me over as soon as he spotted us to give me the news that he had just heard, that my old ship H.M.S. Dorsetshire and H.M.S. Cornwall have been sunk by Japanese dive bombers on the 5th of April, of course he knew that she was my last ship and wondered if I still had mates aboard her, well, obviously I was very shocked, I had quite a lot of mates aboard her including my old friend Walter Fudge who I joined up with way back, but one thing I am most sure about if fate hadn't intervened I would have certainly been aboard her, I suppose that I have the Medical officer at North Shields to thank, the reason for this as I have already explained was because I was taken ill while I was a member of the Dorsetshire crew, I can't help but think about my old mate Walt, wondering if he survived, my action station aboard her after she was a recommissioned ship in North Shields was B Magazine, I wonder what chance I would have had if I was still on her 'not forgetting that I can't swim a stroke', I reckon that it would all depend on how quick she went down as those Magazines are a couple of decks down on those Cruisers and of course there would have been a mad scramble to get back up top, "well, here's hoping you and all my old ship mates survived Walt."

Back on board with not much going on apart from working part ship I have noticed that some of the merchant ships have left in a small convoy.

The second day here and getting plenty of shore leave but the only problem again is money as I have already said we don't get paid very much, a few runs ashore and our money has soon gone, well us Matelots don't go ashore just to see the sights, we go ashore for nothing but a good time being it might be our last, Eh, I'm getting morbid again aren't I. I'm sitting here on the mess looking at old Robbo, he is broke and bored stiff, he can't wait to get back to sea again, you may not believe this being war time but we sailors do get really bored stiff if we stay in harbour too long and really do want to get back to sea again.

But things don't always work out the way that we want them to, we have been here for almost a week so everyone is really browned off (fed up in other words, I don't mean sun burnt,) now after falling in for duty after having stand easy, a hint was dropped by one of the sparks, that we would be sailing tomorrow, sure enough in the morning of the 28th of May "hands to stations for leaving harbor" is piped and Javelin sails out of Mombasa on her own. Now it is nearly half way through the morning watch, I am closed up at defence stations, we have only been at sea a few hours when we heard the news that the Battleship H.M.S. Ramillies has been sunk in Diego Suarez harbour by a Japanese submarine, now how about that then Eh! that could have been any one of us that had taken part in that action 'makes you think doesn't it,' apparently a Japanese submarine had somehow got into Suarez harbour, there is more bad news which we received a few moments ago, there are a lot of casualties.

Here we are out on the high seas. After sailing for nearly a week we arrive at the port of Aden in the Red sea, if there is one place that I never wished to see again it's this one in my opinion it's a terrible place as I pointed out the Incident that occurred when I was here last, it's where the old people are left to die on the roadside so I won't go into it again.

June 3rd 1942 no shore leave has been given and after a very short stay we sailed out of this god forsaken place into the Red Sea once more, a sea so calm it was just like a mirror, now at this very moment I am sitting here at the mess table writing this in my diary and knowing that for certain we are going to the Mediterranean, it just couldn't be anywhere else as we go sailing on into the red sea and not the Indian Ocean, so sailing for three days we are now just entering the port of Suez which is almost at the entrance of the great Suez Canal, I have also been here a couple of times before but I have never been ashore though I would have liked to have seen what it is like, but we have never stayed here long enough for us to get that run ashore, now I have always wanted to know what it would be like to sail down this great wonder of the world but never dreamed that one day I would be doing just that, I had better start believing it because after a few hours stay at Suez on the 7th of June we are actually entering the Suez Canal.

Slowly so as to not make any excessive wash along the banks, a certain speed only is allowed going down the canal, the scenery that we are seeing on both sides of the banks is a sight to behold, sights that you never forget and the fact that I saw my first ever Camel in the flesh for a start, now I could go on about the canal for quite some time but you can't really express in words the feelings one gets when actually traveling down it, you just have to be here to have the remotest idea of what it's like, eventually our journey ends as we arrive at Port Said, which is the last port at the other end of the canal, now as it is nearly dark we moor alongside the jetty and make fast, so it seems as though we are having a night in here, no shore leave is granted but then again I don't think that anyone expected any.

Robbo our killick says that we are not missing anything by not going ashore here, he should know, he says that he has been this way quite a few times before the war, and that unless it has altered a lot there isn't anything to get excited about, the food isn't all that good either, so up goes my hammock ready for an easy night's sleep without any noise from drunken Matelots bumping and barging into it while I am asleep, anyway someone may pinch my place.

Come the morning we don't seem to be getting ready for sea yet but after breakfast the hands are being piped to fall in to start working part ship, for how long? I wonder. Now, that wasn't long because he is now piping again that the ship will be sailing during the dog watches, which is carried out during the second dog watch (don't forget this is the 6pm-8pm,) the Javelin is sailing out into the Mediterranean sea at this very moment.

The idea of sailing into the Med In the evening is taken so as to avoid any enemy aircraft, we sailed through the night in what some Matelots consider to be the most dangerous waters in this war, anyway someone must think so because here we are now. The morning watch is only one hour old and we are at action stations, sailing on we eventually arrive at that great port of Alexandria on the 8th of June 1942. At this moment I am sitting here on the mess deck and I will explain to you about my diary, quite a lot of what I write is scribbled into a note book which I keep on my person at all times while I am on watch, so whatever is happening at that moment I write it down if I can, then I write it in my diary when I get the chance, I also include the everyday happenings, but during any action 'obviously' my diary has to wait until afterwards, although it is sometimes possible during a break in the action to make a few notes, furthermore I have been informed by certain people that it is against naval rules to keep diaries in war time so I have to be as discrete as possible.

Now, what a fantastic sight Alexandria is, it has a great big harbour and all the buildings are white, we have just passed through the boom which is guarded by two boom defence vessels, now the job of these two small ships is to open and close the boom which is a steel wire netting attached to floating buoys, it is in two sections which stretches across the entrance of the harbour and is a great defence against enemy submarines but has to be opened and closed to allow ships to enter and leave, anyway Javelin has now dropped anchor close to the jetty, 'and this is Egypt.'

The big surprise to me on entering this great big harbour is the amount of ships that are anchored here, ships of all sizes from small to Battleships, also tied up to buoys are two very large ships, I am told one is a Destroyer Depot ship and the other a Submarine Depot ship, also noticeable are two big Cruisers and two Destroyers coupled up to one another in the middle of the harbour again secured to buoys, now these are French as I've noticed they are flying the French Ensigns. Our Skipper is about to speak over the tannoy to the ships company at this moment, after his speech he tells us the reason for us being in Alexandria is that we are now officially part of the Eastern Mediterranean Fleet.

In his speech the Skipper made it very clear to the whole ships company to be very wary of the natives, going on to explain a few more issues of things to be aware of when on shore, then said that shore leave will be granted to all the port watch from 16.30hrs until 22.00hrs, cheers went up on the mess decks, I should say that we will have to turn too working part ship for the rest of the day. I am really looking forward to this first leave here in Alexandria Egypt, a place that I had read a lot about when I was a kid at school but never in my wildest dreams thought that one day I would actually be going ashore there.

So here we are, after a day's work on part ship it's shore leave for us the port watch, all dressed up in nice white shorts and shirts, very smart as we walked through the gates of the dock yard, we were instantly mobbed by half a dozen of these native Egyptians. Now, Robbo has already warned us of the tricks that these people get up to so we are reasonably prepared for some of the things, one in particular is about being robbed blind, all our money has been changed into Egyptian currency so we are now dealing in Piastres, so it is pretty easy to see how problems are going to arise working this money out for the first time, which didn't take too long for us to have the first one.

Most of the lads were having the same trouble as us, when at least a dozen Gharries (I think that is how they spell it, they are horse drawn carriages which is the mode of transport to get around Alexandria) are all waiting to take us into Alexandria, the drivers (the Gharry men) were all fighting to get our custom, the same thing is happening to our shipmates, it is getting into a bit of a mess, anyway while we are all having this trouble along came a Matelot who could see that we are having some problems, evidently he had been here for some time and knows how to handle these natives, he sorted us out and told us how much to pay them, also where to go in Alex, so off we went to enjoy big eats with a nice cold beer. For the first time in my life I found myself enjoying a horse drawn carriage ride through the streets of Alexandria with my mate Tom, we also got a lot of information from the Gharry man.

Following the advice of the lad who came to our rescue we found ourselves at the Fleet club, this is where most of the sailors in Alexandria go for a meal, I was amazed when we walked into the place and looked around because you can buy practically anything in here, a great meal for a start is our first priority and with no rationing of any kind, plenty beer of sorts (Stella) sold in cans, it is ice cold, take it from me the only real beer is sold back home in England, you can stay here all day if you want but like the UK they close at night, I reckon that they must do pretty well as the place was crowded with Matelo's. We got talking to a few of the lads who have been based here in Alex for some months now, they put us in the picture regarding the natives and how to handle them. But never go alone anywhere here in Alex and do not flash any amount of money about also remember keep out of the no go areas.

The information they gave us is that this is a great place for a run ashore when you are used to the ways of the natives and their money, but there are some areas which are out of bounds to all allied troops, 'girls and sex' well there is plenty of that here, there are two Brothels one which is actually run by the Royal Navy the other is a public one known all over the world as "Sister Street Alexandria" this has been here way before the war and anyone is allowed admittance in this one, where as the Naval one only allows seafarers to enter and is under the supervision of Naval medical officers, the lads also warned us that Alexandria is alive with prostitutes so 'beware' is their warning, that was the start of our first run ashore in Alexandria.

We are back on board again now after having a smashing time ashore, but there is much more to see, some of the sights here are really something, in the short time that we were ashore I thought the Egyptian way of life is 'amazing' even though we have only seen a very small part of it. After all night in that hammock of mine I certainly feel great, to start the day off we have been told by the P.O. that we will be moving alongside the jetty to pick up some more stores, but it will not be bothering me as I am mess man again today. Broke off writing for a bit as "all hands fall in" is piped as we move from our berth in the harbour and are now alongside the jetty.

Well, I certainly found out how the other half lives today, why is that? you may ask, I was amazed at the events that followed our securing alongside the jetty, for we had no sooner secured when two or three natives came onto our mess deck followed by our killick 'Robbo' who told me that they had been allowed on board by the Captain to take any 'Gash' (left over food) left over on the messes after meals, but the most disgusting and surprising thing that I have ever seen took place right in front of my eyes, they immediately went straight to the gash buckets which are situated at the end of every mess table, they are there for the sole purpose of scraping all the leftover food from the tables, tea leaves, washing up water and cigarette ends, you name it and it goes into the gash bucket, it is then thrown overboard, that didn't bother these chaps though, they dived their hands into the bucket and lifted out all the scraps of floating food depositing it into large empty tomato tins which they carry about with them, this is not the only incident that I have seen that has really turned my stomach either, after we had dropped our anchor they were waiting in boats by the gash chutes and as soon as any of the lads went to empty their buckets down the chutes there was a mad scramble to see what in the way of food was in the water, be it stale bread or meat fat anything floating that was edible was quickly fished out of the water and went into that tin, now that is what I call seeing how the other half live, this style of survival is how a lot of these people have to live, being very poor.

The job of provisioning ship over, we have been here for four days now and the shore leave has been getting better every time, In this short time we have seen more and more Merchant ships enter the harbour, that remark of Robbo's about this looking like a Convoy job springs to mind once more, whilst leaning on the guard rails looking around this lot during the second dog watch I noticed that one or two of the Merchant ships are beginning to get steam up with the amount of smoke coming out of their funnels, although it is usual to do this two or three days before they sail.

Whilst writing this in my diary I have just realized that it's my birthday today, It is 11th June 1942, and of all things I am twenty one years old, Ruddy marvelous eh! It just goes to show how much dates mean to you when you are on a small ship, they have no meaning at all to us as every day is the same, It's entirely different when on the bigger ships because they have Chaplains on board, Sunday services and notice boards which you can't but help notice the dates on them from time to time, anyway what a time to find out it's your twenty-first birthday when the day is almost done, never mind it would not have made a difference anyway because I have never received any birthday cards whilst I have been in the Navy.

A couple of days have passed since I mentioned those Merchant ships getting up steam, today there has been a heck of a lot of activity in the harbour, we have just been told that leave has been stopped for tonight so it looks as though Robbo's convoy remark is coming true again. As the light begins to fade we sail out of Alexandria harbour and lay off the boom, there is also a lot of activity going on out here at the moment, a lot more ships are coming out including Cruisers and more Destroyers, among these is H.M.S. Jervis who is "Captain D" of the Destroyers, that means that he is the senior officer and in sole command of all the Destroyers, which have now anchored and for what? There are Aldis lamps flashing all over the place so that must mean a Convoy (Aldis lamps are a means of communicating between ships.)

Laying off the boom all night as I said, and as dawn comes up the boom opens up as we watch ship after ship come sailing out, all have started to take up formation into a very large convoy, all of the Destroyers started to take up their screening positions all around, 'so now we know.' But what everyone wants to know is where are we heading with this large convoy? Just as we started to get slowly under way an enemy plane appeared high up, evidently this is a spotter plane so Gerry will soon know what we are about to do.

Then comes the pipe over the tannoy that the Captain is about to speak to the ships company, his words were "You are all wondering where we are going with this large convoy of Merchant ships, well I can tell you now, but first I would just like to say that most of you have been with me for some time now, having been in actions before, but my message to you lads who have not seen any action, by Christ you're going to see some this time as we are going to try and get this convoy of Merchant ships through to Malta as the Maltese people need these supplies urgently, also I must tell you that the convoy from the other end of the Mediterranean who has made the attempt have failed, unfortunately every ship bar one was sunk."

After the Captain had finished his speech the ship closed up to action stations, the night passed off peaceful. It's now early morning and the weather is fine, the sun has just broken over the horizon, I am at my action station which is ammunition supply to P1 Oerlikon a fast firing ack-ack (anti-aircraft) gun and my mate Tom is strapped in to the gun by a belt which assists him in swinging the gun around and elevating it, we have received a warning from the bridge to keep a lookout over on the horizon as the sun comes up, for enemy aircraft, but they didn't come out of the sun as expected but from high up out of a clear blue sky, Junkers 88s and Stuka dive bombers (the spotter plane that we saw last night had done his job), with engines screaming they came diving in, the noise was terrible as all hell broke loose, every ship in the convoy opened up with everything they had. Watching those planes come diving in makes you wonder how the hell can they possibly get through all that gun fire without being hit, but they did get through, bombs were dropping all over the place, there was that many planes we couldn't possibly count them, I would say at a guess there was at least fifty, but we were so busy firing at every aircraft that approached or came into our area that we didn't have time to look around, or to see what damage was being done to other ships.

There was one big Merchant ship close on our port bow and we couldn't help but see her receive a hit, as the dive bomber seemed to be heading our way, we banged away at it but it's target was the Merchant ship, we actually saw debris fly into the air as the bomb struck, she immediately began to drop astern of us, a Corvette that was over on her starboard side could be seen going to her assistance but I didn't envy them one little bit, as there is safety in numbers here in the Med, but on your own, well, I wouldn't give much for your chances.

Taken from the Javelin. One of our Destroyers
putting up a smoke screen.

The attack was still going on as the planes kept on coming
in, but not altogether now as they had made their surprise on
the first attempt, some hadn't been able to drop their bombs
so they gained some height ready to make a second attack and
were coming in ones and twos, we saw a small Merchant ship
hit with what looked like two bombs, one of these definitely
landed on her stern but we couldn't see how badly damaged
she was until we started going past her, then we could clearly
see that her back end was just a mass of twisted metal plating,
I reckon that she is unnavigable too as she dropped well astern
of us, two of the smaller escorts dropped out and begin to
follow her.

With all of this going on you might think that we would
have been scared, admittedly the noise that these dive bombers
make when they come diving in is a bit scary, but it's the speed
that things happen, it's all so very quick, so the funny thing
about it all is that you don't have time to be scared, you do

things automatically and carry on doing what you have been trained to do, that is to make sure that if any Gerry plane comes near enough he's going to get everything you've got, you even wish that one does come close enough for you to blast him into the sea, just keep those guns firing, you have no nerve at all. While this lot was still going on my mate Tom said "what do you reckon happens to the ships that drop out of the convoy?" I replied "if they have got any sense they give her all they've got and head for the nearest allied port, but I honestly wouldn't like to be in their shoes."

Well those attacks went on all day long but not continuous as they have to break off when their bombs have gone, some of them even had a go at us with machine guns when they got low enough, sweeping in over the convoy and out again, but this put them at risk, I did see one plunge into the sea after being hit by gun fire. They didn't leave us alone long before they came back again, but not as many as there was in the previous attack, these were the Torpedo bombers and just three of them, they came in as the sun was setting on the horizon, we were having a bit of a breather when the shout went up 'here they come' and not far away and from a different direction this time, then a shout through the headphones "E-boats on the starboard bow," these are very fast motor Torpedo boats which are similar to our own M.T.B's, these are well over on our starboard side and not in range of our guns but like the Torpedo bombers they are a target for main armament as well as the smaller ack-ack guns on any of the ships.

What a sight! As I looked through the binoculars shells could be seen splashing among them, they soon turned away just like the Torpedo bombers, they didn't manage to hit a single ship that we could see although we had the satisfaction of seeing one Torpedo bomber hit the sea and explode, then they all pushed off and we sailed on into the ever growing darkness, by now everybody aboard the Javelin must be really shattered and hungry, we hadn't had anything to eat or drink all day, it had been 'real hell,' nobody had been allowed to leave their action stations to go down to the mess decks. Now that night had fallen the Skipper decided that one man from each section would be allowed to go down to the galley and get each man a mug of soup and biscuit's I have never tried these biscuit's before, they look like those big square dog biscuit's to me, on trying them I found that they are very hard, dry and tasteless, but being hungry you either ate them or went without and like a good dog, er, I mean sailor, we did eat them.

I thought that with it being night now we should at least get some respite from the bombers, after all we still have a lot of Merchant ships left to deliver to Malta, looking at my young mate Tom I can't help but feel sorry for him, after all it's no ideal task being strapped into one of those ack-ack guns swinging backwards and forwards, firing at aircraft that are in and out of your view in a flash, there are quite a lot of young lads aboard Javelin and this must be their first piece of real action, I really do feel sorry for them for I reckon that we have not seen the last of Gerry.

I was going to take the first turn while Tom had forty winks, I thought well we should be OK for a few hours before dawn, but it just goes to show how wrong you can be, although just for a short time, about a couple of hours nothing happened, I had the headphones on as I was keeping a lookout (someone has to be on watch and in touch with the bridge at all times,) we are sailing along when all at once the night sky was lit up as Calcium Flares came floating down from the starlit sky, at that point clearly in my headphones came the message from the bridge, to all Quarters to keep a sharp lookout for E-boats, I could see almost at once that there are a lot of gun flashes coming from well over on the other side of the convoy, so it looks as though they are in trouble once again.

I had to give my mate a nudge and not long after he pointed out a glow in the distance which could be seen clearly against the night sky, which can only mean that another ship is on fire, we have no idea what is going on over there but somebody must be in real trouble, we can see the tracers being fired so they must still be fighting back, here where we are, the flares are beginning to come down and are lighting up the whole convoy, then bombs begin to fall, these are from high level bombers, they are not the normal single or couple of bombs according to the splashes, they are what is termed as a stick of bombs, these drop more or less in a line and they certainly rained down, great water spouts shot up seemingly only a few hundred yards off our starboard quarter.

Now, the problem is that these planes are too high up for our ack-ack guns to have a chance of hitting any, our main armament will not elevate to the angle that would allow us to fire at them either, so there is not a lot that we can do against them as we cannot even see them, what makes it even worse is that you never know where the bombs are going to strike next, It's a different war altogether, meanwhile helpless as we are, we sail on, the air attack is still going on when surprisingly we pull out of the convoy and form up with a few of the other Destroyers and Cruisers, we set off at high speed leaving the convoy to fend for itself for some unknown reason.

I reckon that everybody on board will be breathing a sigh of relief after getting away from those flares and the high level bombers, It is really hopeless as you know that you can't do anything against them, it is just left to the Cruisers with their big high angle ack-ack guns to have a go.

So into the night we sailed with no idea at all as to where we are going or what is going on, that is until the Skipper spoke from the bridge, passing a message to all stations that the reason for leaving the convoy is that a force of Italian warships have left harbour and is at this moment heading towards us for the purpose of intercepting our convoy, so we are now on our way to intercept them just to make sure that they don't get anywhere near our ships at any cost.

As we sailed on we wondered what to expect. I can tell you we are very tired and weary men, I know that I could eat a horse at this moment but I reckon that it will be soup and ships biscuit's if and when we get the chance to eat. It could be a lost cause if we don't stop this Italian force, then again we are certainly not going to let those enemy ships get anywhere near our defenceless Merchant ships, the wording is "at all cost" so that's what it will have to be, this is what is called the British Navy tradition and although we are a far smaller force going into action against a far bigger and heavier force, Go in with all guns blazing and drop your tin fish as close as you can I reckon.

Onwards and ready for a big battle, expecting to hear that call "enemy in sight," after sailing for some time with everybody on the alert, when all at once the Aldis lamps start to flash between the leading Cruiser and H.M.S. Jervis the senior Destroyer Skipper, this could mean that the enemy have been sighted, but no, and we begin to do a full turn as are the rest of the force, nobody could make any sense of this until once again the Skipper passes a message to all quarters from the bridge that we have now received orders to turn back and rejoin the convoy again as a signal has been received from the C-in-C to the Rear Admiral Vian, (who is in total command of this fleet,) that an order has been given for the R.A.F. To send a bomber force to attack the enemy warships 'at last the air-force are going to do something.'

It really is <u>Amazing</u>! Because up to now in the attempt to get these vital supplies through to Malta we have yet to see an allied fighter plane give us some sort of cover, but I hope this is not going to be the case all the way through as I think that we are certainly going to need some help at times, otherwise this is going to be a piece of cake for the dive bombers. Having now turned around I can honestly say that we are very relieved for it would certainly have been some action, that is, enemy Battleships with their big long range guns against our Cruisers and Destroyers.

We have been sailing for some time when the news is passed around the ship that we were less than one hours sailing time from meeting up with the Italian force when we received the recall signal. Heading back to the convoy and making all speed, as we approach, but from a fair distance away we see they are still in a lot of trouble, we can see the calcium flares still floating down from the sky and the tracers from the guns can be seen clearly going up into the night sky. Here we go again, we take up our positions once more screening the convoy, the bombs are still coming down around us and it seems as though there are more bombers up there because it's getting considerably worse, I wonder if we have lost any ships whilst we have been away?

We are told that they have had some respite for almost two hours, joking my mate says "yes they've waited until we got back." It does seem that the flares are coming down more regularly and we can't do a damn thing about it, the problem with the flares are that they come drifting down so slowly, then when they light you up your expecting a stick of bombs to come crashing down on your ship, but as long as we keep on changing course regularly it makes it all the more difficult for the planes up there to get a fix a target.

Once again a message is passed down the phone's from the bridge to keep a good lookout for E-boats, as a search light from one of the Cruisers has just picked some of them up, coming into attack the convoy over on our starboard beam, but they are too far away from our guns for us to have a go at them and in any case we have to be sure of our target otherwise we could be endangering other ships in the convoy, but just because we can't have a go at them doesn't mean someone else couldn't and they are certainly having a battle over there according to the flashes from some of the guns. It all ended with a massive flash of light and explosion, the fading night sky became lit up, 'so what was that?'

The convoy sailed on towards Malta and another day of hell. I suspect with the night now drawing to a close it means that we have to be very alert as the dawn approaches bringing the sun, which will be climbing over that horizon spreading it's brilliance across the sea so bright that it pains the eyes to have to keep on staring into it, on the lookout for what we know for sure will soon be appearing 'torpedo's with their death dealing loads', they will come in low down hugging the tops of the waves and spread out so as to make the targets more difficult, but if we can spot them soon enough the Cruisers will open up with their big guns getting the range, it will force them to drop their tin fish at a distance, then this gives the ships chance to alter course, the torpedo's missing their intended targets we hope.

I can only say that there will be some very tired eyes looking through binoculars as the sun rises over that Mediterranean sky line, It's no joke when you have been staring through these things hour after hour, not just looking at the horizon but also at the silvery water with it's blinding glare for the tell tale periscope of the submarine, this is what makes it so hard and very dangerous every time a ship puts to sea because we have to watch for the enemy not just on the surface of the water but also underneath it and 'of course' the sky, to be attacked by more than one at the same time makes it obviously very difficult, there is no hiding place for a ship in war time, on top of all that we have to contend with very bad weather at times

(I'm not moaning, just stating a fact). At this moment my mate and I are dying for a drink, but before we can think about it anymore the E-boats come in, first on our port side, firing guns at us from a distance, though they would not be allowed to get in range, but they stand no chance against the screening Destroyers 4.7" guns and the fast firing pom-pom also those of the Cruisers, they are soon driven off. I wonder why they didn't try with their tin fish? It could be that they are saving them for a big target perhaps, but while we are pondering these things, the Torpedo bombers came in hoping to catch us out while we are having to watch the E-boats, they don't seem to want to get too close this time because we all (that is everyone that can) open fire, they drop their torpedoes at some distance but I didn't see one find it's target.

It isn't very long after the planes have gone over the horizon that the dive bombers put in their appearance, In they come screaming down from a great height, for some reason they seem to be having a go at the escorts this time, they were more spread out making it a more difficult because you can only fire at one target, one seemed to pick us out as it came around the stern, but then went for a Destroyer just off our stern, he started to dive onto his target and the ship slewed slightly all her guns and ours are blazing away, the plane was hit halfway into it's dive and crashed right on the back end of that Destroyer astern of us, the pilot never stood a cat in hells chance.

It was so close, then, right before our eyes a huge flash, a terrific explosion with smoke and debris flying skywards, some dropping very close to our stern, it all happened so very quickly, in a matter of minutes, straight away Javelin dropped astern to pick up survivors, but there was nothing but a sea covered in floating debris, everyone on the upper deck scoured the water hoping to see lads swimming but we couldn't see anybody, It was a terrible sight, 'one that we will never forget,' to see these horrible things happen right before your eyes is terrible and most of Javelins crew saw this incident, the awful thing is that we don't have any time to dwell on it.

There is so much going on around us, these dive bombers are certainly not going to give us any rest, they keep on coming and are so predictable, they go into their dive so fast with engines screaming and out again very quick after dropping their bombs, there is just a split second to fire that gun. It isn't all going the bombers way though, as I saw some planes hit by gun fire and crash into the sea, one in particular a torpedo bomber which had the audacity to fly low down in between the ships and down the side of the Javelin to get among the Merchant ships, It was plastered by every gun that could bear and blows up then hit's the water, a few of the lads about our position give a muted cheer as the attack is now over. Apart from the Destroyer astern of us we didn't see any other ships actually go down, but we can't see what happens over on the other side of the convoy. Things happen when you are in these actions, you dare not take your eyes off anything and you are looking out for whatever is going to appear in front of you at any moment, you keep on waiting for what you know is certain to come.

While planes are diving at ships, guns are blazing away all over the place 'it seems like a nightmare,' but in our Skipper we have the satisfaction of knowing that we have the best for he's been 'bloody marvelous,' he has slewed this ship all over the place avoiding the dive bombers, I actually saw him once, when we were the target of one particular bomber, pick up a Lewis gun off it's tripod on the side of the bridge and as the plane came diving in at us he held it up like a rifle and opened up, blazing away at the plane, one of it's bombs just missed our bow, falling down the side of the ship, it was marvelous 'what a man.' The problem with these attacks is you just do not know which direction the next raid is going to come from, you could be watching one plane over on the port beam when another one is already coming in from the Starboard side.

We are still living on Kye (another name for cocoa which is made in such a way that a spoon will almost stand up in it), it's real good stuff on a cold wet night also ships biscuit's with occasional mugs of soup. Well, you just dare not nod off, it's a matter of relaxing when you can, that means between raids but it's a hell of a job trying to keep awake I can tell you. As we are nearing Malta the raids are going to get more frequent, I reckon more planes will be taking part as they are nearer to their bases, so we can expect both the Junkers 88s with the Stuka dive bombers together again, but I don't think the lads are caring too much now being really tired out and dirty, I'm sure that in their minds most of them are thinking that we are not going to make it to Malta anyway.

How much longer are we going to have to keep this up? The amount of firing that we have done since we left Alexandria means we must be running very low on ammunition as I reckon most of the other ships will be. As the day drags on we are surprised that we haven't been attacked by quite so many planes, I suppose we can put it down to the fact that the pilots of these planes need a rest just the same as we do. Coming towards evening on this second day the E-boats have another go at us but they don't succeed in getting through the screen and are driven off, no respite for us as the sun is getting low in the sky, in they come, this time from all over the place, dive bombers, just at that moment my mate looked at me and said "well Nick it looks as though this is it."

Almost immediately as the dive bombers come diving in I saw one of our ships a Destroyers receive a hit and she appears to stop straight away, Javelin (being very close to her) goes straight to her assistance, as it is getting towards sunset I think that if she can only stay afloat until it gets really dark then we may have a chance of getting her to Malta, anyway I can see that she is in some serious trouble that's for sure, she is a sitting duck for anything that may come along, so the Skipper decides to take her in tow, 'now we are really asking for trouble,' not only one but two sitting ducks, anyway we receive a signal from the big man on the Cruiser to say "carry on with the tow, make best possible speed and good luck" now, it takes some time to get things ready to tow a ship in normal conditions but this is going to be a heck of a job and we have to do this as quickly as possible, also hoping it's possible to do this during action.

We don't have a clue as to what is going on around us because all we can hear is the scream of the dive bombers and our main armament firing as our guns are blasting away at the Torpedo bombers, while our ack-ack guns are trying to keep the dive bombers away from the Destroyer, which is now lying stationary and swinging around helpless. On board Javelin everything is being made ready for the towing of the stricken ship, the steel wire hawser that is going to tow her is being run out down the waste and we eventually manage to get a line aboard her, so now we can pass them the wire hawser ready for the tow, but after some problems we manage it and set off very slowly after the convoy, which is now some distance away on the horizon.

There is one good thing about our problem, that is it won't be long before it's dark. But crawling at this speed make's us such an easy target for enemy planes not to mention the submarines and E-boats, well the darkness can't come quick enough for me now. On looking back we are in the same position as the poor devils that had to drop out of the convoy way back and we said at the time "poor devils I wouldn't like to be in their place," now we are in a similar situation but no sooner said, a plane appears high up and drops some bombs which actually fall just off our bow, at the same instance the alarm is given of the approach of three torpedo bombers from over on our starboard quarter, surely this must be their last fling, it is a bit of a late surprise to say the least because they usually attack in early morning sun rise, certainly not as late as this. The reason they are here at all is because of the single bomber that sent a signal letting them know what is going on out here. Once again my mate said "how much more are we going to take," 'my thoughts too' as we are in a very vunerable position, crawling along at a slow rate of knots that I can't hazard a guess at, and coming in at us at a very fast speed are three planes with their deadly loads, all we can do is head straight towards them so as to make their target as small as possible, also to give us a chance to fire at them with our main armament as well as the ack-ack guns, fortunately for us, with our shells falling amongst them they must have lost their nerves because they drop their tin fish a fair way off, which missed us by some distance, and in the fading light we didn't see any torpedo's at all.

We are well and truly on our own now, the convoy is now out of sight having sailed on, I don't know if that's good or bad for us, they have left us with one other ship to help, Just as I am thinking about this the tow parts, and I can tell you that every man on board is praying for that darkness to come very quickly. When a tow rope parts it's a heck of a job trying to pick up the loose end again it takes us a long time and some very hard work, so after what seemed hours we managed to pick up the end and get it back on board the other ship, at the same time we are stationary in mid ocean, two ships just sitting here waiting for submarines that could be anywhere, I can honestly say that messing about with a stricken vessel is a very nerve racking job, you get that terrible feeling that anything can happen, you're just helpless to do anything about it, there is nothing more scary for a Matelot than being stationery in mid ocean.

We could get blown out of the water at any second this is one hell of a situation to be in. I am writing this down as I stand here alongside Tom, we don't know what is actually going on aboard the Destroyer, with everybody getting more nervous as the time goes by. We waited a good two hours until we got coupled up again, there must have been a big sigh of relief from everybody aboard when those screws started to turn. In this sort of situation it does really get to you though, but then you get to thinking about the poor blokes on the other Destroyer, what it must be like for them, without us, they have no hope at all.

The Skipper must realize how low the crews moral is at this time, he has a message passed to all quarters, "if we can hold off the enemy planes and E-boats until it gets properly dark, then I will be willing to Splice the mainbrace," well I can tell you that for a tot of the old bubbly 'Jack would walk on water.' We don't have very long to think about it as the E-boats come in for attack, I can only count four of them but once again the barrage that is put down by us seems to do the trick, and they get more than what they bargain for and give up. It isn't a long wait but well worth it and after a short time we sail on into total darkness, and true to his word, the

Skipper orders "Splice the mainbrace" then two killicks come round to each man at his action station and issue one tot of neat rum 'Great,' now bring them on I hear clearly over my headphones which puts a smile on my tired weary face.

During the night the tow rope gives us a heck of a lot of problems, we have to stop again after it parts once more, it is therefore decided to put a double rope on and at last we manage to keep on going until morning. this was going to be the decider for Javelin and the stricken ship, everybody is wondering just what is going to be waiting for us when the sun comes up, It is a certainty that the Gerries are not going to let us tow this stricken Destroyer all the way to Malta, in the state that we are in, so blinking tired and of course very hungry it's going to be a big job. I reckon more important now as old Robbo mentioned when he brought the rum around, we must be almost out of ammunition. I can't believe that we are going to make it out of this mess and if those dive bombers do come back in any numbers this morning, then I'm afraid that we have had it, I know that I am not the only one who is thinking this, even Robbo's passing words might ring true "keep your heads down and your life belt up."

It's so blindingly obvious we just don't stand a cat in hells chance of surviving and that will be two more ships to add to those already gone, I don't think prayers are going to be of much use to us now, it's a far different thing when you can go fast, you can slew these Destroyers all over the place so when the bombers go into their dive you are not there when he gets to the bottom, and a fast moving target blazing away at you with all it's guns is a far more formidable one than one crawling along towing another vessel, all I can hope is that I will still be here tomorrow to carry on with my diary, 'one can only hope.' The daylight arrives and as always here in the Med we can expect a brilliant sunny morning, everyone is alert as much as they possibly can be and expecting this to be "The Day" then of all things that bloody tow parted again.

What a time for this to happen, it is very early yet but we have now got the problem all over again, and for what? there is certainly no time for any more messing about trying to get this ship to Malta which is yet another days sailing away. I reckon that if the convoy does not have any more problems they should be making that harbour tomorrow morning, but not us I'm afraid, if it is at all possible it will take us at least another two days, anyway we are still going to try, we have picked up the tow rope again and in quick time have secured it so we are under way again slowly. Then without warning we are being attacked by enemy dive bombers, there are six and they come in screaming as usual, we open up with everything we have, and how those planes missed us I don't know, the bombs are dropped and they are gone.

I just couldn't believe our luck as bombs that did drop just missed us, 'Christ that was a very close thing,' anyway immediately after the attack, just as we were making some headway again so as to clear this area before any more planes have a go, we receive a signal from the admiral in charge of the convoy ordering our Skipper to take off the entire crew of the of the stricken ship when it is convenient, then sink her. So the message was passed over to the other ship then we had to wait around for some time while everyone got ready for the evacuation, there is one or two injured men to be prepared for transfer and it has to be done as quickly as possible.

So this is a task easier said than done, apparently our Skipper has given them a time limit so that the ships company could collect all their personal belongings, he then sent down one of the leading hands to our mess deck to make sure that everything would be ready to receive them. And so time up, Javelin goes alongside the other ship at a prearranged signal as quickly as possible to start the evacuation, the Destroyer is beginning to list a fair bit now, It is very early in the morning and speed is essential as we are both now stopped in the water, once again we could be in big trouble, for any E-boat could pick us off easy at their speed, in and out very fast, then again there is the U-boat, what an easy target we are making for their torpedoes, what a prize that would be for them just one torpedo that is all it would take to sink the two ships, blow them sky high, all the crews with them.

But our first task is the injured men, well, talking of crews these lads coming on board turn out to be Australians the ship is H.M.A.S. Nestor. 'What do you know' cheekily flying over head is a Spotter plane having a good look, wishing I reckon that he had a few bombs on board because there's two sitting ducks down here but he soon pushed off. After the injured it wasn't long before we had a large part of the crew aboard and as the sun had not arrived on the horizon yet we are pretty sure that we had got away with it, now everyone is off the stricken ship, we stood off a bit and watched as her own charges exploded, then to conserve our ammunition problem the Skipper ordered her to be blown up by firing depth charges at her. I actually managed to take a couple of photos of her going down after our charges had exploded, I could see a fair number of her crew standing in the port waste watching as their old ship sank beneath the waves of the Mediterranean, I really felt for them it must be heart breaking.

H.M.A.S. Nestor being sunk by our Depth Charges.

It is 7am now, with a great sigh of relief we thankfully set off at high speed to join up with the convoy again, now with any luck we should reach Malta by tomorrow morning, that is if they have not had a lot of trouble. After all the trouble that we went through during the night, just what were we expecting this morning? There is no doubt in our minds that we were going to be fighting a losing battle 'against big odds,' which I am afraid that we couldn't possibly have won. The relief is so great, you could tell by listening to the crews conversations on the headphones, I know how most of the crew felt but I just couldn't put it into words, If those German Stuka dive bombers had returned to attack us in any numbers this morning while we were still trying to tow that ship, I am pretty certain I would not be writing this in my diary now . . . That is for sure.

Dying for a rest, just to get my head down and sleep never mind being dirty and hungry, so roll on Malta here we come.

After steaming for the biggest part of the morning and not sighting a single enemy plane the convoy is sighted way over on the horizon just before midday, closing in on them we could see that they are not being attacked so that is a relief, but for some reason they are closing fast on us because they were coming towards us, so now what the hell is happening? it's really unbelievable, the head phones are really buzzing now because no one can make this out but nothing was coming officially from any quarter, so we didn't find out until well into the afternoon, that was after we had turned around when joining up with the convoy, it seems for some unknown reason the Admiral in charge of the convoy had decided to turn back, well we just couldn't believe this, so here we are just a day away from Malta, no . . . It would only have been a matter of hours, all the real tough part done.

So after all that action we had gone through we are returning to Alexandria, now, my mate has just summed it all up when he said "Oh no, we have got to go through all that bloody lot all over again," I'm sure everyone is thinking the same, all I can say is that it's certainly going to be a very close run thing because by now everybody in this convoy must be just about out of ammunition, it's definitely going to be touch and go because the gunnery officer told us some time ago about the ammunition situation, so if the Germans or Italians decide to hit this convoy again on the way back to Alex like they have just been doing for the last few days, then we are finished and that's for certain as we would not last very long at all, I know I have said that a few times while we have been with this convoy, the situations that we are getting into are impossible.

I can tell you now that we are really worried, can you imagine what it would be like if we do run out of ammunition?

We reckon that we were a day short of reaching Malta so now we have got to travel all that way back to Alex. 'Total Massacre' I would say, hundreds of miles and not being able to fire a shot at the dive bombers, E-boats and U-boats, they would have such a field day they could attack this convoy and sink every ship without having a single shot fired at them. What a catastrophe that would be.

But why? for heavens sake, why have we turned back? Everyone is asking, I am beginning to wonder if we will ever get to know the real reason for not carrying on, but no matter here we are having turned around now and on our way back towards Alex with quite a lot of worried seamen aboard all these ships, but let's look on the bright side, you never know they might send out the R.A.F. to give us an escort all the way back 'Joking of course,' sailing on towards nightfall, apart from two lonely planes high up and a fair distance away in the late afternoon, surprisingly we didn't get any attacks, perhaps Gerry is looking for us where we should be by rights? Not knowing that we have turned around and are on our way back, but no, we hadn't deceived them for very long, the sun had set when they finally found us.

Surprisingly there is only four of them this time, although they did manage to get through the screen (conserve your ammunition was the order) they didn't manage to hit any of the ships, but I don't suppose that they would be too disappointed because they had done their job which was to stop these supplies from getting through to Malta, and they had certainly done that. Night fell and we saw some flares come down, they are evidently trying to find us but without any success this time and after a while they soon stopped, we slowly sailed on into the night hoping that at last we could take it easy.

Come the morning and a lot of very tired eyes are searching the horizon as the sun comes up, but it is not from the horizon they come, but from high up once again also split up, about six of them screaming down 'that Bloody noise,' everybody had to open fire and we saw one crash straight into the sea, although some did drop their bombs we didn't see any ships receive a hit and it was over as quickly as it started but we used up some precious ammunition. So we sailed on into the bright morning sun.

Throughout the remainder of the day we didn't have any more attacks, on we go every hour of the nights and days that followed taking us ever nearer to Alexandria and safety, with sore red eyes from lack of sleep and real grubby, forever staring into that blazing sunshine. With no more attacks from the enemy 'it's been one hell of a time,' one that will live on in the minds of all of us for the rest of our lives.

The Skipper was certainly right when he made that speech before we left Alexandria, about seeing some action, I must say that I had already seen some before joining the Javelin, but that lot that we have just come through takes some beating.

Now, my mate Tom has just remarked on my bit of a beard that I seem to have grown these last few days and has asked me if I intend to keep it? I doubt it very much but I will have a "Shuffty" (look) in the mirror when I get the chance, I think that the one thing I am looking forward to is a great big plate full of food 'just bring it on.'

Now, what a sight Alexandria must look to the bridge lookout, even though we were still miles out to sea when he shouted Alexandria off the port bow, now I know that is not the correct way to report a bearing but I suppose in his excitement he just forgot and I reckon that the Skipper will forgive him this time. My mate asked me "what's the first thing you want to do when we reach Alex, eat, sleep or hit the first R.A.F chap you see?" now, that makes one wonder doesn't it because there has been lots of questions asked as to why we didn't see any of our planes during this convoy, I know for sure that a lot of the lads are very angry about this as most convoys get some sort of air support, but we have seen nothing.

At last we eventually sail into the harbour at Alexandria with a sigh of relief as we pass through that boom straight alongside the jetty and tie her up, then the pipe went up around the ship to stand down from action stations, there are some Ambulances waiting here to take off all the injured men from the various ships that have been damaged but made it back to port.

Our first job is to disembark the crew of the Destroyer H.M.A.S. Nestor, who are at this moment filing down the gangway onto the jetty, the officers and men lining up, they then give us three rousing cheers and Javelin's lot do likewise, as they are marched off we watch for a short time as the ambulances further down the jetty are loading the wounded, some on stretchers and a few walking wounded from one of the ships, I reckon that there will be lots more from other ships.

I wonder just how many ships haven't made it, well, we know of one for sure and not one survivor, what a terrible thing that was, it all happened so quickly, we will never forget, but here we are, considering ourselves to be one of the lucky ones. I'm on the mess deck now and looking around at both the seaman's messes, they are full of men but it is the silence that strikes me, this is something that you never get on a mess deck at any time, it just shows what we have been through as when a ship is in harbour this deck is all noise, bustle, talking about leave and lots of other things but this is something different, I know that everyone is dead beat, they have that beaten look on so it's only their faces, after all we have failed in our bid to get this convoy through to the starving people of Malta.

We had been in action on and off for over five days natural that a lot of these lads are taking it badly, as I said most of this ships company had never been in action before, it will take a day or two before things begin to return to normal, but I am starving and I reckon that what all these lads want is a great big plate of hot food and a couple of days sleep. Now, when that food did arrive there was very little talk for some considerable time, and I can also tell you something else, that is, if I never see another ships biscuit well, it won't be too soon for me, I reckon that will go for most of the lads on the ship. After that first full meal for a week and as I said eaten in almost dead silence, these lads are still sitting here on the mess and some fool has just mentioned shore leave.

This might have been a normal topic of conversion but not at this time, one of the lads threw a pillow at him and I can't say that I blame him, no shore leave for me thank you, I'm going to sling my hammock alongside old Robbo who already has his slung, turn in and sleep until Christmas "now, I must be joking" I should have said I should be so lucky, anyway at rise and shine the next morning there are still a few hammocks occupied when hands to breakfast is piped, just shows you how tired the lads are, but ships routine doesn't stop after an action, it goes on just the same and after breakfast everybody has to fall in on parade and no one is excused, that is unless they are sick, tired because you had a troubled nights sleep due to enemy action doesn't come into it, so the Killick of the mess has to see that those late hammock risers are duly tipped out of their warm comfy beds.

Anyway today we have learned the price we paid in our attempt to get a convoy to Malta, our losses although unofficial at the moment are two Cruisers sunk, three damaged, three Destroyers sunk and one damaged, one Corvette damaged, the news of the Merchant ship losses is not known up to now, number of them damaged for sure, some are believed to have made it back to Tobruck, we now know that one of the Cruisers which is H.M.S. Hermoine was sunk by torpedoes from a submarine and has suffered a great number of casualties, the Cruiser H.M.S. Newcastle has been torpedoed but her fate at this moment as yet is unknown.

We do know that the Newcastle should have made harbour shortly after we did yesterday, but on looking around the harbour here, as yet there is no sign of her, but with being damaged she might have gone into Tobruck, the cruiser H.M.S. Birmingham was hit by dive bombers and has also got a lot of casualties but is here in Alexandria, so all in all I reckon it was a bit of a disaster. We have just been informed of another convoy heading for Malta at the same time as us, from the other end of the Mediterranean to us, sailing out of Gibraltar, although they were attacked it wasn't on the same scale, they did manage to get a ship or two safe into Malta, so in a way I suppose I will have to change my mind and say it was a success after all.

I have just come from up top (upper deck) this morning where I had a good look around the harbour to see what damaged ships did make it back, on looking through my binoculars I spotted the merchant ship that had been hit on the stern, that is 'ruddy marvelous' and looking at her she seems to be lying OK but how she got here I'll never know, as for the others that we saw hit well, I can't see any, the only place near to them for safety would have been Tobruck but

I wouldn't like to have to stay there very long, but of course they could have gone on to Port Said and I would think that they would be pretty safe there, still I don't suppose that we will ever know.

The 17th June 1942, which is a the day after arriving back from taking part in "OPERATION VIGOROUS" which was the code name for the convoy, we are really taking it easy or I should say have been, the Skipper gave us all a Make and Mend after our morning work. Sitting here now on the mess with most of the lads writing letters home, no doubt answering the letters that we received this morning from England, this is all air-mail letters, we haven't received any sea mail since we were in Madagascar. The dawn of 18th June arrives and we have been designated Duty Destroyer, as we are alongside the jetty we are about to ammunition ship, how about that then, after that take on stores (probably lots more ships biscuit's). Both those jobs completed and a very busy morning over, we are now about to move out into the harbour.

Refueling is the next job before we go to our buoy, then I reckon that we will be ready for whatever is out there again, but it just reminded me of my twenty first birthday again and what a way to spend it eh, but that is one thing that I won't forget in a hurry. So we are now ready for sea at a moment's notice no chance of any shore leave for anybody tonight and here's me waiting for that slap up meal in the Fleet Club again and one big cool beer please. It's also about time my mate and I started to look around for some female company again, I know that he doesn't have a girlfriend back home because he told me when we were in Durban.

We didn't get called out on duty yesterday but have moved back to the jetty again and a surprise awaited us, the sea mail has actually caught up with us at last, the last time was when we were in Madagascar, there is three letters for me, the first one I opened was form my cousin and I got the shock of my life, his letter began with the news that Joyce, she was my ex girlfriend had been seriously injured in an accident while at work and had been asking for me in hospital. Well, this news really shook me because no matter how I tried to forget her she was very often in my thoughts, now, why would I have that great big photo of her hanging on my locker door? This same photo has been with me in every establishment and was also on my locker door on my last ship the Dorsetshire, the small photo is what I carry on me at all times in every action that I have been in, so I wasn't really kidding anyone but just trying to kid myself. all my mates had their wives and girlfriends photos hanging on their lockers, although you might say that I probably didn't want to be left out, no it was no excuse because I had loved her so very deeply and you don't fall out of that sort of love so very quickly, but in his writing my cousin had failed to include the hospital's address that Joyce is in, so I can't write to her, of all the rotten luck.

In this sort of situation it has been known to get leave on compassionate grounds, and although she was no longer my girlfriend I had to try and do something if she was that ill, so I put in a request to see the Captain to see if I could possibly get some leave, but I knew how the Navy handles these sort of things and it was no surprise that the request didn't get any further than my divisional officer, I should have guessed that I wouldn't stand much chance, but after reading my request he sympathized with me and said that it was impossible for me to get home on the grounds that I had requested and that only for a wife or parent could this be granted, sometimes even these requests failed unless the situation was right, then he gave me a lecture on my position in all this, warning me against jumping ship as lots of men had done in similar positions and whereby made for the nearest R.A.F. base then hitched a lift on a plane going home.

Most matelots including myself knew about this dodge, but I had no intentions of deserting, but there was no doubt about it though the news had certainly shaken me straight away I sat down and wrote to my mate by air-mail explaining the position that I was in and telling him the reason why I couldn't get home to be with her, but to give her my love when he saw her and tell her to please get well for me. Now I had promised my mate that we would have a run ashore tonight, so despite the bad news we are off with old Robbo's words ringing in my ears, "there is nothing that you can do about it now so go ashore and forget it." well I can't forget, but life is too short and dangerous for us at the moment and his parting words "Get out there and enjoy yourself and live for today because your tomorrow may never come" were wise words from an older man.

He is right you know, so it's look out Mothers here we come, lock up your daughters cause we're after some fun. We went straight to the Fleet Club and that slap up meal was the first thing on the agenda with the beer afterwards, well things begin to look a little brighter and we started to spread out a bit away from the Fleet Club exploring a few of the high spots of Alexandria, although quite a lot of the city is considered dangerous for matelots and is out of bounds, but there are plenty of places to have a good time here. We staggered back on board that night after a great run ashore, we had one more run ashore before sailing out past the boom again, thankfully we are on our own so no convoy this time but we didn't go out of sight of land and I couldn't believe it, we are out here to do gunnery exercises as though we haven't had enough practice over the last few weeks.

Fortunately the practice only lasted a few hours and we are soon sailing back into Alex anchoring straight away. Now one of my first jobs on entering harbour as ships side working party is to grab a tin of white paint and hop over the side onto the anchor chain (cable we call it) and paint each link of the cable right down to the water line then swim round the side of the ship to the gangway wearing a life jacket 'don't forget I can't swim a stroke,' we take great pride in our ship and like to keep her looking smart or tiddly in Jack words, when we left England we had a smashing black and white camouflage which made Javelin stand out from the rest of the Destroyers very tiddly we thought, but when we arrived here in Alexandria we had to change it to battleship grey (some jealousy on the part of Captain 'D' we suspect) but even now she looks a damn sight smarter than these others.

We don't seem to be doing much in harbour these days, it's mostly general routine. my job as I've already stated in harbour is painting, where ever any painting wants doing, be it the funnel, mast head or over the side, you name it and that's my job, it's a job that I like very much, some of the lads are cleaning guns while others are washing my old paint work down. There is plenty to do on board a ship but if it so happens that if you haven't got a job don't worry the Petty Officer will soon find you one, It does get very boring, though at times even if a thing is very clean well sometimes it's just 'clean it again.' Luckily though we are getting plenty of shore leave to know our way around Alex a lot more now, there's no doubt there is so much to see and if you have the money you can buy anything you want.

That is one of the problems, as I have said quite a few times before, Jack doesn't have or I should have said get a lot of money to spend and going ashore every chance that you get it's soon gone, then all you want to do is get back to sea again, we have only been to sea once since the Malta run, you might not believe that a matelot gets tired of being stuck in harbour all the time and wants to get back to sea, sometimes the danger doesn't come into it at all.

Here we are on the 27th June. We are at sea once more having just sailed out of Alex, escorting the Battle Ship H.M.S. Queen Elizabeth the second in company with a few other Destroyers, we are escorting her to Port Said.

Sailing out of Port Said after only a short stay and returning to Alexandria, but no sooner had we dropped anchor securing the ship than we were getting ready to go to sea again, sure enough out we go, this time we are escorting a small convoy of Merchant ships the destination is Port Said once again, on arrival we go into harbour. This place is not anywhere near as big as Alexandria, our Killick who has been ashore here before doesn't reckon much to it, but we didn't stay long enough to get a chance to see what it was like, only staying for a few hours before leaving the harbour and making speed back to Alex, this time we go straight alongside the jetty and secure up to the bollards.

As it happens a mate and I were soon over the side doing a bit of paint work and got talking to a couple of Army chaps who were doing some sort of patrol on the dock, during the conversation they were telling us that Tobruck has fallen so that things are not looking too good in the desert, now that puts us in some danger here in Alex as the word is that the Africa Corps have now pushed our lads back as far as Mersa

Matru. If this is true the Germans are now only seventy miles from Alex and we reckon that there must be some truth in the rumours because now and again the odd German plane has been over the harbour here, so it was no surprise to anyone after hearing the latest news that things are getting even worse that the C-in-C orders the total evacuation of all Naval personnel.

So the big movement began in earnest with the announcement of all personnel on shore and on ships based at Alexandria to start the evacuation at once on the 1st of July 1942. So very quickly things begin to move with the Javelin and the rest of the Destroyers, with all the big Depot ships H.M.S. Woolwich, the Resource and the smaller H.M.S. Reliance ready to move in a very short time, now all three of these ships are a bit on the ancient side and as their job was mainly repair work as well as supplies they don't have to use their main engines much because they are always in harbour, some are tied up to buoy's and taking this lot in convoy is going to be a very slow escort job.

But we sail out of Alexandria 2nd July 1942, our convoy consist of three of the big depot ships, H.M.S. Woolwich, Resource and the smaller H.M.S. Reliance then following on behind in a smaller convoy with Wrens on a transport, all the other smaller crafts and the submarine Depot Ship H.M.S. Medway, all of us heading for the same destination Port Said. We did see just two enemy planes on our way but they were high up, when we all opened fire at them they soon pushed off and didn't even try to attack the convoy. We arrived at port Said without any trouble of any sort and they told us that they had just had an air-raid by some high level planes but had sustained only slight damage.

I suspect that the planes that bombed Port Said were the same ones that we fired on when we were out at sea. The whole convoy had gone safely into the harbour, with being very big ships this took a little time, while we were standing by we received some news that really shook us, the convoy traveling a few miles astern of us had been attacked by enemy dive bombers and H.M.S. Medway has been sunk, that sounds unbelievable but it's true and what rotten luck. We sailed out of Port Said on our own only an hour after arriving, we had only been sailing a short time when we passed the small convoy that the unfortunate Medway had been a part of, the convoy is still heading for Port Said, evidently the Bombers had gone for the biggest target.

On we sailed arriving at Alexandria, the first thing that struck me was the emptiness of the harbour, that is except for those French ships which surprisingly are still here, most of the lads thought that they would have done a bunk when they saw all the British ships leave, but it might be that they don't want to go, the problem I would think for them is where could they go, anyway we went straight alongside the jetty finding that the Army had taken over the place, a few of them asked us "what the hell are you doing back in Alex?" of course this time we just don't know, one of the lads casually asked them the same question and we got the shock reply that they are here to blow this jetty and all the warehouses here sky high.

It was then at that moment that the Army Officer in command appeared and asked for permission to come aboard, he came up the gangway onto the Javelin and was shown down to the Ward Room to meet with the Captain, I reckon that he would of had a tot or two of the wet stuff after telling the Skipper what he and his men intended to do, however apparently before he did the job they had come to some agreement between them, to allow us to enter these Warehouses for a certain time to take out anything that could be of use to us on the mess, but it would not be a free for all and that everything had to be done in an orderly fashion under the supervision of his men.

Talking to one of the soldiers before we knew that there was going to be any raiding of these warehouses, he told us that the places were stacked out with all sorts of stuff some that is worth thousands of pounds and in his words "it is all going up," so we got news of what had been arranged, which is by orders of the Army Officer, one rating from each mess would be allowed on shore in an orderly manner to take whatever they think is of use, all thoughts of being able to take just anything had been rescinded by the Captain and that we are to only bring back on board anything that could be of use on the mess, however after the Army Officer had gone the Sergeant said that it would be OK for two men from each mess to go into the warehouses but a time limit had been agreed with the army officer and we would be escorted by a Corporal who would say when the time was up.

The problem as to who was going to be selected for the job was left entirely to the Killick of the mess and old Robbo picked me and one of the younger lads of the mess, so off we went when everybody was ready, now this was exciting stuff and when we went into the first of the warehouses I was taken aback by the sight of at least half a dozen brand new cars, then foods of every description stacked right up to the roof on wooden pallets, but we didn't have a lot of time so we had to search all these huge warehouses, there was so much one of the lads in passing said "what a Bloody waste of money, all this going to be blown sky high" I just thought then of the value in money that must be here, hundreds of thousands of pounds and more.

Well, I grabbed a couple of sack bags and the last shed that we went into contained food of every description, so on searching among the stacks I found sugar and tea in large quantities so into the sack it went, the lad with me went for biscuit's, sweets and chocolate of all kinds it made your eyes pop out to see this stuff, stacks and stacks of it all in neat order just waiting for us to take our pick. so by now my sack was really full and very weighty so off I went back to the ship, Robbo and some of the lads were waiting for me at the guard rails ready to take the stuff off me and back I went again hoping that the time had not expired, the other lad in our mess passed me staggering under the weight of his sack.

I arrived only just in time as some of the other lads were coming out saying the time is up, but I shot into the first warehouse to carrying on filling my sack until the Corporal came in and said OK that's it, as I walked to the door I passed a crate with some material on it and I just picked one up tucking it under my arm, walking back alongside the ship I lobbed it over the guard rail on to the deck where one of the lads off our mess picked it up for me (I wouldn't have been allowed on board with that material,) anyway, between us we had managed to get a nice feast of biscuit's plain and mixed, sweets, some chocolates of all kinds, tea and sugar that would last our mess for weeks. as for the dress material, that is what it turned out to be, well it would come in useful to someone I bet it's worth a bit.

Talking to one of the Army Sergeants a bit later and he was saying that all these warehouses are now wired up to high explosives as is the jetty that we are alongside, nothing is going to be left for the Germans, to top it all when we leave this place the whole harbour will be mined, we shook hands with these chaps wishing them luck and one hour after the C-in-C's gear, his staff and the last mail arrived on board we sailed out of Alexandria for the last time probably. We sailed on arriving at Port Said where we dump the lot and for now this looks like being our base, date 3rd July 1942.

So here we are and what a grim outlook faces us if what Robbo says about this place is true, but we will soon find out as shore leave has been granted and as the Starboard watch are the duty watch, we (the port watch) are off ashore. We are told that the natives ashore here are just as bad as those in Alex and will if you are daft enough to let them 'rob you blind' but we are wise to most of their tricks by now, it is very obvious that these natives don't like us very much despite the fact that we are putting a lot of money into their pockets. The beer is reasonable I suppose and the food was not a touch on the Fleet Club but it was edible. I think that I have found out the reason that these people do not like us very much, I've been told that they are having a lot of air-raids.

I suppose that we can't blame them on that score as I am sure that if we didn't use their harbours to berth our ships they wouldn't be getting any air-raids. they say that they had a big raid only this morning before we arrived, the bombs were dropped in the harbour area, but very little damage was done and no ships were hit, just slight damage was caused to one or two of the buildings, unfortunately there are some civilian casualties. After the run ashore the verdict from the lads is not too bad, Robbo says that the place has altered a lot since he was here in 1938, there is one thing that I noticed, that is that your money doesn't go very far here, I put that down to the fact that the beer here is dearer for one thing, but I suppose it was an OK run ashore. So back on board and most of the lads are wondering how long we will be staying here, so the daily ships routine continues and we have this mornings Captains rounds.

This is a signal for every Killick and his mess man for that particular day that they have some work to do, all this starts after breakfast when the rest of the hands have gone to work part of ship, first off the mess table is scrubbed down with hot water then the oilcloth which is a plastic material is scrubbed, when dried out it is laid out just partly unrolled on the near end of the table, all the pots and pans which have to be washed then polished with all the cutlery, polished again and then laid out very neatly on the oilcloth, everything on the mess deck has to be stowed away, the deck washed down and dried off before the Skipper makes his inspection, although he always does his rounds in the morning you don't know just when he is going to turn up, that's Captains rounds.

So the runs ashore continue as the days pass by but there's really nothing to write about here apart from the air-raids, we have had quite a few of them but they are mostly night time raids and it gets a bit unnerving being stationary when the bombs start to come down, we have also had a couple of daylight raids but apart from one ship being set on fire there hasn't been a lot of really bad damage. Thankfully we sail out of Port Said on the 15th July and after a few aircraft scares we arrive at the beautiful Island of Cyprus, docking at Famagusta on the 16th July, shore leave is granted within the hour, once ashore we notice that nearly all the buildings are white and everything is so clean with grapes growing in abundance. The grapes hang over walls in great big bunches and we actually picked some as we walked along the road, I must say that I have never seen so many grapes before growing wild. The people here made us so very welcome especially the girls. I reckon that here is everything that a matelot wants on a run ashore, restaurants with plenty of big eats, the food is well prepared and is very good with plenty of wine also fairly cheap at that, they warned us not to drink too much as it is very strong stuff. I must say what a very beautiful place Famagusta is and my first run ashore here is one that I won't forget, I only hope that we will be seeing a lot more of it.

However it all ended far too soon and we are back on board before we know it, the girls waving to us through the gates as we sail out of Cyprus. the next day very early during the morning watch we arrive at the port of Haifa on the Palestine coast on the 17th July, we secured alongside the Cruiser H.M.S. Cleopatra who has the famous nickname of H.M.S. Pepperpot, she got that name when she was in a convoy while being attacked, she was very badly damaged so much so that her hull and Superstructure was full of holes hence the name Pepperpot, this ship has been in quite a few actions and is a well known. We have just received some fantastic news from ashore "the Captain has been promoted," the message has been passed on by the signals branch. I don't think that there is one sailor aboard this ship that would say that he hasn't deserved this promotion and rightly so, of course if this is true then it's more than likely that we shall be losing our Skipper in the very near future which will be a very sad loss. Leave has just been piped for both watches which is strange too but why worry, very shortly after, my mate and I are soon strolling through the streets of Haifa which also has an out of bounds area, out of bounds areas are places that are considered dangerous for 'Jack' and are patrolled by the Military Police, but now is the time to find out if Robbo's tales about this place are true it certainly looked promising, before we had gone very far, the first place to look for is one that sells beer after that food.

It didn't take us very long to find the beer, once again this stuff is an insult to beer, but all I can say is as before it's drinkable but the food I thought was very good and plentiful. On walking around here 'well, it's amazing' the things that you can buy, really lovely things that your girlfriend back home would just love to have only they cost money, "now how many times have I said that," we have found out that this place has quite a few white girls living here and as with one or two other places that I have visited a lot of these girls work in the Brothels, apparently just like Alexandria Haifa is notorious for these.

One of the private places here is noted for it's exhibitions of the sexual kind and is certainly no place for a naive young sailor. now you innocent people back home wouldn't know what these are (and I'm not going to tell you) but suffice to say that when you have been to one of these, you've seen it all and I can tell you now that I am not in the least bit shocked at the things that some women do in these foreign ports. I was an innocent young lad when I joined the navy but my word not any more my eyes have been well and truly opened, to think that this is the sort of life that some of these people lead or how they earn their living and have done for years, England well there is no comparison, things that go on here would never be allowed back home. Anyway we had a smashing time ashore and went back on board a lot wiser in the ways of the world than we did when we went ashore.

We spent another three good days here in Haifa before sailing out again during the forenoon watch, arriving back at Port Said on the same day. For the next five days we lay alongside the harbour wall it was mainly working part of ship every day, but we do manage to have a game of Housey— Housey aboard the Kelvin (one of our other Destroyers) a couple of nights when we didn't go ashore, but when we did go it was more or less to stretch our legs as being on a small ship we don't get much exercise, anyway, Port Said is not Alexandria or Haifa.

We keep on having these 'Red Alert' air-raids but nothing to really worry anybody, when they happen during the night there is not much sleep for us as we have to man the guns, just the same as we would if we were at sea, what Gerry wants to bomb this place for I will never know as I wouldn't think that the few ships that are here at this moment are worth the trouble, just two small merchant ships apart from the Destroyers. We sail out of Port Said harbour on the 23rd July during the first dog watch, joining up with quite a few Destroyers and four Cruisers then sailed on into the Mediterranean, after steaming for some considerable time we all turned heading straight towards the coast just as it was getting dark, we went to action stations and we knew that we must be getting close when the order came through to take up our positions for bombardment.

Once in position and the order is given to open fire all hell broke loose, our target was Mersa Matruh port installations, when those guns opened up the night sky was soon lit up with fires breaking out all over the place, one very big fire started in the harbour which must have been fuel of some sort because it lit up the whole area, this is a very heavy attack with both Cruisers and Destroyers joining in, on completion all the ships joined up again, got back into formation and set off at speed leaving Mersa Matruh well and truly lit up. The fires could be seen burning when we were miles out at sea, after steaming for some time the Cruisers left us with just a small escort of Destroyers, the Javelin with the remainder of the Destroyers returned to port Said and we copped for Emergency Destroyer.

So no shore leave for the port watch, but I don't think many of the lads would have gone anyway as we have been warned that there might be an air-raid later, although that raid didn't materialize until the next day during the morning, this was evidently a reprisal for the attack on Mersa Matruh, but although bombs were dropped they were mainly out in the harbour, there was no damage done to any of the ships and only slight damage to the harbour. So after a busy morning we prepared for sea again just before dinner and sailed out of Port Said during the afternoon watch, the starboard watch are closed up at defence stations, the rest of the Destroyers all came out at the same time.

Once again waiting for us are the Cruisers and the rest of the escorts as usual, we all formed up and off we went again sailing on into the night once more heading for the coast 'this is getting a bit boring' yes it's Mersa Matruh the same old routine, shells hammering into the harbour a lot more fires and one or two explosions this time, then back we go at full speed and enter Port Said harbour during the morning watch. This is repeated all over again the following day, we sailed during the second dog watch this time with the same Cruisers plus one more making speed heading for the coast once more again, yes it's Mersa Matruh I can't believe this but it's the same thing all over again.

This time we fired star shells into the harbour so that we can see if or what damage has been done, we really plastered the place this time, although I thought that we must have caused a heck of a lot of damage the last time, anyway we leave Mersa burning brightly this time, there surely can't be many more targets there for us to fire at so back we speed to Port Said when once again, the Cruisers and most of the Destroyers split up on arriving probably leaving just a few of us to suffer the air-raid that we will no doubt get this morning

27th July, fortunately for us we have only been in the harbour a short time when out we sail once more this time it is for a submarine that has been sighted on the surface.

It was suspected that this submarine would probably be waiting for any shipping coming out of Port Said, but despite searching for most of the day and carrying the sweep on well into the night we picked up nothing, the U-boat was probably charging his batteries ready for his run back through the Mediterranean or to his base and for this purpose they have to surface to do the charging. It seems as though we are always at sea these days, but after this boring search the Skipper has just told us that we are going into Haifa for a boiler clean and that the news has just come through with the results of the raids on Mersa Matruh, the special reconnaissance reports say that the port is now a wreck and that the entrance of the harbour is blocked by the wreck of a sunken ship also there's total devastation of the port installations.

So instead of returning to Port Said we sail on entering the harbour at Haifa, here we go straight into the dry dock for a boiler clean. After securing ship the Captain announced over the tannoy that both watches are being given 48hrs leave and that he has made arrangements for the crew to visit either Jerusalem or Tel-Aviv, it was left to the choice of each individual as to which place they wished to visit, now all our watch decided on Tel-Aviv my mate and I were among the first to vote, so the whole of the ships company was abuzz with the idea of visiting these fantastic places. the reason I didn't pick Jerusalem although it must be a fantastic place, was that I thought that we had seen enough of the Arab nation and I reckon that being Jewish Tel-Aviv would be very different from most of the places that we have visited before, their way of life would be entirely different.

So off we went arriving in Tel-Aviv after a very smooth journey we were dropped off at a small hotel right on the sea front which was already booked for us, it was a lovely place all paid for by the Royal Navy I presume. My mate and I dumped our gear setting off straight away to view the sights and after just a short walk we were amazed at the beautiful things that you can buy here, that is if you have the money, and things did seem to be on the dear side, some of the jewellery and the decorative stuff was fantastic but quite beyond any ordinary sailor's wages, the food was very good and not too expensive, we soon settled down to a grand feed. but there was something about these people that was a bit puzzling though, the way that they acted when we spoke to them was as if they didn't like us very much, it was even more noticeable when we were walking though the city and we tried to make some conversation with the girls but they just didn't want to know, Just passed us by.

The great thing about Tel-Aviv are the sights and we did our sightseeing on a horse drawn carriage, one thing that we noticed on our ride round this place was the amount of our Army personnel that could be seen walking about. It was fantastic so we decided to stop at what would be described as a big restaurant for a meal and we got talking to two army chaps the conversation turning to why these people were not very sociable, they told us that very few of them have any knowledge of the English language and wouldn't understand a word that we said and that only the well to do have that privilege, however like my mate I thought that there was more to it than that, but we didn't intend to let it spoil our leave here anyway just being ashore here made a change from being at sea all the time.

Photograph of myself on shore leave in Tel-Aviv

So with our first day in Tel-Aviv behind us despite a few problems we had a great time after drinking some of the local wine, another big dinner we retired to our rooms and had a good night's sleep. Here I am now back in my room in the morning after writing this in my diary after having had a good breakfast and raring to go for another day out to see some more of this beautiful place, that is if I can get my mate out of that very comfortable bed. So being a little wiser on the citizens of Tel-Aviv off we went for our last look around the city although we decided to skip the horse and carriage this time, we did really enjoy ourselves and the time went all too fast but we did manage to get a smashing photograph of us taken together as a memento of the time we spent in Tel-Aviv, we probably won't come here again and I still think that we chose the right place as I don't think that Jerusalem would have been our cup of tea.

Me and Tom

With our forty eight hours leave over, back to Haifa we go and on arriving back on board the first thing that we hear is that the aircraft carrier H.M.S. Eagle has been sunk at the other end of the Mediterranean, I know a lad aboard her who came from the potteries, we both got drafted at the same time when we were in Pompy Barracks being on the same mess, now I wonder if he survived, still that's what this lot is all about it's no good thinking about it now. Just my luck I'm duty watch today and with the boiler clean now over I reckon that it won't be very long before we are back at sea again, so part ship working for us today and it's my turn again for the cooks job, I dodge the painting or whatever it was that the P.O. had got lined up for me.

On duty watch now and this is the day after we arrived back off leave, the dry dock has been filled during the early morning so out we sail into the harbour during the forenoon watch, we are going to refuel first then to anchor but only for a very short time before a movement among the remaining Destroyers and Cruisers set in motion and a move towards the entrance of the harbour, so we hoist the anchor and join up with the escorts outside, then an announcement by the Skipper over the tannoy passed the information to all hands that our mission is a very important one once again, this time it was Rhodes a very heavily defended Island belonging to Greece but now occupied by the Germans.

This is where we think that all the bombers and E-boats come from that attacked our convoys on the way to Malta, so we are going out to give them a taste of their own medicine. The date is 12th of August. After sailing for some time we eventually sight land in the darkening light and after closing in, orders are given to open fire and every ship began the bombardment, this is a sight that everyone wants to see, Cruisers and Destroyers are really hammering that Island

and very soon the place was lit up with fires all over the place, really big fires in some parts but it is all over very quickly as we turned away making all speed from what must be a really battered Rhodes, after only sailing for a short time we picked up a contact on a submarine and went straight into the attack dropping depth charges and really hammering that Submarine.

Attacking the Submarine with Depth Charges.

We pressed home the attack for some time and we didn't intend them getting away, no sailors can have any feelings at all for these submarine crews because when you have seen ships that are unarmed blown out of the water by these Subs without any warning at all, and some of the crews fired upon while helpless in the water and in life boats, then nothing is too good for them "Give them hell" says my mate I don't think that there is a man aboard this ship that wouldn't agree with him, what everybody wanted to see was that submarine come to the surface so that we could blow it to pieces, so after a very long wait after continually dropping our depth charges sure enough paper oil and clothing came floating up to the surface in large quantities, the Skipper had us throwing buckets over the side to catch up some of the oil that was floating up to the surface for the purpose of taking samples, I reckon that, seeing the amount of the stuff on the surface, we are going to claim this one for sure.

After the excitement had died down and everybody had finished talking about what might be our second submarine sinking we had sailed on.

We arrived back in Haifa on the 14th August, now what do you know! We had only been in the harbour a few hours and here we are on the move again with the Starboard watch on duty taking us out through the boom, it looks like some more escort duty as the Cruisers Cleopatra and Arethusa follow us out of the harbour straight into what seems to be the making of some bad weather, but it doesn't stop us from doing anti-submarine sweeps.

Our next port of call is Port Said, we wait outside the harbour while the Cruisers went in then H.M.S. Coventry and Dido came out. We sailed on straight into some really rough weather, a gale of some force and I don't have to tell you what it's like aboard a Destroyer in stormy weather, anyway we battled on arriving at Haifa on the 16th August, going straight alongside a tanker for refuelling, on completion we sail straight out to sea again doing anti-submarine patrols, way out all day before returning to harbour at Haifa on the 17th. At last shore leave is granted but not for our watch but at least we can relax a bit apart from the watch keepers who will be on duty, the rest of us are going to take it easy after the liberty men have gone ashore.

Today is the 18th and I'm working part ship, however due to one of our lads on the mess being sick Robbo has asked me to do the mess man's job today, so it's my job once again to prepare dinner for this hungry lot on one mess, that means laying all the plates knives forks and spoons in their respective places where each rating will sit for his meal at the mess table, then at the pipe of hands to dinner I will proceed to the galley call out my mess number to the cook who will hand me said dinners on a large tray and proceed back to mess where Robbo will assist in dishing out a fair share to each hungry rating, when all have finished I will wash every plate, cup and piece of cutlery then wash down the table, leaving the mess in a dry clean tidy condition 'sounds awful doesn't it,' the thing that I am looking forward to is that shore leave tonight so that we can eat someone else's cooking for a change.

So dressed in our white shorts and shirts all neatly pressed, down that gangway we go and for once we got a surprising remark form the duty Petty Officer as we passed him at the gangway head "Make the most of it" he said, now I wonder what that was all about my mate remarked and for once it got us both a bit worried because it was a funny thing to say, I wonder if he knows something that we don't? well let's get ashore and have a good time as it may be our last, who knows and who cares, beer, big eats and girls in that order if you please ask any matelot and you will get the same answer, myself I always look at these runs ashore like that, as the waters that we operate in have the big reputation of being the most dangerous in this war and when looking at it from our point of view I don't think that they are far wrong because it's just like sailing up a very wide river with the enemy occupying both banks so you are in constant danger from either side.

The E-boat bases are very well known as is the notorious 'Bomb Alley' which has the reputation of being the worst place to pass though in the whole of the Mediterranean, so there you are, we are hearing every day of a ship being sunk with the enemy so close to us, but that's it live it up as I am always telling my mates and Haifa is one place where you can certainly do just that, there is so much here and it turned out to be a great run ashore, so much so that we had to practically carry one of the lads from our mess up the gangway on going back on board, luckily for us there was no officer of the watch on the Quarter deck when we got to the top of the gangway, only the bosuns mate and a leading hand otherwise we might have been in some trouble.

So it turned out that we managed to get our drunken ship mate up the waste and onto the forward mess decks without being seen by said officer, I don't think that he will be in a very good state for duty in the morning, he will probably report sick. Well, it looks as though we are going to be here for at least another day as my first job this morning is going over the side to paint the ship's number or Pennant, G61. It's a job that has to be done on the outboard side by sitting on a stage slung over the ships side, alongside the jetty it is a lot easier, the pennant is done by painting the entire thing in black and finishing off with a white strip all around the letter and numbers to make it stand out more. I really like this job being ship side it excuses me from having to work under the watchful eye of a Killick or Petty Officer as ours just details us off for the job then leaves us to it.

Why I said we would be here for another day is that if we were going to sea very soon I wouldn't have been painting that Pennant, so it's lucky starboard watch who will be going ashore tonight. I have got a couple of letters to write then another game of 'Housey' on the Petard who is lying alongside. 20th August and there will be no shore leave for me tonight because here we are out at sea having sailed out of Haifa during the morning watch in company with Captain D and the other Destroyers, this time we are escorting a small number of Troop ships, our destination we are told is Cyprus. Now, we have just heard some more bad news that an old favourite of mine, the Princess Margarete has been torpedoed and sunk by a U-boat while being convoyed from Port Said to Haifa.

This is a terrible loss as the Princess Margarete was considered by some to be a grand old lady, when I first saw her she was in Alexandria, although she was old she had just had a refit and looked really great but now she has gone, we played Housey-Housey on her once so we feel the loss a bit, the buzz is that there are very few survivors so the Mediterranean claims more.

Sailing on we eventually arrive at Famagusta safely on 21st August this time there's no shore leave. We can see that lying here in the harbour there are quite a few merchant ships possibly waiting for escorts, so we do just that as we sail out from Cyprus during the first watch escorting most of these ships and arrive at Haifa on the 22nd straight to an oil tanker and part refuel then go alongside the jetty, the pipe goes while we are at dinner "leave is been granted to the port watch."

Now, if I am to get ashore tonight I will have to get a sub because I am stone broke and the only person that I know who might lend me a bit is my Oppo at defence stations, I've done him a few favours in the past. I forgot to say that leave is from 1700hrs to 2200hrs but before this I have another job to do that is to wash and iron my shirt and shorts, so it means that I will have to take them down to the engine room to dry quickly before I can iron them, a job I should have done before now. Well, my old Oppo. came good with the sub, so

I'm all set for a good run ashore with just enough money for two of the B's (beers and big eats) I'm afraid this time.

It wasn't a bad run ashore, we soon got into the mood of thing's, we had a few beers and stretched our legs.

So here we are another day but of course we are on watch aboard, I've been washing down paint work as usual but we do get a bit of news today because the mail turned up again this morning, once again one of my letters must have been in a fire because nearly half of it is burnt and unreadable, although this is not the first time that this has happened as on my first ship in Freetown I received mail that had been in the water also one or two that had been damaged by fire.

A job to do tonight before slinging my hammock.

24th August and we are at sea and the port watch are on duty closed up at defence stations. We sailed out during the forenoon watch, this time we are escorting a number of Troop ships and after sailing for a short time we are suddenly attacked by about a dozen dive bombers, bombs again all over the place we had some very near misses, but the barrage that our lot put up was fantastic and we did see three enemy bombers shot down this time but once again we were very lucky, the way that these bombers caught us out so soon after leaving harbour makes you think that they knew when we were coming out, we hadn't seen any spotter planes so how the hell did they just pick us up like that.

Sailing on, we had no more attacks on the convoy and arrived OK at Cyprus, the Troop ships sailed in and remained alongside while we sailed straight out again having an untroubled trip back to Haifa.

Again after a very short stay to pick up the mail out we go again meeting up with Captain 'D' and H.M.S. Jervis doing anti-submarine patrols, after sweeping for a considerable time and not picking up anything we finally sailed on arriving at Port Said eventually on 27th August. Shore leave was piped for the port watch but as my mate and I are short of cash this leave will be passed over, not that I think that we would have gone ashore anyway as Port Said is certainly not Cape Town or Durban.

28th August, part ship working today and some more letter writing for me as I must write to my mate back home to ask him what has happened to Joyce my ex girlfriend, as I have not had a reply from him in answer to my last letter.

29th. We have been designated as duty Destroyer today so we will not be going ashore tonight, perhaps this has come at the right time for me and my mate as we are still short on the money side, this does happen very often as you go ashore in these fantastic places it's so very easy to spend more than you really should, but while I have nothing to do and it's after tea here aboard the Javelin, I have talked about anti-submarine patrols but not said just what this means aboard a Destroyer, so now to explain, first off I think that they are a waste of time as they rarely turn up anything and we have been on so many, now most ships have 'Sonar' and a rating specially trained on this equipment he sits in a small compartment down below decks, wearing headphones and sitting in front of a screen.

When the Sonar is switched on it sends a signal down into the depths of the ocean in the form of a single 'ping' noise this carries on until such time the signal sent down strikes an object and the 'Ping' echoes back to the ship and records on the screen, the operator immediately reports to the bridge by phone that he has an 'Echo' contact and gives the bearing which is showing on his screen to which the Skipper changes course towards, as the ship keeps on that course it approaches the target and the 'pings' from the Sonar get quicker, once over the top of the target the operator then reports that he is getting a continuous echo and then the order is given by the Captain to fire the depth charges, sometimes these echoes can be misleading and turn out to be nothing more than a shoal of fish or even a sunken wreck, that is all part of anti-submarine patrols.

A walk on the upper deck before turning in and I have noticed that the wind is getting up a bit looking outside that boom, I can also see that there's quite a lot of shipping in here and there also seems to be a lot more activity than usual of ships coming and going, some of these ships are loaded with Tanks and a hell of a lot of equipment such as guns aircraft parts and Army lorries of every type, I reckon that this stuff must be going into the desert for Monty's Desert Rats and from the news that we have been getting our lads have stopped Rommel's advance and are now beginning to build up their forces, so the amount of material coming through here can only mean one thing Monty is about to go on the offensive.

Now, I did mention about a lot of activity yesterday, well funnily enough this activity has now gone into working at night, the unloading of a lot of these ships suggests that there is a lot of ammunitions on them, less risks from air attacks I suppose but I wouldn't want to be anywhere near one of those ships if it went up, but there I go again it's a job and someone has to do it. One other thing is puzzling me and that is the amount of ships that are now passing down the canal and out into the Mediterranean, where the heck can they be going to?

It's got to be Cyprus or Haifa awaiting Montgomery's call, when that comes I reckon that we are going to be very busy.

But it doesn't seem to be happening yet awhile as we have been doing nothing except these boring anti-submarine patrols every day, out then back in again at night, then have to put up with the occasional air-raids so we haven't been getting much peace. I know the Destroyers are expected to do more sea time than most other ships and Javelin has certainly done more than her share just lately.

I must say that there hasn't been much excitement in the early part of this month of September, things seemed to have quietened down, that is until the early morning of the 9th September a very bright sunny morning too, we weighed anchor with the rest of the Destroyers sailing out of Port Said with all the Cruisers following, this time we thought that this is going to be another bombardment job but as we sailed on we realize that we were wrong, as there on the horizon for all to see was Alexandria.

'Wow' it was great to see, on passing through the boom I was amazed to see ships in great numbers, with old Robbo standing beside me I remarked that this is where all those merchant ships have been heading for and not Haifa or Cyprus, then he had to go and spoil it by saying "Convoy Again" but it's so amazing to see Alexandria again and untouched, because we never expected to come back here and see it just as it was (just as we left it). anyway into dry dock we go for some slight repairs, now the definition of a dry dock which I should have mentioned before is an enclosed dry basin built for the purpose of repairing and refitting ships which can sail straight into it, then the water is drained out after the gate is closed and the ship is shored up by huge timbers and sits on a Timber bed.

On completion the dock is refilled and out you go. A dry dock is also very useful and handy for personnel who have to work on ships of all kinds, all their gear can be taken up the gangway off the jetty or slung on board by crane, none of these things are possible of course if you are out in the harbour, well, here I am going on about work when I should be thinking more about getting ready for shore leave, yes leave has been given to both watches on our first day in the dry dock and for once I don't have to borrow any money as we were paid while we were in Port Said and I would sooner spend my money here than in that place. So once again we take that run ashore in this very exotic place and the three 'Bs' might be tested tonight.

The run ashore was fantastic, it's the morning after now and we have just moved out of the dry dock and are alongside a Tanker refueling. 12th September, at the moment it looks as though we could be going to sea again soon. Yes, it wasn't long after leaving that Tanker that we sailed out of Alex once more, after steaming for some hours we arrive at Port Said of all places, It appears that we've just missed a big air-raid, a couple of ships have been hit and are badly damaged at this very moment, fires can be seen burning from the upper deck down the far side of the harbour, could be some buildings on fire.

So after picking up the fleet mail including our own we hope, we soon got out of Port Said and meet up with a fair size unit of the Eastern Mediterranean Fleet, after forming up we sailed on up the coast and after travelling some distance we split up into two halves, the first lot leaving us early, the rest of us carry on further up the coast, the port of El-Darba is our target this time. When we opened up the bombardment it was really something as there are more Cruisers and Destroyers in this action and we really plastered the place, I tell you when we broke off this action there must have been total devastation on shore, fires burning in the harbour, the docks area was all lit up with flames shooting high into the night sky. I wonder how the other lot got on? apparently their target was Tobruck so we were told which is not so far up the coast as El-Darba.

I reckon the other lot should be half way back to Alexandria by now having done just as good a job as we have, this is certainly softening Rommel up for that big occasion when it comes. As we sailed away from El-Darba the fires could be seen for miles out at sea. We sailed on at speed arriving back in Alexandria very early during the morning watch, I reckon after a good nights work well done, now we expected to see the other part of our force already at anchor in the harbour when we arrived but of course they could have gone on to Port Said and I thought no more about it, that is until we sat down for breakfast, the word came from our own signals that they had not gone to Port Said.

So now we all began to suspect that something was desperately wrong 'disaster' was the word being bandied around. Unknown to us at the time, disaster was certainly the word for it as the half we left heading off for Tobruck last night had met with a shocking loss, this news was broken to the ships company by the Skipper, in the attack on Tobruck the other unit's came under heavy fire from the shore batteries and were also attacked by E-boats, the news is very bad, we have been informed that this small force has been sunk or so seriously damaged that they couldn't escape and had to be abandoned.

The Cruiser H.M.S. Coventry and two of the Destroyers I know very well, but the Tribal class Destroyers H.M.S.

Zulu and Sikh were also among those who were sunk but I couldn't say who the other Destroyers were, at this time there is no news of any survivors, they are saying that the Cruiser Coventry went down very quickly and at this moment there is no news of the other Cruiser the name which I also don't know, this is a terrible shock so many ships, the whole ships company are talking about the rotten luck, It only goes to show how lucky we were as that could so easily have been us yet we went a lot further up the coast than them and blew the hell out of El-Darba we never saw a thing, my what a 'Bloody' costly piece of action that turned out to be and to say that the lads are depressed is putting it mildly (12th September).

Here we are on the 14th September, we are Emergency Destroyer and at anchor in the harbour, things seem to have quietened down with just the normal working part ship and this was the routine for the next few days as the C-in-C has gone a bit easy on us since that catastrophe the other night, one thing that has to be realize now is that the Eastern Mediterranean Fleet has certainly been weakened by the loss of those very gallant ships and their crews, all have seen such a lot of action in these waters. The mail has arrived I have received just two letters one from my sister and one from my mate back home, this one has evidently crossed with the one that I sent back to him previously, In his letter he said that he has visited my ex-girlfriend Joyce in hospital at Stoke-on-Trent and that she is now on the road to recovery, the surprising news is that she now has another boyfriend which he didn't know about when he wrote to me before. He explained that I wouldn't be hearing from him again for some time as he had received his calling up papers and was joining the R.A.F. Well, that was some news wasn't it, I was a bit puzzled as to why my ex-girlfriend should be asking for me when she had already got another boyfriend, to think that I went to all that trouble to get compassionate leave it's a good job that I didn't get it wasn't it, I would have looked a right fool, although this is news that I really didn't want to hear, so despite all my feelings for her and the photo on my locker door I reckon that this means that I have got to put the past behind me, but that photo will still stay on my locker door.

We have been getting plenty of shore leave and are now getting a bit more used to Alexandria, also beginning to handle the natives a lot better and feeling easier when we do go ashore, but there I go again speaking too soon as we sail out of Alex, this time we are escorting two Cruisers and arrive OK at Haifa on the 19th September, expecting to get some more shore leave here but <u>no</u> the Cruisers go into the harbour and we and the rest of the escorts turn straight round back out to sea we go in a very short time. We arrive back at Alexandria, just in time to be the Emergency Destroyer again so no shore leave tonight for the Starboard watch so we can but hope that we are still here tomorrow night for our run.

Well, we are still here, nothing happened yesterday or during the night to take us out to sea and we have moved alongside the jetty again so that's a good sign. After falling in to work part ship this morning I went to climb the steel ladder to get to the pom-pom gun deck and my wrist watch fell off and dropped onto the steel deck, unfortunately it now keeps stopping and I don't know why, now I do mess about with watches a bit in my spare time having learned a little bit about the trade from a messmate on my previous ship who spent nearly all his spare time repairing the crews watches aboard, to which he earned himself a lot of spending money, it is a good hobby and a profitable one when you know how.

So my first job on going ashore tonight is to find a watch repairer or it might be a jewellers shop I don't know for sure, I can tell you that after walking round for some time we did eventually find what I was looking for and it wasn't all that far from the Fleet Club, we went in the shop and 'Wow' she is beautiful, dark hair and eye's I thought she was smashing, I explained to her how I came to drop the watch also that I did know a little bit about them, she then asked me if I was in the watch making trade to which I replied that I wasn't, then had to explain to her how I had got my knowledge about them, this got us into some sort of conversation and we seemed to be talking to each other quite naturally, It got round to her telling me that she is the shop manageress and that there is an older woman and a young chap working as assistants, the owner has another shop in the centre of Alexandria, I then asked how long it would be until I could collect the watch and she said that the watch would be ready in three days but I had to explain that it may take me longer to pick it up.

I didn't know if we might be at sea or not although it worked out that the 22nd was shore leave for the port watch again also the fact that my wrist watch had got to be paid for the following day, then the real fact that I wasn't too flushed with money, so I decided to give the run ashore a miss this time, yet all I was thinking about was seeing that girl again hoping to get more acquainted. The 24th arrived and shore leave for the port watch was piped during the dinner hour and tonight couldn't come quick enough for me, my mate had lent me a little cash so over the brow we went, he knew what I was up to as we had arranged to separate when I got to the shop, if things didn't work out we would meet up again at the Fleet Club later.

We parted and off I went straight to the shop, she said that the watch only needed a good cleaning and was now OK so I paid straight away and we began to chat again, although she seemed to be a little on the shy side we did make some form of conversation, she told me that it would soon be time to close up and would I like to have a coffee with her before she went home, now I just couldn't believe my luck and the invite was accepted, we went into a little room at the back of the shop where we had that coffee, the conversation between us was quite good and it came to me that this girl has taken a fancy to this tall blond headed sailor, my this sailor had certainly taken a great big fancy to this dark headed girl, I don't know what it is, but we chatted away in that back room without realizing that the shop closing time had gone some time ago, during that time we exchanged names and before leaving I plucked up the courage and asked her if I could see her again, I was over the moon when she said that she would like that, she gave me her phone number there and then so that I could ring her on the first day that I was free, I had explained to her that I am on a ship and only allowed ashore at certain times. I left that shop walking on air 'fantastic' I just couldn't believe that this thing had happened so quickly, now back on board and I have just written this incident with the dark haired girl down straight away as I feel so excited about it.

But that date was not going to be yet because today is the 25th and as the duty watch we have just closed up at defence stations as we are about to sail out of Alexandria, it looks as though we are going to be escorting some Cruisers, and yes we did but only so far out as all they have been doing is gunnery exercises. We returned to harbour just before nightfall going straight into the dry dock again, we are told over the tannoy that this is for a boiler clean and that both watches have been granted 48hrs leave. so now is the problem of where to spend it most of the crew decided on Cairo this time, well who wouldn't want the chance to visit this most wonderful place, my mate has decided that this is going to be the leave of all leaves.

I can only hope that he is right because this is something that I'd never dreamed of, as we are not going to set off for Cairo until the morning I can actually get ashore tonight and meet that girl, so to get to the nearest phone and make that first date and I only hope that she will understand when I explain to her about our trip to Cairo, the phone on the dockyard is very convenient and the date was made, we arranged to meet at the Fleet Club and I can't wait. Without my mate tagging along I met her outside the Fleet Club, she looked great and I took her inside for a meal and a look around the place, we had a drink or two at the bar and we had a smashing time together, when the time came for me to return to the ship she said that it had gone all too quick, she surprised me when she asked "when we can meet again" now this is where I explained about the trip to Cairo and was pleased when she said "you go and have a good time but don't forget me," 'WOW' how about that then.

So the morning came for us to set off on our leave, it wasn't long before we stepped ashore in Cairo, the first thing that we did on our arrival was to take a Gharry ride around the city, the Gharries here they are almost the same as those in Alexandria except they are much larger and have covered tops, we stopped a few times at different bars or dens I suppose you could call them, some of the girls we saw in them "well I can tell you something if they dressed like that back home they would lock them up" but they did a lot for the poor sailors eye sight, anyway we kept on stopping at all the different places for a beer or a bite to eat. The sights were fantastic you wouldn't see anything like these anywhere else in the world, there was so much of it to see but we would need a lot more than our time would permit to see the whole of this city.

We managed to find a place for the night, it wasn't too bad and the breakfast was great. For our last few hours here we just went walk about and I wouldn't have missed this for the world, just to go into one of these places at night where these dancing girls are, the atmosphere is something that you never forget and these places are the most crowded that I've ever been to, you have to be very careful how you act, enjoy yourself without trying to be too boisterous I think is the word as I think that they can turn pretty rough and there is a hell of a lot more of them than us.

There are also parts of Cairo that are very dangerous, not only were we warned by the Military police but even some of the Gharry drivers told us never to go to these area's as they are officially out of bounds to all the forces, but for us the run ashore in Cairo was perhaps the best ever but you certainly needed a lot more than the 48 hours that we have to cover the whole of this place, those hours start from when you leave the ship and ends when you arrive back on board and you had better not be adrift, you go to a place like Cairo and you see a little of the things which you never forget for as long as you live, Egypt is a wonderful country and it's capital does it proud 'Ah, Cairo we won't forget you.'

So with my leave over, here we are back on board ship and some very sad news awaits us which is that the Skipper is leaving the ship tomorrow after his promotion had been announced officially, most of us knew that it would come to this one day and so it is decided among the lads that we should have a quick whip round of the whole ships company, the money collected was handed over to one of the Petty Officers who is going ashore with postie so that he could buy a suitable gift which would be a going away present, to be presented to the Skipper when he leaves as a token of our respect, another idea was to present him with a photograph of the whole crew.

We have been told that the Skipper is going to command a Flotilla of Corvettes and I don't think that he is going to like that very much, most of the lads are surprised at this as well as this is certainly not the sort of Command that a man of his standing would have wished for, I am not alone in thinking that he deserved something much better, my we are certainly going to miss him, even now sitting here at the mess table you can hear from certain lads that they'd have gone anywhere with him, now what sort of man is going to try and replace him on board this ship surely they wouldn't be sending a rookie, it's got to be somebody used to the sort of action that we get here in the Mediterranean, but if it's a new one then we are in big trouble.

There will be a lot awaiting the arrival of this new Captain when he boards this ship and if it turns out that he is a new one then I for one would want to say goodbye to the Javelin pretty quick. So the morning came when our Skipper is to leave us, we presented him with his gift and the photo of the crew, although he didn't say anything I think he was a bit moved, but he did tell the Chief Buffer to thank the crew and wished us good luck, as he went down the gangway our Killick Robbo standing alongside me said "there goes a great Skipper, he is going to be sadly missed" and I couldn't have agreed with him more and back we went to the same old routine working part ship.

The 28th September there is some work being done on the upper deck but with the man at the helm gone nobody seems to be really bothered, but at least we are going to get some more leave and it's our watch ashore tonight, I can't wait to meet that girl on shore and give her the small gift that I bought her in Cairo, but first I must get to that phone in the harbour to let her know that we are back and I am coming ashore tonight. It's the morning after seeing her and I must write this down, I did phone her and she said that she would meet me at the Fleet Club again, but imagine my surprise when walking through the harbour gates with quite a lot of the lads, she was there waiting for me but when I walked up to her didn't I get some stick from the lads, wolf whistles the lot, she apologized thinking that I might be annoyed but I was really pleased and told her not to be sorry hoping that she wasn't embarrassed by it all.

That run ashore really cemented our relationship and once again we had a great night at the Fleet Club, this time she wouldn't let me pay for anything when I gave her a present from Cairo she kissed me (It was a beautiful silver heart shaped locket) so I guess things are going on fine as we have already made our next date, but I am also getting a lot of stick from the lads on the mess now after that little scene at the gate entrance but I don't mind. Here we are once again it's the 8th October and having sailed from Alexandria during the morning watch (I had to break off there as action stations sounded) just as I was going to say how I went on ashore last night with my girlfriend.

We had only been at sea just under an hour when we were attacked by two dive bombers screaming down like hell, the first bomb went down our starboard side but we blasted away at them, although Jimmy, the one who is was in charge of the ship did a good job. We arrived safely at Port Said and was made Emergency Destroyer straight away and again on the

9th and the 10th. On this last day we were told that the new Captain would be coming on board, so there was a bit of a rush round to get everything ship shape, he arrived on the morning of the 11th October, funnily enough I took an instant dislike to the chap and I haven't a clue as to why, but there is something about him, Robbo said maybe it's his red hair but my mate says it's the way he speaks anyway the general opinion on the mess decks is let's wait and see.

We left Port Said on the 14th October and I have not been ashore once, anyway we sailed out on exercises, we reckon to let the new Skipper get the feel of things and find out just how good his crew are. 'Well, he soon started,' we were at defence stations when we left the harbour which is the normal routine and after sailing for a short time, all of a sudden the alarm bells went off for action stations and everybody closed up at the run to their action station thinking that we were being attacked, on arrival we started the usual searching for whatever it was that had caused the alarm, going through the procedure loading the guns ready to open fire and were really ready to go, then to the surprise of every man on board the Javelin this new Skipper spoke over the tannoy system and said that this had been an exercise. This was really and truly the worst thing that he could have done to get any respect at all from the lads aboard his new ship, the words being used down most of the head phones are too much for me to write down here, but a mild one was 'What a Bloody Cheek' and I can't say that I can blame them at all, we had seen more action in just a few months than he would probably see in the whole of the war (didn't I say that there was something about him that I didn't like) we certainly didn't need him to tell us how important it is in getting to our action stations in double quick time as we had had plenty of practice, anyway we stayed at sea doing different exercises and after a really bad day we arrived back in Alexandria with most of the crew in a bad mood I reckon.

Too late for any shore leave so this made the mood even worse, come the morning I am working part ship once again and back over the side painting the pennant, it had to be a quick job which is a difficult enough one at the best of times but out here at a buoy even more so, the amount of paint work being washed down and guns being spruced up I reckon that this Captain thinks that the Javelin is not smart enough, it makes me wonder just what his last assignment was, but I suppose that we will never know but probably straight from a training establishment or ship.

The 19th October it's our turn for shore leave and I'm really ready for it, although I am seeing my girlfriend on a regular basis now on occasions I have met up with one or two of the lads when I've been out with her and of course the ribbing on the mess has got worse, the leg pulling is a regular thing now every time I get ready to go ashore but I know that some of them are envious. The last time that we went into the Fleet Club there were quite a few of the lads from my mess there and my word she didn't half get some looks but 'She's mine' fellows go find your own, but I do really like her very much and I think that although we have not known one another very long I think that the feeling is mutual, so much so now that she will not let me pay for anything when I am on shore with her and I have also been invited to her place, I haven't taken her up on that offer yet, but who knows let's say that I'm thinking about it although Robbo says "what is there to think about" anyway there is plenty of time as I reckon that we will be here for a long time yet, although you never know, anything could happen as Monty is definitely preparing for something in the desert.

But now my shore leave tonight well I must get to that phone first and let her know that I am back and really looking forward to seeing her, that was done OK and off I went with the rest of our watch once again surprised to find her waiting for me at the gates, this time old Robbo with his mate passed me as I was almost at the gate and 'Lucky Devil' came out, I reckon that I was but I was just thinking as I walked up to her that she was one of those very nice girls and not one of the ordinary every day run of the mill tarts that sailors usually pick up that hang around the dock yard gates, and it showed as she was still a little on the nervous side but we are getting on fine really, becoming more close to one another as the days pass by. It was once again a great night ashore but it all went too quickly for us but everything is OK now and we both can't wait for the next time.

Here I am back on board and I have just written this nights shore leave down, apart from a couple of drunken matelots trying to sling their hammocks and doing a lot of swearing because they keep on dropping to the deck, I am now going to climb into my hammock that is hanging just over my head and dream sweet dreams of a lovely dark haired girl (Got it bad haven't I). The morning has arrived and I have just finished my breakfast of sausage and egg (just making a point which I forgot, breakfast is drawn from the galley and you have what is going 'no choice' but tea as I have probably said before is from the food that a mess man draws from the stores and it could be tinned fish cheese corned beef bread and butter is issued every day). The Bosuns whistle is calling for the hands to fall in so must dash.

After mustering the next call was special sea duty men to their stations, so that means that we are off to sea again and out we sailed during the morning watch 20th October, we are on our own doing a sweep for enemy submarines all day, we sail back into harbour during the second dog watch so the starboard watch will get no shore leave tonight. The morning of 21st and would you believe it we are once again designated Emergency Destroyer so there will be no leave for me tonight 'I can't believe this,' but the 22nd comes round and out we sail again this time we are escorting two Cruisers who are doing Gunnery exercises while on the way to Haifa and into the harbour we go during the afternoon watch, shore leave has not been granted, but lets hope this may change tomorrow.

23rd October, I'd arranged to see a film with my mate at one of the cinema's tonight, we had seen one film and were about ten minutes into the second one when a message was flashed onto the screen recalling all the crew of H.M.S. Javelin, we were to report back to the ship immediately so there must be an emergency to be called back to the ship like that, so back to the ship we dashed, we were on board a couple of hours before we sailed and nobody seemed to know what was happening but there is one thing that I am sure of and that was the fact that we sailed with a few of the crew adrift, two from our mess that I know of have not made it back on board, it's not everybody who gets to know about these recalls then again some that do just ignore it.

What was the recall for in the first place here we are sailing on into the night and all through the night just patrolling we certainly weren't looking for anything, we didn't see anything either, well most of the lads reckon that this was another training exercise on behalf of the new Captain, perhaps he was looking for some action, anyway he would be disappointed because we were out there all night and we didn't see as much as one flying fish, we sailed back into Haifa on the 24th going straight to an Oil Tanker to refuel, then went to anchor where we remained until the second dog watch then sailed for Alexandria doing an anti-submarine sweep on the way.

25th October after arriving in Alex we went alongside the jetty and took on some fresh provisions, there was a bit of a buzz going round that Montgomery had started his offensive in the desert that it had been a real big one with hundreds of tanks involved, so our guess was right about all those tanks, aircraft parts and all the big army lorries that were going through Port Said well we did say that it looked as though Monty was getting ready for a big attack, so I reckon that we will be doing a lot more sea time now. I am jotting this down in the diary not having anything else really to write about at all, for the simple reason that we have been at sea for the last two weeks day in and day out, just continuous patrols at sea all day then into harbour at night. I must mention that on the night of Montgomery's big push a naval force consisting of Cruisers did night bombardments on the coast at the same time and all returned to base, one that we missed for once. I did manage to get a message to my girlfriend before all this started telling her that I may be away for some time and not to worry so now this has come out she will know the reason why I have not been ashore, funny thing though there has been a lot going on not very far from here yet when we have been out on these patrols we haven't seen one enemy plane.

GERMAN FIELD MARSHALS

Rommel

I suppose that with such a lot going on in the desert he is more than occupied trying to drive back those 'Desert Rats' who we now hear are driving Rommel's crack Afrika Corps back, so now we are pushing our naval patrols further out into the Mediterranean. While we were off Tobruck this morning 8th November 1942, news has come through of the landings by allied forces on the North African coast, now I reckon that's going to cause the Germans a bit of a problem because Rommels troops which are retreating fast are at some time going to have allied troops behind them also in front of them, this news has also caused a bit of a panic in Alexandria because we have been recalled from patrol with some urgency.

The problem seems to be with those French Warships in the harbour, our lot are worrying that these ships might try to break out and head for North Africa probably making a lot of trouble for our lot, so our orders are to wait outside the boom well in sight of the French ships just to deter them from doing anything silly, but we needn't have bothered as they did nothing so back into the harbour we went on November the 9th and went straight alongside the jetty finishing off the job of provisioning ship. The harbour is now beginning to fill up with Merchant Ships again and this morning we saw some Destroyers come into the harbour escorting those two big Depot Ships, so that is a sure sign that things are getting back to normal here.

The news on the radio sounds pretty good in the desert, our lads are still pushing the enemy back and they say in some parts that they have got them on the run, but the forces in North Africa have met up with some stiff resistance but are still driving slowly forward, well as things are beginning to get a bit easier in the desert so it seems are things getting easier for us here, today has passed so very slowly as we only worked until dinner time when quite surprisingly during the dinner the pipe 'Hands to make and mend' well now that means that we have the afternoon to ourselves, I don't know if I have mentioned this before but the term make and mend comes from way back in the navy and is given so that a sailor could repair any of his gear, but these days it's usually spent writing letters back home or getting your head down on the mess deck, well this is the first make and mend that we have had. My make and mend was spent washing and ironing my gear getting ready for that shore leave tonight hoping to make up for all the lost time, now I have failed to mention very much about my girlfriend apart from the fact that I think that she is lovely and just a few other little bits of information so now it's about time that I did, first off her name is Irene and she is a year younger than me at twenty, I know that her father is from Greece but I think that her mother is Egyptian but not sure, she has lived in Alex since she was three and been the manageress of the jewellers shop where she works for just over two years now and has a place of her own, oh she speaks near perfect English, I'll say it again 'I think she is great.'

Again I was met at the gates of the harbour but this time there were other girls there waiting for their boyfriends off ours and other ships, I took her to the Fleet Club again just for a drink before we went to watch a film that she wanted to see 'we had a great time' she has once again asked me if I would like to visit her home at some time and I have agreed, things are moving along nicely now and I am certainly not going to push it too fast, not that the lads in the mess will let me forget her either as I am getting my leg pulled constantly, but I'm old enough to take all that there is, one thing that I have over them while I've been going out with Irene is since I first met her I have seen a heck of a lot more of Alexandria than they have and with her being able to speak the language certainly helps a great deal also I don't get ripped off like they do.

We are really hitting it off now and she's a lovely girl, the lads on the mess say that I am a lucky so and so, I know I am, to have a girl waiting for you every time that you go ashore after being at sea is something that is really worth looking forward to, so much so that I am no longer putting off visiting her home and have phoned her asking her if it will be OK the next time I come ashore, she is really pleased, so it became possible that my first time fell one Saturday when my leave started at 1300hrs, I rang her early in the morning soon after breakfast, she was over joyed and arranged to pick me up at the gates.

So that was how it started and she was there waiting for me, it was only a short journey to where she lives not all that far from where she works, it's a lovely little place and it's her own, she said that if I would like to I can go there straight from the ship, any time that I want and further more offered me a key just to prove how much she trusts me, 'Now, how about that then,' what a nice position to be in, especially since she has told her friends all about us now. Our first time really alone together was lovely, I also found out that she can cook too. We talked quite a lot, something that we have not been able to do before, so that was my first time spent with her in the privacy of her home and she seemed to loosen up and lose some of her shyness.

Well, when I showed Robbo the key to that little place he was amazed, then out it came "My, Nick, it must be love" and when I jumped into that hammock that night I couldn't sleep for some time I just lay there thinking about her, wondering a lot because of things old Robbo said a few days ago, "have you thought that we may not be staying here much longer and could move to another area at any time then how are you going to manage and I don't suppose that she knows that this is something that you will both have to face in the near future." When I woke the next morning I was really worried as I must have fallen asleep with this lot going through my mind, the thing is that I have never even thought about this before and I certainly dare not say anything to Irene about this now.

Things certainly seem to be looking up everywhere now, we sailed out of Alexandria and waited outside the boom while four big Merchant ships, a lot more Destroyers and a number of Cruisers came out of the harbour, the Captain has just announced over the tannoy that our destination is Malta again. 17th November 1942 and I have noticed now that there are four Cruisers and a fair sized escort this time a big screen of Destroyers, 'so here we go again', we close up to action stations straight away but let's hope that this time there is not too much of the ships biscuit's and Kye (Cocoa) business like there was the last time.

I should also have said and not so much of the bombing please but if it comes it comes, we shall have to try and deal with it like we did the last time anyway with things going like they are in the desert I would think that Gerry has a lot more on his plate this time to be bothered by one convoy going through the Mediterranean, so sailing on with everyone on the alert, but there was no alarms on the first day and the morning of the second day arrived with everyone waiting but the expected didn't happen until later during the afternoon watch, with the sea beginning to get a bit rough and everyone was watching the setting sun but we didn't have long to wait, in they came Torpedo Bombers low down, there was quite a few spread out and torpedoes were dropped all over the place, everybody was scanning the sea when all at once the bridge lookout spotted one heading straight towards us off our port beam, I picked it up in my binoculars as the ship was slewing hard over at full speed so as to move our stern out of the way. Those that could see that torpedo watched with bated breath as that tin fish passed our stern by only a few yards and actually ran through our wake, both my mate and I had a grandstand view as it passed out of our sight and carried on for what seemed only a few seconds then there was an almighty explosion! The torpedo struck the Cruiser H.M.S. Arethusa just forward of her port beam, she was on fire and in a bad way that was plain to see, Javelin being nearest to her altered course straight away to give her assistance and I could see that she was well and truly on fire and stopped now, H.M.S. Jervis Captain 'D' who was also on her port bow raced to her aid but there wasn't much that we or anyone could do apart from giving her cover while she tried to put out the fire.

The weather is going to cause some trouble because it looked like a storm was on it's way, that's all we need at this time especially as she will certainly have to be taken in tow, while watching this, one of our escorts picked up a submarine echo and started to drop depth charges at the same time, my mate nudged me and said "she is moving again" but the smoke was pouring out of her and there was a huge hole in her side. The convoy sailed on into what was a fading light now, as far as we know there was no-one else hit and here we are once again this time with two other Destroyers and a stricken Cruiser, the Javelin might have a part to play again, but I was very pleased when the job of towing was assigned to H.M.S. Petard, all I can say is good luck to her as she is surely going to need it.

I haven't forgotten that load of trouble that we went through in towing the Nestor but this is something different, a Destroyer towing a Cruiser and it will be a very slow speed, I can't imagine what it's like aboard that stricken Cruiser at this moment it must be terrible, of course she has the job of trying to keep afloat and put the fires out then there are all the casualties to contend with and most of all get safely back to harbour in this rotten weather, I don't know for sure but the grim solemn task before that of burying her dead comrades while still at sea, although I don't like to say this but on looking at their damage there must be quite a few.

Now, as for the attacking torpedo bombers I understand that two of them were shot down but we didn't see any of this as they were on the starboard side, but those that were on our side dropped their torpedoes a long way off and so kept well out of gun range, so with night drawing in fast hopefully there will be no more attacks unless it's by E-boats, so the Arethusa should be OK, it has been decided by Captain D that we and the Jervis are going to be the escort for the Arethusa and the

Petard, so we have now turned round and are heading back to Alexandria, it's going to be a very long slow journey with possible problems on the way back, it turned out that during the night the Arethusa was finding some difficulty of some sort while being towed forward and it was decided to try Stern first. Apparently this was of some help so that was the way that we left them when we received a signal during the morning watch telling us to break off and steam back to the convoy, so we left the Jervis and the Petard still pushing on with stricken Arethusa slowly a long way from Alexandria. The storm had broken during the middle watch and ploughing through heavy seas we dashed off back to join up with the convoy again and I can tell you this if you have never been on a Destroyer in a force eight gale well you have never been in the real navy. 19th November we finally arrive back at the convoy still sailing on towards Malta, from a signal that we received they had just beaten off an attack by a number of dive bombers and without any damage to the four Merchant ships. The weather is really bad now if anything I think that it had worsened during the morning watch and looking across at those big Merchant ships I could see that they were taking a real buffeting, but ploughing on at a steady rate of knots and hoping that we wouldn't be getting any more attacks when all of a sudden out of a laden sky twelve fighter planes came diving in over the convoy! wings going in salute, 'what a relief' they were ours and great cheers went up all around the ship, they had flown out of Malta to give us some escort the rest of the way to the harbour, so we had actually made it at last and as the convoy would be arriving at Malta that evening a lot of the Destroyers were ordered to turn round 'their job well and truly done.' In this very rough sea doing a turn was going to be a hell of a job as by now we had got to do this turn into mountainous waves, it was almost the end of the Javelin as we almost capsized as she keeled right over onto her side, with the amount of sea water that came inboard we lost two of the lads over the side, 'I consider myself extremely lucky,' we had changed from action to defence stations now that we had air escort, the starboard watch were on duty and I was just about to go down the starboard waste outside on the upper deck when she suddenly went over on her side and I grabbed hold of the nearest thing to me which happened to be the pom-pom deck ladder and the sea sweeping down the side of the ship whipped off my sea boots! 'That was a real scary moment I can tell you.'

They say that we did a sixty three degree roll but a lot of the lads say that it was more than that, one or two of the old three badge men reckon that they have never experienced anything like it, but when I went back onto the mess decks it was a complete shambles, broken crockery and stuff everywhere amongst the sea water, I had to paddle through this lot to get back to my locker so that I could find something to wear on my feet, the problem was there was so much stuff down, lads all trying to sort something out of all the mess that for quite some time I was better off walking about bare footed, now I said that it was a scary moment for me well if I speak the truth I reckon that this lot had scared the living day lights out of most of this ships company it was a very close thing.

It turned out to be that bad that the Skipper had to take emergency measures and ordered an empty tank to be filled with sea water to act as ballast, after that she seemed to settle down a bit, but sitting here now writing this I can say that if the Javelin had gone down nobody on this ship would have stood a cat in hells chance of being picked up or surviving in this weather, I certainly wouldn't like to be where those sea boots are now. It's the morning after and I reckon that not many of the lads got much sleep last night that included me as it turned out to be a terribly wild night, later on in the day this incident was put down to the fact that we were very low on fuel, now I wonder who's fault that was. I would just like to say "those poor lads that we have lost over the side wouldn't have stood a chance."

We sailed on and after some hours we left the rest of the ships, we went into the harbour at Tobruck which was now back in our hands again and went alongside a Tanker to have the water pumped out of our fuel tank, some time later the tank was topped up with oil and while this was in progress the alarm went for action stations while an air raid was taking place on Tobruck. Although bombs were dropped on shore none fell in the harbour and whilst all this was taking place we had a visit from a number of our M.T.B.'s asking for any spare supplies also passing on the good news that the convoy had arrived safely in Malta.

Out we sailed hopefully on our way to Alexandria and who should we see just as we approach the boom but H.M.S. Petard behind the Arethusa who was now being towed in by tugs, I reckon that they must have had some trouble with the bad weather, on entering the harbour we secured at the jetty as the Arethusa tied up at the far end, I wasn't surprised to see ambulances waiting on the dock side, I'm wondering just what number of casualties she did sustain, for that information I didn't have to wait very long as the Petard tied up alongside us and passed on the news that unfortunately '156 officers and men lost their lives' the number injured is not known at this moment but they say that there must have been quite a lot, this incident was just sheer bad luck for Arethusa as she would not have seen that tin fish coming towards her so no chance to steer clear.

What a terrible tragedy it was and what must it be like for the rest of the crew, many who have lost their mates but then again we grieve for all our lads, when you see these things happen you can understand why sailor's have so much hatred for all submarine crews, they do their dirty work unseen, it has also been known for them to surface after sinking a vessel then machine gun the lifeboats and men swimming in the oily water, this is something that never happens aboard a British submarine. 22nd November at Alexandria, we have received a message from the C-in-C to all ships that took part in the convoy to Malta on the 17th November "Well Done" and every ship was granted 24hrs leave.

Yes, very nice indeed but little consolation for the crew of H.M.S. Arethusa who had just lost all their mates or for that matter all those ships and crews who took part in the previous catastrophe to Malta, didn't their efforts against all the odds deserve some words of thanks, we went through some real action in those six days, we lost some good ships and crews but I suppose that because we didn't make it to Malta it wasn't worth a mention, so the only good thing to come out of all this is the 24hrs leave which I think that every ship in the Eastern Mediterranean Fleet deserves. Most of the lads off the Javelin are planning another trip to Cairo but not for me thank you I intend to spend mine with my girl friend and just as soon as I get the chance I'm off to that dockyard phone.

It wasn't until later that I managed to get ashore to that phone, Irene was already at home when I told her the good news, she was really pleased and said that I was to go straight to her place when I get ashore, so now I must start to get my kit ready for tomorrow I know that my mate is going to Cairo again but I don't think that twenty four hours gives you enough time to really enjoy yourself there, but for me it's all arranged so for now it's out with the soap, out with the old bucket and get dhobying (that's washing in civvy street) my gear I can't wait for 1300hrs tomorrow.

The 23rd arrives and off I go straight to Irene's place, to my surprise she was there to meet me and had actually taken the time off work for my leave. The time that we spent together was great. we had talked so much and things were now perfect between us, she just asked me out of the blue to stay the night as I hadn't even made any arrangements, in fact with being in a hurry to see her again I hadn't even thought about it this I explained to her but she said that it was settled then. The night turned out all that we wanted it to be, neither of us wanted this short 24hrs to end but end it did in the most unusual fashion. early in the morning on the 24th the military police are all over the place on the road outside, some in small vehicles shouting through loud hailers for all Naval personnel to report back to the their ships immediately as they drove around, the noise that they were making I am sure woke everyone in the vicinity, well what about that for a let down, so what had been a lovely day and night is certainly spoilt for us, just to say that I am furious would put it mildly, so very reluctantly I dressed and as I kissed Irene she was shedding a few tears, I was so very sorry that I had to leave her like that, it is only 0700hrs, the only thing that I could do was to promise that I would make it up to her, so back to the ship I go and on the way meeting up with quite a lot of lads all heading back to their ships.

So here I am now back on board and have been here nearly all day waiting for men to come back off shore leave, it's quite obvious that we're going to be very short on crew as they are coming aboard in ones and two's. Now here I would just like to say thank you very much Sir for the 24hrs leave that you gave us and we didn't get. We sail out of Alexandria late at night on the 24th, there are still quite a few of the lads missing which is natural as I know for sure that most of our lads are still in Cairo, there are three off our mess alone so what chance have they of finding them? Being in Cairo how many of them will want to be found? After all 24hrs leave should mean 24hrs, not 15.

We are escorting a large number of Merchant ships, the escort consists of four Cruisers and quite a few Destroyers, I just wonder how many crew members are still missing off these other ships. What do you know we have just been told over the tannoy that our destination is Malta once again, well we knew that we would be going back to Malta but nobody expected it to be after only a few days 'really,' we haven't hardly got over the last one but that's the war for you. So what can we expect this time well Monty is still driving Rommel's army back and according to the latest news it's ongoing, we said last time that the Germans would be having a lot to contend with in the desert to bother about a convoy and look what it cost us, sailing on and what we expected never came about, we sailed on up that Mediterranean sea like it was a peace time cruise and we didn't see one enemy aircraft. What a relief it was, so for once a convoy goes through to Malta from Alexandria without a shot being fired. When we sailed into the Grand Harbour at Malta on the 27th November 1942 we are met with something really special, you would have to see it with your own eye's to believe it, 'thousands of people,' I have never seen anything like it in all my life they must have known that this convoy was on it's way here, Malta Valleta harbour itself stands back very high up it surround's the Grand Harbour and the roads have walls all the way round them, it is here that the sight of a life time is being displayed because these walls are jam packed with people everywhere, cheering, shouting and waving flags of all sorts, the noise from the harbour walls and the few ships that are in the harbour sounding off with their sirens and hooters as we enter is something that's brought a lump to my throat, this is a fantastic sight.

The grey sandstone walls all draped with bunting of every colour, the buildings that had stood everything that the Germans could throw at them like the people, defiant to the last and don't forget these people have really suffered, the bombings must have been terrible at times and at what cost, they have been almost at starvation point but at last it is all over for them now and this fantastic reception will not be forgotten by any of us Navy lads for a very long time, I can honestly say that this lot brought tears to a good many sailors eye's and that included mine. This convoy although smaller than the one that had to turn back is by far the biggest in ship size that has reached Malta yet and the quantity of food that they carry will no doubt improve life a little bit more but I suppose it will be a long time before Malta gets back to anything like normality again. Javelin went to anchor at last, with satisfaction we have finally made it to Malta, I just couldn't believe our luck, we have been made Emergency Destroyer straight away.

Well, we might have known, as it is getting towards nightfall let's hope that we will not be required for any call outs as we have only this one nights duty. The air-raid siren went after being here a few hours but they are high level bombers having a go at the air field so we're told by one of the P.O.'s, although now that Malta has her Spitfires I wouldn't think that Gerry will be very successful and so it proved as the siren went for the all clear after about one hour. Shore leave is granted to the port watch, my mate and I decided to have a look around just to see what Malta really looks like at least be able to say that we have been ashore.

Back on board it won't take me very long to write these few words before slinging my hammock, I can only say it's a shambles at the moment but then again we didn't expect it to be anything else not after the hammering that Malta's had although I reckon that it must be a nice place in peace time, at the moment it's how you would expect somewhere to look that has really been in the wars, how they managed to stick it out in those conditions well only they know that but things will get better in time, on looking at all the damage here it's going to be a very long job, it's going to take a lot of hard work to get things moving as there are a lot of wrecks in the harbour and loads of damage to make good.

Well, with that out of the way and my hammock slung I can now write some letters while there is some peace on the mess deck as most of our mess are still ashore, my first one must be to Irene back in Alexandria who I don't suppose I shall be seeing a lot of in the future, but I don't know for sure just guessing, I am praying that this is not so but I don't think that there will be very much activity at that end of the Mediterranean now that Malta has at last been freed, I won't be able to tell her anything in this letter just hope to see you soon I reckon, when we had our long conversation at her place I did explain that this sort of thing could happen, we just hoped that it wouldn't.

Anyway here goes for a nice long love letter to a lovely girl, I must try to explain to her not to worry, that I am OK and lots more that I am not going to tell you about, I will have to break off there as the sirens are going, the duty watch gun crews are heading for their action stations but I don't think that they will be of much use as once again it looks as though they could be the high level bombers and the ordinary small ack-ack guns would be of no use at all with the range being too far for them to have any chance at all, I just hope that there are no lights showing on the jetty where they are unloading those big Merchant ships that we brought in, it would be a terrible shame if anything were to happen to them now.

It was amazing to see the number of men unloading the first two ships that went alongside, it was only a short time after we had anchored. I reckon that they will be working throughout the night too and will need to as it will take some days to unload all four of those ships. I've heard a few bombs drop while this air-raid has been going on but it sounded a long way off not anywhere near the harbour area of Valetta. Where we are anchored is not actually in the harbour but way down at the other end, up what I think is what the locals call a Creek which is partly obscured by trees on either side. we are not the only ones here so I reckon that we should be fairly safe, anyway the all clear is sounding off again so that wasn't a long raid so we might get a good nights sleep for once and hope that tomorrow doesn't bring another duty watch for us.

We sail out of Malta on the 29th November, in company with Captain D and two other Destroyers, the Kelvin and Tribal class H.M.S. Nubian and we are now doing patrols off Malta, after sailing for some hours at sea lights are sighted on the horizon and we all turned towards it making speed and as we get closer in the dark we see it's a ship on fire, getting nearer we all get in line closing to her stern, finding that it was a small liner or a passenger type ship towering above us as we passed up her port side, then we were that close that we could see in the light of the fire people leaning over the guard rail and pointing down at us as we went past.

She was well and truly on fire and stopped in the water, as we steamed around her bows a searchlight was switched on by H.M.S. Jervis picking out what appeared to be an Italian ship, a Destroyer was alongside the stricken vessel taking off survivors there was also another Destroyer with a number of smaller ships at the scene but standing off a bit, well, we all opened up! In a very short action one of the Destroyers had been sunk some of the smaller ships were either sunk or left on fire, I can only hope that the smaller ships were not loaded with soldiers or civilians, the one other Destroyer escaped as soon as the firing started, he was away and although fired on he did manage to get away.

We left the scene of this action with the liner still burning fiercely, probably a lot of people still on board, it wasn't going anywhere was it, only to the bottom of the Mediterranean in time. We carried on with our patrols searching for any more enemy shipping but despite a big search throughout the night no more were picked up so we headed back to Malta after what was a very successful operation. On arriving back into harbour we were given some news that I didn't want to hear, "As of the 29th November we are now based here in Malta" so we should have been told that yesterday now with this news I got my first piece of sympathy from old Robbo because he could see that I was very disappointed when this news came through while sitting at breakfast, his last words were "I warned you didn't I."

What rotten luck but I should have guessed that this would happen some day but I did hope that it wouldn't be for a long time yet, now there's my girlfriend all those miles away and I may never see her again so yet another letter, but still I can't disclose what has happened as I have explained before that all our mail is censored, I suppose that she is anxiously waiting for our next meeting but there is nothing that I can do about it although I am sure that she will realize that after a time that something has happened to keep me away from her, she will then get the message, but I am hoping that it will not be the last time I'm certainly going to miss her and this would have to happen just when we were getting on so well together. I have written to Irene now, it was a very long letter and with all the love that I have given to her I think that she will get the message.

We are now in the month of December and have not had much shore leave, from the 4th to the 7th we have been at sea each day meeting convoys out at sea and escorting them back into Malta or out on patrol doing anti-submarine sweeps even escorting empty ships down the Mediterranean and leaving them with their original escorts then returning to base. There is so much activity going on now at Malta with the blockade broken there are ships of all sorts and sizes arriving every day with much needed supplies, so Malta is beginning to get back to some normality now, the place is packed with sailors of all nationalities so there should be money pouring into the shops and bars 'that is if they have got any decent beer to drink yet.'

After coming in from patrols on the 7th December we have been alongside the jetty doing a boiler clean of sorts, each watch has been granted 24hrs leave but my mate and I are not taking this up but are going to do just the normal run ashore mainly for the beer as we have been told that they have now got some draught beer as well as tins of new stuff, so as there is nothing else to spend our money on at the moment that will be our run ashore and back on board after to sling the old hammock. The run ashore we did finding that they did have some new beer and it was as they said not too bad at all but there is still no real night life or entertainment yet but I'm sure that I will sleep a lot better in my hammock than I would have if I was on shore.

The boiler clean is completed and out to sea we go on 10th December, on patrol we did have a bit of excitement as a submarine was spotted on the surface but far too late for us to ram her and she had dived long before we got to her position and despite getting a contact dropping some depth charges nothing came of it and we soon lost the contact all together, so carried on with our patrol but we were never near enough to the enemy coast to really meet up with any opposition, so back into Malta we sail and we had hardly the time to anchor before the sirens sound off but luckily it was beginning to get dark, but I say luckily as the bombs began to fall into the harbour this time evidently they are now after the merchant ships that are bringing in all the supplies, they evidently know that there are plenty here now.

This was a real go this time, I could also hear the crunch of bombs falling in the distance and dropping on shore so this might be the air fields again, there was a hell of a noise from the guns ashore, they reckon that a lot of these are the Navy 4inch high angle guns and they take some beating, but once again when the morning came I could see no damage to any of the shipping or any in the harbour area, no bombs dropped here in the creek, yes I've found out that we are at anchor in 'Selima Creek' that is the proper name for it. While we were at sea yesterday the mail arrived for us and I received two letters one I had really been looking forward to from Irene, I think that I must have read it at least half a dozen times since I opened it, as it is such a lovely letter.

I guessed right when I said that she would realize what had happened, she doesn't know where we are but knows that we are no longer in Alexandria, enclosed is a smashing photo of herself and has had the photo that I gave her of me enlarged and kisses it every night before she goes to sleep, she is praying that this is not the end of our love and that she is missing me very much, she begs me not to forget her and to please write more often to ease her worry, I shall have to write straight back today when I get the chance.

The month of December has been fairly quiet oh I know that we have been doing all these patrols and have been in action a few times but a lot of the danger seems to have dropped off apart from the air raids here.

It does seem funny though to think that every time that we go to sea we always seemed to be looking up into the sky or searching the horizon at sunset and dawn of every day for those bombers and the E-boats, now they aren't there any more, but don't get me wrong we are still very diligent, always on the lookout not intending to be caught out as we know that there is always some sort of danger out there, and as Robbo says "don't count your chickens just yet" wise words from an old hand, but we have been doing these patrols now nearly every day and Malta is getting back to strength day by day with more and more ships arriving with things beginning to move onshore, even some shops are now open so it can be seen that things are slowly getting back to some form of normality.

I have just mentioned the word normality, well how about this, the 25th December 1942 and it is Christmas day and the one day in the whole year when every sailor in the Royal Navy likes to let his hair down a bit, here H.M.S. Javelin is lying at anchor in Malta harbour with a force eight gale blowing outside with H.M.S. Jervis Captain D emergency Destroyer and the Javelin is the standby duty Destroyer, now surely there wouldn't be anyone foolish enough to be out at sea today in this lot, not if they could help it, so we reckon that we should be OK to enjoy the usual Christmas festivities, of course the matelot's on both of the ships really looking forward to their turkey, Christmas pudding, the tots of rum the sippers and that drop of rum that most matelots keep in a bottle for special occasions.

Everyone was having a great time and it was as if there was no tomorrow, the great Christmas dinner has been eaten the pudding well there was enough rum in it to make your head spin and toes curl, I am sure that if someone had put a match to it the ship would've blown up 'only joking though,' but our Christmas pudding is made with rum mostly and very little water is used that's what we call some pudding, 'what a great Christmas,' now, I had already slung my hammock in anticipation of getting my head down after the dinner, some of the lads were already lying down on the lockers the worse for wear (rum wise), It had certainly taken it's toll, when all at once in the distance it seemed some fool was having us on and piping "Hands to stations for leaving harbour all the port watch close up."

"Get off" or such words someone shouted but when the Killick sitting next to me said "come on Nick that's us" I knew it was no joke, I just couldn't believe this, but close up we did and out we sailed following on just behind H.M.S. Jervis into that force eight gale. Having closed up I reported to the bridge 'P1 Oerlicon closed up' (everybody has to report to the bridge when closed up at their stations) but I think that everybody is like me expecting to have some information passed down to them as to what was going on but nothing was said, I could hear through the head phones the same question was being asked by everyone, on we sailed into the really wild storm and after sailing for some time we spotted lights off our starboard bow, they seemed to be flashing all the time.

Action stations was sounded and we expected to be in action at any time now but I couldn't make out what these lights were except that they didn't seem to be getting any nearer and after some time began to realize that what we were looking at was lights on land, a message was passed down from the bridge to keep a sharp lookout, from then onwards we just patrolled back and forwards all the time keeping those lights in our sights all through a terrible night. In the morning we found out that we had been patrolling off the coast of Sicily looking for anything that we could sink but the problem was that even the Germans had the good sense to enjoy their Christmas day and not be so bloody stupid as to deliberately go to sea in a force eight gale when he didn't have to. What made it even worse is that we never saw a sign of any ships at all, as my mate says "well we did see some pretty lights flashing on the sea wall outside Sicily harbour" so ended our Christmas for 1942, wet through and tired we sailed back to Malta during the morning watch going straight to anchorage, it was then that we found out what this Christmas day charade had been all about, the Skipper on the Javelin had been ashore in Malta and seen some big wig at Naval HQ and had asked for permission to go to sea in other words he had volunteered to go to sea on Christmas day, but the whole ships company knew that as the Captain of the duty standby Destroyer that if he got that permission that he surely must realize that H.M.S. Jervis who was the Emergency Destroyer would also have to sail out with us and her Captain was the senior Officer, I wouldn't think that this had ever been done before. Now, I wonder how Captain D would be feeling about that! 'Bloody furious' I reckon, what about his crew? not only was our Christmas ruined but we also ruined theirs and I know for sure that this is going to cause some trouble the first time we step ashore, our lads are not very pleased about that in fact everybody is furious to think that two ships companies had a perfectly good Christmas ruined by one man, well things on board got even worse during the day so much so that the Captain was finally informed by one of the Officers of the whole ships companies feeling's about this affair and that we are very angry that he had actually volunteered to go to sea and by our actions had forced another ship to go to sea with us.

The consequences of which we will soon find out the first time we step ashore and meet up with the crew of H.M.S. Jervis, as we know that there will be trouble no doubt then obviously some complaints from the Maltese authorities, well all the lads were wondering what his reply would be to this and it wasn't long in coming, "the Captain will speak to the ships company over the tannoy" was announced by the Bosuns mate as he went around the ship piping his message just after the first dog watch and before any leave had been piped, his message to the ships company was "I know that it was Christmas day but I thought that the best way to celebrate Christmas was to go out and meet the opposition, they started this war, I and others want to see it finished as soon as possible." I can only say that if he could have heard what all the lads on the mess decks thought of that idea, as everyone was saying what a load of old rubbish in loud terms and that he didn't care a stuff for the crew or their Christmas, speaking for myself I am very pleased that we didn't meet any of his so called opposition because I'm pretty sure that I would have had a job to focus on anything, my mate who is younger than me was in a far worse state and he would have had to fire the gun, I know that quite a lot of the lads were just as bad and if it had come to any action they would probably have sunk the Jervis let alone any enemy ships, but old Robbo summed it up proper when he said "Thank the lord that we didn't run into any of the Italian Fleet" and from one of the lads "Bring back the old Skipper he wouldn't have pulled a stunt like that."

I would just like to mention here that we didn't have much trouble when we went ashore the first time after the 'Opposition Farce', but we did have to explain to some of the Jervis crew that we on board the Javelin were just as upset over this incident as they were and that we had shown it on board the ship by having the Captain explain his reasons for going to sea.

Malta harbour 1943 the weather is still very bad outside, no ships going out and none coming in, it's been that way since Christmas Eve, we even had a force nine gale blowing on Boxing Day so we just escaped that but it does seem to be bating a little now. 4th January and here we are again out at sea having sailed during the forenoon watch into what is still heavy seas, ploughing on we eventually arrive at the port of Tobruck once more this place has certainly been done over since we were here last.

Looking around this harbour there are one or two wrecks that were not here before so they must have been sunk here in a very short time as the last time we called here there was just one which had been there from the very start and that was almost in the entrance, Tobruck it'self seems to have had it's share of air raids as the place looks a shambles now, although I think that Tobruck has seen some of the most fiercest fighting of the desert campaign up to now so I suppose it should show a lot of scars, we didn't stay long before we were sailing out again arriving at Alexandria on the 7th January going straight alongside the jetty leave is piped for the port watch that evening, now I was really excited and looking forward to this leave more than anything but first I have to get to that phone and give Irene a wonderful surprise. I can hardly wait to see her again and of course it shows, I am having quite a lot of the usual leg pulling from the lads on the mess but I couldn't care less we are back in Alexandria that's all that matters, I have just a few moments ago made that all important phone call and she squealed when she heard my voice on the end of the phone, she is going to be there at the gates to meet me and is over the moon, I can't wait that call for liberty men to fall in it can't come soon enough for me, the working day of part ship seemed as though it was deliberately taking it's time but it came at last and there she was smiling as though it was only a few days since we had parted.

As I got closer to Irene I could see that she had tears in her eyes and it really hit me hard I did what I couldn't help doing and kissed her and off we went, we had a few wonderful hours together it was something to remember for both of us, and before we parted I thought it best to explain to her what our situation is now that things had altered in the desert, heart breaking as it was I had to tell her that there was always a chance that I might never see her again as we could be stationed at Malta for a long time or even be transferred to some other part of the world and that there was nothing I could do about it, I'm afraid this news really broke her up and I was at a loss as to what to do except to hold her close.

It was a long passionate last hour, after a lot of talking neither of us could say what would happen, the only thing is to wait and see and just hope, I also had to say that we wouldn't be staying in Alexandria very long I couldn't hazard a guess as to when we would be coming back again so the embrace and the kisses were far more longer and passionate this time, I left her feeling very sad, writing this now after coming back on board with almost everybody turned in except me, I was really feeling this. after working part ship today the 8th January I am still full of the talks that Irene and I had, but can't help but feel sorry for her, but there is hope as I have been told that we may not be leaving here just yet. he starboard watch went ashore tonight and I can only hope and pray that I might get another chance ashore tomorrow.

The 9th dawns and we have been working part ship all morning, nobody seems to know just when we are sailing again, having just finished dinner it won't be very long before we will know one way or the other, it didn't come until stand easy was piped "Leave to the port watch" I managed to get to the phone just before tea so it was one more time of togetherness and was over all too quickly for both of us. Back on board again I got the news from Robbo that we are sailing tomorrow, the 10th January out we sail during the morning watch, after doing an anti-submarine patrol we entered Tobruck again on the 11th.

We stayed in Tobruck overnight then sailed out again during the forenoon watch we are evidently heading back to Malta, on the way we received a signal that H.M.S. Packenham had sunk a submarine off Malta whilst doing anti-submarine sweeps 'great news again' and we enter the harbour anchoring in our usual place on the 14th January, sail out again on the 16th at night during the first watch Javelin in the company of H.M.S. Packenham, we were doing a sweep for any enemy shipping and this time we sailed a lot nearer to the African Coast and after some considerable time we struck lucky in picking up a large Merchant ship (when I say picking up I mean we picked it up on our radar screen), she started to make a run for it heading for the port of Tripoli but she stood no chance, after a short chase we both closed in on her both ships opened fire and within a very short time round after round were finding their target, very soon she stops and we fire Star Shells (these are Calcium flares that float down on a small parachute I think I've mentioned that before somewhere,) anyway these light up the whole scene and it's plain to see that she is now on fire and is as we suspected a fair sized Merchant ship, men can actually be seen standing at the guard rails and as we are watching these men we can see some jumping into the sea. From my position on P1 Oerlicon the ship appeared to be sinking slowly, now the fire was definitely getting a real hold and lighting up the night sky, she seems to be listing over to starboard I reckoned that it must be getting very warm on that deck, my mate had also pointed out that in the light from the fire he could see men swimming in the water towards us, soon after, the order was given from the bridge to lower the scrambling net and standby to pick up survivors, as they climbed up the lads are there to help them over the guard rail and onto the deck, it is noticeable that some of them are in need of help as they are injured and also assistance to get them down to the mess decks.

Quite a few of the survivors are OK but wet and really shaky, very nervous too, anyway we managed to pick up twenty eight and despite scanning the water for some time we didn't see any more men, but I suppose that the Packenham could have picked up some of them as there must have been a lot more in the crew than these few and of course there would have been some casualties, well we soon found out that they are all Italians and after the enemy ship had gone down we did another quick search of the area just in-case there's the odd one or two still swimming around but no more survivors were picked up so we turned away and headed back to Malta.

We went from action stations to defence watches, I made my way down onto the mess decks and one of these Italians was sitting at our mess table he was also sitting on my locker, the lockers on Destroyers are fixed to the bulk head acting as seats on one side of the mess table, anyway this chap had a terrible wound to the top of his head a piece of shell fragment had struck him just above his nose on the front of his forehead and passed right through his scalp from front to back opening a very nasty wound it was a horrible sight, the poor bloke just sat there in a daze and I am sure that he must have been in some terrible pain, well I felt really sorry and sat down beside him, one of the lads made some tea and I gave him a cup and started to try and talk to him so as to settle him down but he didn't understand much English, he got out some photo's and began to show me and the lads some snaps of his wife, baby, home and parents.

One or two of the lads in our mess were really shook up about this chaps condition and I say it again he must have been in terrible pain yet he didn't show it at all, one of them put some rum in his tea and he seemed very pleased about that, I was really touched and it made me realize once again these people are after all human beings just the same as us, as we sailed on towards Malta our lads were wondering what would become of these men after all they were only merchant seaman, as most of the crew were feeling very sorry for the chap with the scalp wound we asked if it would be possible for us to have a check or a progress report on how he gets on? The medics on shore said that if it is possible they will get a message back to us.

So all the survivors were landed ashore during the morning watch on the 17th January, we arrived while there is an air-raid on and it seems that the air fields are the target, we have also been told that there could have been some mines dropped in the harbour during the night as a Corvette had heard some splashes 'What a Joke' anyway it didn't stop us from leaving harbour as soon as we had landed our survivors 'mines or no mines' doing our usual anti-submarine sweep and having a very rough time out there, being on a Destroyer in bad weather you know you are at sea, but on the bigger ships there is some rolling and pitching but nothing like the smaller ships.

On our return to Malta at night we could see the gun flashes when we were some way off the Island, it was touch and go if we would be able to get into the harbour at all then to top it all we received a signal at the entrance that some mines have been dropped for certain in the harbour, that was going to be a problem for us as we had to get across to the other side to our anchorage somehow, but how do you do it when it's dark and the mines are there somewhere, yet not knowing just how many have been dropped, so it was going to be pot luck for us, we started to move very slowly but then it was decided that we would anchor for the night then move to our regular sight in the morning, so when morning came a Mine Sweeper appeared and started to sweep for the mines and after some time passed we were allowed to move to our regular berth, no one was allowed in or out of the harbour while these mines were being swept and that took all morning.

In the late afternoon we weighed anchor and went alongside a Tanker to refuel then alongside the jetty to take on some more ammunition and back to our anchorage, now, you might think that after all the sea time we have been doing just lately we would be getting some shore leave . . . but not likely.

9th January 1943 we weighed anchor once again and join up with H.M.S. Kelvin sailing out of Malta and it's another night time patrol again, the last time we were lucky, well Kelvin is the leading Senior Officer and all that stuff, we sail straight for the coast once more as reports have been coming in that Monty is only forty miles from Tripoli so the Germans might be trying to send through some reinforcements to Rommel who by now must be very short on supplies.

So here we are closed up at action stations and have been going up and down this coast for some time expecting to find some kind of shipping, but it's now well past midnight. I forgot to mention in my diary that on the 18th there was some changing round of action stations, I am actually sitting here writing these few notes down in my note book on a magazine hatch which is open, as soon as any action starts I will be down in that magazine. I am now writing this after some action, when I said that it was after midnight we finally struck lucky when we picked up on our Radar screen a fair sized convoy of ships moving away from Tripoli so we turned towards them going straight into action.

Now, I wasn't going to see any of this action, oh, I was going to be in it that's for sure but not from behind a gun, no it was in the worst possible place to be when in action and that's down in the magazines, I was partnered in there with the lad who I used to be with on defence stations on the starboard ack-ack gun, "A" magazine was now my action station and Fletcher my mate is also on my mess now, our job is to keep the guns supplied with shells and cordite by putting them onto a hoist which carries them up to the gun platforms on the upper deck, from down here we don't know about anything that is happening up top, all we can hear is when the guns fire and the revving of the engines as the ship speeds up or slows down then it goes quiet again, then off it goes again, one thing about these magazines it gets really warm and it's no light weight job either. Both the shell and cordite cannisters are fairly heavy and to top it all when you go down into the magazine you are fastened in with the clips on the hatch cover, this is done for the ships safety if it catches fire, why? you might ask, well to save the ship from blowing up, the magazine is flooded and I can say with all honesty when that hatch closes after you and your mate and the the clips go on it's pretty scary, the men down there deserve a bloody medal, oh it's all right for them up top if the ship gets hit they stand a chance but down there in the magazine on a small ship not much chance at all. As I said we only know when the action is over when the hoist stops working and everything goes quiet, the banging of those guns seemed to go on forever, we were both soaking wet with sweat, then all at once the noise stopped and for some minutes we just waited to see what was going on then a kind person up top remembers that we were stuck down there and opened the hatch cover, we climbed out to find what all the noise was about, we found that the ship was abuzz with the news that between us Javelin and Kelvin have sunk 'Eleven' enemy ships only one managing to get away, Robbo told us that we were throwing depth charges at them again, well all I can say is that me and my mate Fletcher were only too glad to get out of that sweat box by the time the action had finished as it was really warm down there, it wasn't until later on that we found out we had been down there in that magazine for just over three hours.

No survivors were picked up after the action this time but some of the lads said that they heard a lot of shouting coming from the water and I pity them because the sea isn't a nice place to be swimming about in especially when it's dark. We sailed on and with a good nights work well done and arrived back in Malta in the early hours of the morning the 20th and went straight to our station, for once we had no duties, just working part ship as usual but for some of the lads that are getting some more ammunition on board, a thankless job at the best of times, the pipe by the Bosuns mate for shore leave went during stand easy and it's leave to the port watch who are off duty so my mate and I decided to have a run once again.

Onshore we quickly noticed that there had been a lot of improvements made since we last went ashore, one thing that we noticed straight away was that a tea room had opened up so in we went just to see what was on offer and were quite surprised, we actually got something to eat with our cup of tea so things are looking up but the night life doesn't seem to have altered much yet although the beer seems to be a lot better, I suppose given time everything will return to normal, after all the battering that Malta has taken and what the people have had to endure will get really back to anything near normal for some months to come, we must not forget the state of this place and all the bombed out buildings, but life is beginning to get back to some sort of normality as we noticed that one or two sailors and a soldier or two had girls for company now, I suppose that we couldn't expect them to be too sociable at first, although there has always been a fair amount of different services stationed ashore here, all through the siege.

It is food and respite from the daily attacks of the bombers that all these Maltese people want, after all this time they have it now and they certainly deserve it, it seems that the air raids are getting fewer and the ships entering harbour are coming in a lot more frequently, bringing in all the needs of the Maltese, the days of going hungry are now over, but it's not just food that is being brought in as I have seen one ship unloading medical supplies. The 21st and it's back to a sailors normal chores, mine today is touching up some paint work on a couple of the gun shields, after I have finished this I must do some letter writing to Irene tonight as I received a fantastic letter from her and have yet to answer it.

Today is the 22nd and the letter to Irene should be well on it's way by now as the day is almost done and we are preparing to go to sea again. Out we go during the first dog watch, we are doing escort for two Cruisers H.M.S. Cleopatra and the Eaurylus, the Destroyers—Jervis, Kelvin, the Tribal class Destroyer, H.M.S. Nubian. We appear to be heading straight for the African Coast again as it is getting dark, our destination this time is the port of Zuara. The bombardment commenced as soon as we arrived, only it was the Cruisers that were doing the firing this time, it was the port and the surrounding coastal area that the big guns of these Cruisers targeted. I'm watching from my defence station to see what damage had been done and if there was any shipping in the harbour, I could clearly see the fires and the explosions, some very large as though they had hit some ammunitions.

Star shells were fired over the harbour but we could see that there wasn't any shipping there, just as we turn away there was a huge explosion that lit up the night sky, we assumed it must have been the ammunition dump going up, now that was something really worth seeing and as we sailed away into the night away from Zuara the sky line was alight with fires so there must have been a huge amount of damage, that should certainly help those desert rats of Montgomery's, at the rate that they are going I reckon that the war in the desert will soon be over, anyway we sailed on arriving back in Malta on the morning of the 23rd and went straight to a Tanker and refuelled again, we seem to be doing this regularly now.

We sailed again immediately 'no rest for the wicked' this time there are just two of us, we are at sea with the Destroyer H.M.S. Nubian, sailing on down the Mediterranean we eventually arrived at Benghazi on the 24th, once again we see the total devastation ashore and the ship wrecks in and outside the harbour almost blocking the entrance, looking around it amazes me how these places managed to carry on as long as they did and they have certainly taken a battering, well believe it or not we are here for the purpose of ferrying R.A.F. Personnel, 300 of them between the two ships, 150 each and transporting them to Malta, 'comes to something now hasn't it, we are a ferry now,' anyway out we go once we have embarked all our lot, they must thank their lucky stars because the weather is good. We arrive back in Malta on the 25th and go alongside the jetty disembarking the R.A.F. lads, then to our anchorage.

We sailed out of Malta the next day on the 26th during the morning watch and turned east, for four days we were just breaking waves. 30th January 1942. At last we arrived at Alexandria, we went straight into the dry dock and a well earned rest after twenty seven days continuous sea time, I reckon this will be a proper boiler clean, not halfhearted like the one that was done alongside the jetty wall. Sure enough the announcement was not long in coming with the Bosuns mate piping the good news that 48hrs leave to both watches has been granted today 'Wow' now this is something that no-one expected when we sailed out of Malta, certainly not me, leave is to start at 1200hrs so it's now a mad dash to get all my gear ready to make that all important phone call to Irene.

As expected the mess deck is a hive of activity with everybody dashing about sorting out, some trying to borrow irons to get the creases out of gear that has been folded in lockers since they last went ashore and all the other things that go into making a sailor look so smart when he steps ashore, I must make that phone call right now so that I can let Irene know what time I will be going through the dock yard gates, I am really looking forward to this leave probably more than any other time, 'great' it's done and I will be spending all my leave here in Alexandria with my girl, once again it's all arranged after I gave her that wonderful surprise phone call, I must say that even though we have not been able to see each other as often as we would have liked her letters have meant quite a lot while we have been in Malta, in her letters she says that she can't get enough of me so that must mean something.

'Big head' you might say but what about having a girl that won't let you pay for anything when you are ashore with her, many a sailor would give up his rum ration for a girl like her, no kidding though I know that I am very lucky, I'm off now. As usual she was at the dockyard gates waiting for me, you can call it what you like but this is love. She told me that she had got the time off so that we can be together, so I don't have to tell you where I spent the whole of my leave, as I have said before it's only a small place but it's lovely and all her own, we spent most of the time together indoors and didn't go out except to shop for extra food.

I find that this is a life that I could really get used to, I can go around Alexandria seeing the sights with someone who understands the language and knows her way around, but there is another thing now, she is beginning to worry about me when I am away at sea 'What a girl,' she says that if anything happened to me she would never even know about it, but that is something thing that I can't help, anyway our time together was not interrupted by noisy M.P.'s (Military police) this leave. And so I spent all of my leave with her.

Here I am back on board after spending a smashing time together, she is looking forward to lots more as for me well I certainly can't wait but once again I had to explain to her not to get her hopes up too high as we are in a tricky situation and it could be that we sail out of Alex one day and I might not be able to let her know what is happening, but she doesn't want to hear this.

I have also told her that I don't want to leave the Mediterranean not while I have her to love and this really brings on the tears, but we parted at those gates both praying that there will be lots more of these 48hrs together.

The boiler clean was completed on the 5th February 1943. I have managed to see Irene three more times, just the normal nightly shore leaves but I had to be back on board by 2300hrs, now each run ashore is better than the last, you know I really don't want to leave her now and she doesn't want me to go either but there is a war still on.

As I expected we sailed out of Alex on the 6th February during the first watch, yours truly is on duty closed up at defence stations.

Cruisers and Destroyers are the escort, among these twelve Merchant ships there is one big Troop ship and it's loaded with soldiers, we have sailed out into a gale with a very rough sea which is going to slow this convoy considerably, straight away I feel very sorry for those poor soldiers aboard that Trooper because they are in for a very rough passage where ever we are going to. So sailing on with nothing much to write about except to say that we have been making very slow progress due to the weather on the first day, on the second day out of Alex it started to rain very heavy, H.M.S. Jervis exploded a mine seen bobbing about on the surface so another thing to watch out for in this bad weather.

Still in very rough weather we arrive off Tripoli during the early hours of the morning watch, six of the ships left us and went in to the harbour the rest of us carried on, if anything the weather got even worse has we sailed on towards Malta, just before we entered the harbour the Destroyers H.M.S. Petard and Nubian joined up with us, it's now the 11th February and with the gale still blowing hard outside we go to our usual anchorage. The 12th and 13th we are still in harbour, for once we are very glad to be out of it, on the 14th we are made Emergency Destroyer and are at one hours notice for sea, then to top it all we were made E.M.D. again on the 15th, then on the 16th we sailed out of Malta with the rest of the Destroyers escorting two Cruisers H.M.S. Orion and one other the name of which I don't know as there are two or three of these Cruisers that are exactly the same.

The Cruisers are out here doing gunnery exercises. We returned back into harbour at 1500hrs and shore leave is granted, lucky port watch are the off duty watch, my mate and I decided to give it another go and were very surprised this time to see how well the improvements had come on, and it wasn't a bad run ashore at all, one other thing that we can't help but notice is that Malta had become a lot quieter now, the Spitfires can be seen everyday doing their patrols around the Island now that they have got the fuel and at times we have seen them sweeping low over the harbour heading out to sea, evidently they are no longer on the defensive but out there looking for any enemy that they can attack. We sailed out of Malta on the 17th of February doing a ferry job again, this time we have quite a lot of civilians on board and the weather is beginning to get a bit rough again.

Arrived at Tripoli on the morning of the 18th during the forenoon watch with no problems, we went straight alongside the jetty to disembark the passengers then given two hours leave, I think that everybody on board was eager to see what this place looked like so there is a mad dash to get ready as we only have a few minutes before we are due to fall in ready to go ashore, but despite all the rush, when we get ashore it is very disappointing because we haven't have the time to go far, what we see is a place that's been battered a lot, buildings where shells and bullets had hit them, there is lots of rubbish lying around on the outskirts, shell cases and burnt out vehicles pushed into the side roads but that's about as far as we get, but the most noticeable thing about Tripoli is the amount of wrecks in the harbour and around the entrance.

Talking to some of the Army chaps onshore we are told that those that are sunk at the entrance are being worked on by engineers and are going to be blown up as are those in the harbour, but giving my candid opinion of Tripoli as a whole, well, I don't reckon much to it, I am sure that my runs ashore here if and when will be very few, but I suppose like a lot of other places that have seen a lot of this war, it's probably a nice place in peace time but it's definitely not Alexandria, we sail out of Tripoli at 17.30 into a fierce gale and push on into heavy seas heading back to Malta and arriving on the 19th, no shore leave is given so it looks as though we will be doing the Emergency Destroyer duties again tomorrow.

It's morning, sure enough as we expected Javelin is now at one hours notice for sea, working part ship all day without any problems. The night passing without turning out so I was very pleased as it has been a wild night out there. 21st and it has been a normal working day as we are the duty watch, there has been no chance of any shore leave so I am going to write a letter to Irene before I turn in. At sea again on the 22nd, so you see that the war doesn't stop just because of the bad weather, once again our destination is Tripoli where on arriving there is a noticeable difference at the entrance as most of the wrecks have disappeared so the Army Engineers have been very busy and in a short time too.

That was quite a surprise as some of those wrecks that were here a couple of days ago have now vanished, probably the small ones have been towed out into deep water and sunk, although there is still a lot of work to do inside the harbour, we go alongside the jetty and leave is given, split three hours to each watch, the port watch has the first session, although the weather really spoilt it I'm afraid that I haven't changed my mind about Tripoli, I reckon that it doesn't compare with the likes of Haifa or any other place that we have visited it's just a typical war torn City and a very poor one at that, although we haven't had the time to visit the City Centre so maybe that is entirely different to the outer parts but I don't think that I would want to spend my hard earned money here, I would rather save it on the off chance of going back to Alexandria.

Talking of Alex I have received a lovely letter again from Irene and as usual she is praying that we can be together again very soon, she has sent me another beautiful photo and that one has gone up on my locker door alongside that other big beautiful photo, I am going to say this, even though I now have Irene I still think a lot of that girl on that big photo, well you don't love someone so very much for so long and then just forget all about them, but here I am now thousands of miles away from her and she has someone else now and life goes on. We are now preparing to embark Maritiouse troops straight after the starboard watch come back on board and we sail during the second dog watch, once again I feel for those pongo's (Soldiers), I suppose that it is terrible weather for them to endure and I bet they thought at times they were dying.

Some of these soldiers are down on the mess deck but quite a lot of them are lying about on the upper deck on the port waste, they look terrible, being on board the Javelin makes it even worse for them as she rolls and pitches all over the place in this bad weather and we have had to warn them to keep away from the guard rails when they are being sick as there is a danger of them going over the side, you feel sorry for them but the annoying thing is that you can't really do anything to help, we think how lucky some of us are, as I have said before I still haven't been sea sick yet and have never had the feeling either, yet you get sailors who have been at sea for years and are sea sick every time they leave the harbour wall, it's really embarrassing for them.

We eventually arrive at Malta on the 24th February and went straight alongside the jetty and disembarked the troops, from there we went back to our old mooring place and are designated E.M.D. again so no shore leave but a nice quiet night in, the morning of the 25th out to sea we go again and still pushing into some bad weather, I don't suppose that we will see anything of the enemy in these sort of conditions, sailing on we arrive at Benghazi during the afternoon watch where we had another surprise as there doesn't seem to have been anything done yet to get this place sorted out, if anything it's in a worse state than Tripoli, but probably too busy pushing Rommels lot back beyond Tripoli, there are a lot of our soldiers here and we are about to embark a large number of them.

No shore leave was granted but then again who in their right mind would want to go ashore here, now as these Troops started to come on board it was obvious that these lads were our own British soldiers all 180 of them and as they descended onto our mess deck with their gear they were laughing and talking, of course it wasn't long before we got to talk with a few of them, I found that two soldiers came from Derbyshire area, one from Burton-on-Trent which is very close to my small village and a place that I know very well, the conversation got around to Malta and what is it like? well I could tell them that it has certainly improved a lot over the last couple of months and is getting better all the time and that they wouldn't have to worry about the air-raids as they had just about finished now.

Food, beer and girls was the main concern and in that order I think, also what was it like when we first went ashore? and quite a lot more things which we all tried to give them the answers to the best of our knowledge, we found out from asking them a few questions that they had not been in any of the desert battles and that they had only been in Benghazi for a few weeks but some of their mob had been sent up to Tripoli and although they were going to Malta they had no idea why, well I reckon that Malta needs plenty of help all round, I suppose that the main thing is unloading ships in the harbour that must be one of the most important things at the moment, anyway we sailed out of Benghazi at night, thankfully the weather has improved a lot.

We arrived at Malta OK on the 27th during the morning watch and went alongside the jetty to disembark all the troops.

Now we are alongside the jetty we have started working part ship but only for a short time. Yes, we might have guessed it we sailed straight out again during the first watch, in company with other Destroyers and have closed up to action stations, we have been told that we are heading for the Pantelleria Strait's and that we are doing a sweep for any enemy shipping, now, this has always been a very dangerous place for British War Ships but despite searching into the night we had no luck this time so we sailed back to Malta arriving during the morning watch on the 28th February.

Still not satisfied we sail straight out once again, almost before the wake from our stern had the time to settle down, we are again in company with other Destroyers and one of the Cruisers is H.M.S. Orion, we push off during the morning watch and this time we are traveling at high speed, really making the spray fly, we arrive at Alexandria in quick time early on the 2nd March we go alongside the jetty and start to load provisions, now what I want to know is are we going to get any leave? but Robbo thinks that doing the chores which we have just done, we may be sailing late this evening, however during the stand easy in the afternoon leave was piped, I knew that it wouldn't be for my watch as I was pretty sure that we were the duty watch, and so it proved.

Lucky starboard watch was the one that was going ashore tonight, well I was at the point of going to give Irene a ring to let her know that we were here in Alex but old Robbo persuaded me not to, like he says we don't know for sure if we will be here tomorrow and I think that he is right as it would have only given her false hope, I certainly didn't want to do that as it would hurt her terribly. Ah well I've just got to keep my fingers crossed and hope for tomorrow which can't come soon enough for me. The morning comes and we have been working part ship, here I am now just after dinner sitting on my locker writing these few notes before we turn out again for the afternoons work, at the moment no-one knows what we are going to do, even the lads on the mess can see that I'm getting a bit anxious.

And so it was old Robbo who came to my rescue not long after we had fallen in for the afternoons work, he came up to me and gave me the news that I was dying to hear, he had asked the Petty Officer in charge of our part of ship if he had any idea as to when we would be sailing again and then he dropped it "well we certainly won't be sailing today for sure," for that news I promised him my next tot of rum, to say I was over the moon would be putting it mildly and at the first opportunity I'm off to that phone but it wasn't until hands to tea had been piped that I get the chance to nip down the gangway, that takes some doing as there's always the Officer of the watch and the Bosuns mate looking out for that gangway, but the Bosuns mate is someone that I knew so there was no problem.

It was wonderful to hear her voice again, she was very excited and will pick me up at the gates 'I can't wait' and so a lot more leg pulling from the lads on the mess, oh I tell them "you're only jealous" but I've made the mistake of telling them her name some time ago so it will go on, with the order "Liberty men fall in" I was down that gangway like a flash and there she is I just grabbed her and kissed her in full view of quite a lot of number 1 mess amid a chorus of the whistles and shouts, off we went and we had a smashing time together on this run ashore, Oh, I know it's only a few hours 'but just to be with her,' I know that she doesn't want me to go because each time that we are together she thinks that it may be the last.

We are making the most of our time together and loving every minute of it, though we know that we are in for a no future ending but trying not to think about it, now, don't get me wrong, Irene is definitely not one of those good time girls as she has never had a boyfriend before and it was a long time before she got over her shyness, it was rather funny when I first met her in the shop and made that casual remark about how I became interested in watch repairing, I never dreamed that it would lead to us becoming so close as it just seemed at first like the shop keeper taking an interest in the customer, but being a sailor I suppose that it made it a bit more of a surprise despite that shyness as Irene has told me since I was so easy to talk to, well back on board again thinking once more how lucky I am to have a girl like Irene, while slinging my hammock I am wondering if I might get another chance ashore.

The morning of the 4th we turn to working part ship, there doesn't seem to be any sign yet that we are leaving when the Bosuns mate came round piping hands to dinner and leave to the Starboard watch from 1700hrs to 2300hrs, well that put us out of our misery but I thought that I would give Irene a call just to let her know that we are still here and as yet I can't say if I will be ashore tomorrow night, if I don't ring then she must assume that we have sailed. Lucky me here we are on the 5th and I'm going ashore again and just as soon as the dinner was over. While stacking empty paint tins into a skip on the dockyard I flew to that phone very quickly and gave her the good news.

Writing this on the 6th we are out at sea, just a few words to say that I had another fantastic time ashore last night, when we parted she begged me to keep on writing as often as I can, she gave me a little present with the instructions that I wasn't to open it until we had sailed and here I am not wanting to go to sea now, this situation is really getting to me now (I should have listened to Robbo in the first place).

She was so sure that we would be seeing each other again that she gave me a long lingering kiss and said it was to last until we meet again.

We had sailed during the afternoon watch on the 6th March after spending five lovely days in Alexandria, we are now escorting a convoy of four supply Merchant Ships and after four uneventful days we arrive at Tripoli once again on the 9th, as we arrived late there is no chance of anyone getting any shore leave so it's a night in, so sling that hammock early and my chance to open that little package that Irene gave me. 'Didn't I get a shock' for wrapped up in tissue paper was the heart shaped locket on a gold chain that Irene wears around her neck, when I opened it there in miniature in the back is a snap of her, the one of me was still on the front, now I have never seen Irene without it, she has worn this locket ever since I gave it to her and there is also a lovely letter with this which brought tears to my eyes (good job I was in my hammock) but I am not disclosing what she said that brought on the tears anyway I can't wear it around my neck but I will keep it in my inside pocket.

The morning of the 10th arrives we are still here in Tripoli and during dinner, leave was piped for both watches but only for a few hours, as we had nothing else to do my mate and I decided to give it another try.

We did manage to get into the more lively part of Tripoli and found that this was not as badly damaged as the outskirts of the dock area which is a shambles, although there wasn't much trading going on, in any case we couldn't buy anything with the money that we had but it would have been nice to get a souvenir of some kind, looking at the harbour area when we first came we noticed there has been quite a lot of improvement and I was surprised to see the amount of ships that are lying at anchor, evidently Monty had received loads of supplies for his Desert Rats now they had managed to clear the wrecks. We stayed here during the night but sailed out of Tripoli during the morning of the 11th, it was a long drawn out affair as we had to wait for all those ships to come out (eighteen of them) I suppose that most of them were empty.

We sailed at a very steady speed for five days, we didn't sight a single plane then would you believe it just as we sighted Alexandria at least twenty R.A.F. planes flew straight over our heads flying low, well I can't write down here just what most of the ships company thought about that, we sailed into the harbour on the 15th and went straight into dry dock for some minor repairs, now this was something that I was really looking forward too but never expected lots more leave, although we are too late for anyone to get any shore leave tonight and it's the Starboard watch who are ashore tomorrow night so I will have to keep my fingers crossed and hope that we may be here for a day or two.

However it was not meant to be, we came out of dry dock on the 17th and went straight out to sea, still in sight of Alexandria we began testing our guns doing torpedo trials, then of all the rotten luck after the completions of the tests we anchored outside the boom all night, then in the morning we up anchor and sail back into the harbour on the 18th, yes, I might have known we are once again designated Emergency Destroyer, well I just can't believe that this has happened of all the rotten luck even more so when the next morning arrives, the Bosuns mate piping "hands to stations for leaving harbour" all the Starboard watch close up and this was just after we had finished breakfast on the 19th.

So out to sea we go with the Jervis and the Kelvin escorting the Cruiser H.M.S. Orion, we had only been at sea one day when the Jervis left us and we sailed on arriving at Malta late on the 21st no shore leave was granted for the simple reason we sailed straight out again, this time with more Cruisers and we know that we are bound for Alexandria again.

Being at sea again for just a day and who should join up with us but the Jervis, in company with a few others. sailing on we arrived at Alexandria but no chance of any shore leave once again before we were ordered to sea and this time we are escorting three big Troop ships all loaded with soldiers, now, I wonder where all this lot are going to because there must be quite a few hundred aboard these big ships, surely not Malta unless they are relief for the garrison, but with this fair sized escort of Cruisers and Destroyers we arrive at Tripoli on the 28th, we then left straight away on our own and arrive back in Malta later on the 29th.

We weren't in Malta for long and off we go again on the 30th, you might notice that I have not been adding any casual notes in my diary of late, well this is because when at sea most of the time there is nothing to write about as we are always on duty except for the breaks between watches, then we are working part ship, it works like this we come off a four hour Middle watch at 0400hrs then get our head down and wake at 0700hrs have breakfast and back on watch at 0800hrs until 1200hrs come off watch and have dinner then a short time after this you may get a break but you are back on watch at 1600hrs until 1800hrs then tea and back on watch again to do the first watch at 20.00hrs until midnight, this carries on the whole time that you are at sea so there's very little to write about as it is a continuous routine and doesn't change.

We have been escorting three big Transports and have been travelling in blazing hot sunshine down the Mediterranean, we arrive at Alexandria once again on the 3rd April, once more we go into dry dock, this time it's for a boiler clean and what do you know we get some great news it's 48hrs leave for both watches, but this time it's split the Starboard watch are to go first on the 4th April and of course the port watch are duty watch, but now that I know what leave we are getting I can give Irene a ring and give her the good news in plenty of time for her to make any arrangements, I wasn't able to get to the phone this time until very late on the first day here, she must have been out as I couldn't contact her at home so I will have to try again tomorrow.

So, with the Starboard watch having gone ashore on their leave the 4th, I have still got to get to the phone but working part ship now it's all painting for me with the leading hand watching over me all the time so I still haven't been able to phone, I am jotting these notes down just after dinner and the chance comes when I have to use the heads (toilets) on the dockyard, I rang the shop and she was really excited about the leave, well it didn't seem very long before I was walking down that gangway onto the jetty, I was looking forward to this leave like all the others I suppose but I don't have to tell you that all my leave is being spent here in Alex, although most of the lads are on their way to Cairo again but not for me I wouldn't miss this leave here in Alexandria not for a month in Cairo not when have a girl like Irene here, when I see her standing at the gates waiting for me I know that I'm not going to miss Cairo, but it is beginning to get very hard for me knowing all this has got to end one day.

I was greeted with the usual kiss and off we went straight to her place it just seemed so very natural now. I can honestly say that now I am back on board that as usual my 48hrs leave was great, we had a lovely time together even though we spent most of it at her home we only went out once, I thanked her for the beautiful locket and the lovely letter that came with it, I stressed that I want to replace that one for her at the first opportunity, although she didn't say anything I haven't forgotten that tomorrow is Irene's birthday and I have got to do something about it though I haven't got a lot of money but with what I have got plus some that I must borrow I want to buy that locket for her, my leave is over all to quickly on the 8th of April.

Now, I have managed to borrow some cash off Robbo but we are watch aboard today I and somehow have to get ashore to get to the Jewellers in the Fleet Club to buy that locket, so I had to come up with some idea to get off the ship for a short time, then it suddenly came to me, after I had been to get some paint out of the foreword locker I found that we were getting very low on grey paint, now this was after dinner and I was getting desperate so I went to the Petty Officer in charge of our watch to report the fact that we had almost run out of this paint, his reply is "you had better get down to the paint shop on the docks and draw another drum," but first I would have to wait while he got the chit signed by our store man, so in my overalls away I went, in just over the hour I was back on board with a drum full of ships side grey paint and a beautiful locket on a silver chain in my pocket, crafty eh!

I am hoping that there will be shore leave for us tomorrow with a bit of luck as we are still in the dry dock, there is still some activity going on down below so it doesn't look as though the job is finished yet so it's fingers crossed. 9th April and still painting the ship, I am hoping that during the dinner time break the Bosuns mate will be coming on to this mess deck piping some leave for us. Well he didn't let me down but it is after we had finished dinner and were being piped to fall in on the port waste for the afternoon work on part ship, so once again I had to make that phone call which turned out to be no problem, when the time comes I will be one of the first down that gangway, I have taken a lot of ribbing from the lads as I let it slip that it is Irene's birthday today, but as our Killick is always telling me "Enjoy it while you can" I have to admit that I never want this to end It's just that I can't see what we are going to do, it's an impossible situation.

He is very cynical is old Robbo but I suppose that he might have been in the same situation that I will find myself in the very near future, once again back on board, what a fantastic night we had and she didn't think that I would have remembered her birthday, when I gave her the locket that I had bought she was over the moon with it and even tried to give me some money so that I wouldn't be short but I wouldn't have it this time after all it was a present, she put it on and said that she wouldn't take it off again, as I left her by the gates of the dockyard and walked those yards back to the Javelin which is still in the dry dock, I was once again thinking how lucky I was then Robbo's words came back to me as I settled down on the mess to write these last few notes before slinging my hammock and turn in. It was still on my mind when I finally dropped off to sleep. The morning of the 10th we are still here finishing off the paint work in the dry dock but for how much longer? Leave has just been piped again for the Starboard watch as we sit here during dinner, and although the boiler cleaning crew have finished there's no sign yet of us moving out of here. It wasn't long though the next day on the 11th just after we had finished our dinner when the pipe went for the Starboard watch special sea duty men to their stations was called and so out of the dry dock we go and into the harbour before anchoring, I guess that I wouldn't be going ashore again tonight as we can't be staying here for much longer or we would have gone to a buoy.

We finish off painting then we got quite a surprise when a big lighter came alongside and forty soldiers came on board, of course this started the buzzes going around the ship but perhaps they are only taking passage to somewhere like other times when we have been a ferry, perhaps though the rumours that have been circulating the ship recently that we would be doing some landing exercises with troops could be the answer, we only got the real answer when we got talking to some of the soldiers and they could only tell us that they are aboard the Javelin as far as they knew for the sole purpose of an exercise, but they couldn't say when or where the exercise was going to be, so it is believed to be the real thing and we are supposed to be training with these troops ready for a landing on an enemy coast somewhere.

To make it even more likely that this is a beach landing, a few hours later some inflatable dinghies and a load of gear came on board so what more proof did we need, our Killick said that he had been talking to one of their Sergeants and apparently this exercise is being carried out by other groups of soldiers on quite a few more ships over a period of time, even they didn't know what it was all in aid of, we did get some real information later the exercises are to get ready for a landing on the Greek coast but not for some weeks so it looks as though we are going to see a lot more action but of a different kind this time.

We sailed out of Alexandria on the 12th April escorting a small convoy, so that is my chance of another night with Irene gone, our third day out at sea we receive a signal that the Paladin and the Packenham have been in some action off Tripoli, they have sunk two Italian Destroyers but unfortunately the Packenham has received a lot of damage and is on fire. We sailed into Tripoli on the 16th, leave is given to just one watch, only and that's Starboard, we are only staying for a short time. We sail out again escorting just one big Merchant ship.

Arrive at Malta on the 18th, it's here that we receive some very bad news and that is the Packenham has gone down, she had to be dispatched by the Paladin after trying to tow her as she was very badly damaged and is still on fire. We also received some further bad news that there are quite a few casualties but no reports of how many.

Well no more Housey-Housey aboard another of our very old ships 'she will be sadly missed' as she has done a hell of a lot of good work in the Mediterranean and elsewhere but that's how it goes sometimes. Here in Malta we had another surprise not long after we had gone alongside the jetty all forty of the Army chaps their gear and the inflatable dinghies have been disembarked and up to now no-one knows what's happening, as soon as the troops had left so did the Javelin, we sailed out with the Cruisers Orion and Cleopatra the Destroyers Paladin, Petard and Nubian, and are doing manoeuvres and proceed on our way, now I wonder what that was all about? On the morning of the 20th we sight two T.L.C.s (Tank Landing Craft) we escort them into Tripoli, as usual we sail straight out again, we are now escorting a small convoy of enemy prisoners and arrive at Alexandria on the 24th of April.

We have to go alongside the jetty to land these prisoners and we have to standby while each of the ships disembarks it's prisoners, they are being received by quite a number of Army vehicles, watching these prisoners they didn't seem to be too bothered in the least as they were laughing and talking to one another as though they were going on a picnic, some of these were Italians, I suppose that they were glad to be out of it as I reckon that the majority of them didn't want to fight in the first place, but we could see the difference in the German prisoners or Africa Corps as they like to be known, as they went down the gangways onto the jetty there was hardly a sound out of them, one or two did talk but there was no laughter at all.

It wasn't long before I was laughing because shore leave was being piped for tonight and it was my watch for a change, I'd had plenty of time to get ready but no time to give Irene a call in any case she would be at home now having finished work so it was going to be a surprise this time, down that gangway

I go heading straight to Irene's place to give her another lovely surprise. Once again we had a fantastic time, there is so much that I could write in my diary about the times that we spend together but I would need a far bigger diary, apart from that it's all very private. I did meet her twice more as we stayed for almost a week, it was evident that the reason for staying so long is the amount of shipping that arrived here in that time and would be needing escort to somewhere.

The escort we are a part of is a big convoy of twenty three ships as we sail out of Alex late on the 29th April, amongst them are one or two Yankee Liberty ships and a Troop ship with soldiers on board, we have a very large escort this time, after this lot had finally got into some sort of formation which certainly took some time we pushed off, sailing for two days without any problems we are just off the coast and the port of Benghazi, feeling quite safe with Montgomery having full control of the desert from Benghazi right up to and beyond Tripoli, 'Wrong' as usual, they came screaming down about a dozen or more they really did catch us by surprise with things having been so quiet of late, out of the sun they came diving in before you could bat an eye, bombs dropping as always all over the place, everybody opened up but the surprise factor had already paid off and some of the planes are already through the screen and out again.

The Tanker was the first ship that I saw hit and in a matter of seconds it seems, the flames were shooting sky high everything was happening so quickly that we didn't have the time to close up to action stations we were far too busy firing at these aircraft, plain for all to see was a ship on the other side of the convoy receive a hit due to the amount of smoke spiraling into the sky, at the same time we heard someone on the bridge who was in direct communication with all the guns by head phones shout "That's the Troop ship on fire," there is another ship also on fire that we can see however this one didn't seem to be as bad, now the planes had gone and the Tanker was being abandoned, the crew had already taken to their life boats none too soon as the ship exploded in a fire ball, we are told that the Troop ship is also being abandoned because she is sinking, we have no idea how many casualties there are or how many Troops she is carrying.

Well, the surprise certainly worked but the lads said that they did see at least three of the planes shot down, not much of a loss though when you compare our losses alongside those of three enemy planes, one Tanker and one Troop ship sunk, another Tanker badly damaged but making headway, but there you go for the past few months we have been traveling up and down this Mediterranean Sea and we have not seen any enemy planes at all, this certainly wasn't expected as this was a one off, completely out of the blue attack, still, there is the worrying thing at the back of it all, what never fails to amaze me is how the hell does Gerry know about these convoys? because we have never seen any of their spotter planes 'Makes you think doesn't it.'

We arrived at Tripoli on the 3rd of May 1943 having had no more attacks, we do a refuelling job here as does the Kelvin, this is the first time we have managed to do this here so things must be looking up and as we are both leaving the harbour we got a message to say that there had been a lot of casualties aboard the Troop ship, the Tanker that blew up most of the crew managed to get off but there are a number of men unaccounted for but 'hopefully' they might have been picked up by other ships, the other Tanker that was hit received only slight damage by fire but has a number of wounded men but fatalities, we saw her going into the harbour at Tripoli and she didn't look too bad although her bows were badly damaged, I reckon she was very lucky.

We have been at sea for four days and we arrive back in Alexandria on 7th May and lucky port watch are given shore leave, as it was only dinner time I had to work part ship this afternoon so I will have plenty of time to think what I am going to do tonight, I haven't had the chance yet to ring Irene so I can only hope that she will be at home, but I needn't have worried though (I didn't get to that phone) she was there when I arrived and for a change we went to see a film. We only saw about three quarters of the first film and was really enjoying it when it happened again, yes, up on the screen flashed a message "all H.M.S. Javelin and H.M.S. Kelvin crew are to return to their ships immediately" yet another recall, so once again I had to leave her and dash back to the ship and two hours later we sailed with the Kelvin again making speed. on the third day out we met up with a small convoy off Tripoli we then turned around and sailed back the way we had come from, after a day with the convoy we were attacked by six E-boats but although they tried to get through the screen we drove them off. Sailing on and what do you know it's Alexandria again! However it's just before night fall so too late for any leave on the 12th May 1943.

13th May and it turns out to be a very sad day for me, this morning I am sitting here on the mess writing these last few notes and really looking forward to my leave tonight but I was called to the Chiefs office with another rating and we were both handed draft chit's, now I was really shaking when I went back into the mess, I told old Robbo and the rest of the lads the bad news, after all I have been through with my Oppo's here on the Javelin, this is something that you never expect . . . just straight out of the blue no warning at all, I just couldn't believe it why me? That is all I could think as I was one of the first few rating to join the ship back in England and apart from about seven others I've been aboard this ship longer than anyone, now it looks as though I am going to be the first to be drafted off her, so I've emptied my locker, packed my kit bag and hammock, all I have to do now is to say goodbye to my mate Tom, old Robbo and the rest of the lads on the mess, there was a lot of head shaking, for like me they couldn't believe it.

Here I am aboard my new ship just jotting this down, I had to wait around for about an hour on the Javelin before I found myself in the liberty boat with the other rating (a stoker) to be drafted, then we sailed towards the ship that we are on now which happens to be the big Depot ship H.M.S. Woolwich, as I write this I can only say that I'm really going to miss the lads on our mess and my old mates, in this war you never know what is going to happen.

Greetings from H.M.S. "WOOLWICH"
Meditteranean XMAS 1943

Now I have got the hard part to do all over again, to start with a whole new routine as this ship very seldom goes to sea, I am going to miss that too, but I suppose that the only good thing to come out of this is that I am here in Alexandria and I know someone who is going to be over the moon when she hears the news. I suppose that it will console me, knowing that I shall be seeing Irene a lot more often. The first piece of news that I've heard on my second day on board here is that the Javelin is heading back to England, well what rotten luck and I've been through such a lot on that ship, the lads certainly deserve to be going home, but I am wondering what old Robbo would be thinking about my situation now with Irene after all our talks together perhaps he will be saying "well good luck to you Nick but you have got a hell of a problem now and it's going to get even harder for you."

The 15th May 1943, I have just come down from the upper deck after watching the Javelin sail out of Alexandria for the last time with tears in my eyes, my whole way of life for almost two years has gone, it's an entirely different routine altogether aboard this ship of course this will not be of watches as there will not be any night work to do it's all day work. 7th May, four days have passed since I left the Javelin, time has moved on and I've already made a few more mates, one actually comes from Derby which isn't all that far from my home, surprisingly the thing about this ship is that there are not a lot of seamen aboard but what few there are seem to be on one mess, the rest of the ships company are mostly made up of skilled men, they have to be as this is a Destroyer Depot ship and does quite a lot of repairs, also catering for the needs of all the Destroyers in the Eastern Mediterranean Fleet.

She carries loads of spares of every description that a Destroyer would need, both Electrical and Mechanical, also the experts to use them for mainly minor repairs so a ship would then come alongside the Woolwich for repairs, but all the major repairs are all done in the dry dock, one other main function of this ship is that she is also the main signal station for the Admiralty here in Alexandria, it's also very big so there is lots of room. We still have Port and Starboard watches but not in the same sense that a ship has at sea, this way it just breaks up the ships company into two for leave purposes and there is no middle, morning, afternoon and dog watches as such it's more like a day job, no dive bombers or submarines and E-boats, no riding the waves in a force nine gale or going down below off watch at 0400hrs soaked to the skin or standing behind a gun shield trying to get some shelter from the wind and waves that are breaking over the ship, no I think that this will do me till the end of this war.

I've dropped in very lucky aboard this ship I reckon because I've got another one of those 'cushy numbers' that I mentioned when I was on board the Dorsetshire, well now this one is just as easy, it's called Signal Distribution Officer's (SDO) Runner, the runner part is my job distributing messages or signals around to all the Officers, Chief Petty Officer's and cabins and there are a heck of a lot, to do this job I have to be in the rig of the day which is always white shorts and shirt, black stockings and shoes, by doing this job I get to know all the latest news as hundreds of signals come into the Woolwich every day, through this I found out that I wasn't the only one to get drafted off the Javelin with the stoker, six went off at Malta, six in Tunisia and the same number at Algiers, I have also heard that there was some crew trouble when they arrived at Malta and that the Military police had to be called. Now, I don't want to make any real comment on this but I am not surprised because the Skipper wasn't very popular with the lads, but all that is in my past now as I have settled down well on this ship also getting to know the Officers and I'm really enjoying my job, the lads on the mess though few are great and we have no Killick in charge, now for the long awaited best part about being on the Woolwich as it means that now I am ashore regularly and I am seeing Irene all the time, she is over the moon just like I knew that she would be, when I first told her that I was on another ship and it was stationed here in Alexandria and that I wouldn't be going to sea again, well at first she wouldn't believe me but I managed to convince her when I started to arrange to meet her every other day and had a long weekend with her in the first month.

Really, things couldn't have worked out better for me, week in week out no problems at all, I've spent time at Irene's place while she has been at work, at weekends mostly so many more long weekends with her over the months. I have seen such a lot of Alexandria too, more now do old Robbo's words keep on coming back to me that this is going to be one of those impossible situations in the long run, so the time came when we were together one week end and everything had been fantastic, as we sat together I brought up the subject of what are we going to do, marriage was out of the question the Navy would not allow it, although we are in love with one another now but try as we might we couldn't find a way, we both realize that a time would come in the end when neither of us could stop the inevitable, when I sail from Alexandria for good, the real problem was that neither of us would know when that is going to happen that is the hardest part about it and though she cried we vowed that we would still carry on and make the most of every day that we have together, who knows what might happen, I must say that our times together after we had that talk are great and I never miss a day when I have the chance of seeing her.

Things are moving fairly quickly in this war, I have been aboard the Woolwich six months now, Mussolini has resigned on the 26th July and Sicily fell to Allied Troops on the 17th August, the invasion of Italy took place on the 3rd September. Now there you have a few dates, I hope that I haven't' got any wrong because all days and dates seem the same in the Navy, I have been on shore with Irene tonight and she has told me that the news has been given out that the Italians have stopped fighting, so now the Germans have got to fight all of this part of the war on their own, so I reckon that the war in this part of the world will soon be over as they can't fight everybody and they have no chance of getting any supplies through by sea now, of course the newspapers are full of it the following day and my trips ashore to see Irene become harder as the days go by as she begins to notice the change ashore in Alexandria as there are very few sailors about, both Navy and Merchant. This is more obvious on looking around the harbour here as the ships numbers decrease, I could see that things were happening very fast and apart from those French Ships today there are no warships of any kind, the news on the radio this morning is that the war in the desert is going our way. I've just come off the upper deck after watching a big Merchant ship going out of the harbour and she is 'sailing on her own', my how things have changed over the last six months what with that and other signs like no warships coming into Alex any more and very little activity going on shipping wise. Well, the writing looks very much on the wall to me if that signal that I read only yesterday is anything to go by, that said that all Royal Navy personnel attached to the Eastern Mediterranean Fleet were all being transferred to the Far East bases.

A couple of weeks have now passed and things aboard the Woolwich have been getting pretty hectic making preparations for leaving Alexandria and I've finally had to break the news to Irene that our departure was imminent, she has taken it very badly, breaking down into tears which certainly upset me, 'what a flaming mess' I know now how much I love her or I wouldn't be feeling the way I do, it is so heart breaking to hear her say she loves me, and there is nothing that I can do about it and should have known this all along, she has begged me to keep on writing to her, I said that I will because we never know something might come up, but on that particular night I couldn't tell her that this would probably the last time that I would see her, which was almost a certainty for there is no reason at all for the Navy to stay here any longer as the war here in the Mediterranean is almost over.

I know where we are going but not when, now before I left Irene the last time she had asked me for some special keepsake that I cherished, well on my Identity disc, the one that all service men have to wear round their necks, I have a plastic shaped heart and inside it is a four leaf clover, it is one that I bought off a Fortune Tellers in Skegness and I always wore it as she said that it would bring me luck, anyway to get ashore once more to give it to her I had to change with one of the lads on the mess, I told her that I had changed my watch so that I could see her one more time and when I left her she was in a very bad way, it was once again heart breaking for me to see her upset and I will always remember her and the times that we spent together, I did really love her, it is just as heart breaking for me as it was for Irene.

So it turned out that the big day came all too soon and I didn't get the chance to see Irene again as all leave had been stopped a few days before we sailed out of Alexandria for the last time on the 7th December 1943. We are heading for that far off country of Ceylon at a steady 13 knots and my action station is the Transmission Station (T.S.), the job briefly is to send all the information that it gets from the Director to the guns, I have already explained the function of the Director before, but just briefly the Director is situated at a very high point on the ship plotting every movement of the enemy which is passed down to the TS who then passes it to the guns, it's a bit of a complicated thing and would take some time to explain in detail but all I am hoping is that we don't meet up with anything because at the moment it looks as though we are doing this journey on our own.

A big ship fairly slow not heavily armed is a very easy target for a U-boat, this is a really frightening trip for me being so used to fast moving ships, I'm just going to make sure that my life belt is blown up ready and keep everything crossed until we reach safety, anyway I am looking forward to Trincomalee in Ceylon as this is another place that I never dreamed that I would be seeing, there is one thing that I forgot to mention before I go on and that is the day before we left Alex my mate from Derby was drafted off the Woolwich and he is on his way home to England but I know that he had been out here for over two and a half years so he had done his time. We sailed on and arrived at Port Said, well if there is one place that I will not miss and that is this place! Old Robbo was right when he said that it is a dump, we didn't stay here very long before we sailed heading down the Suez Canal moving very slowly. We eventually arrive at Port Tewfic on the 19th December.

We stayed at Tewfic for just one night and sailed on the 20th into the Red Sea making our way slowly to Aden where we arrived during the morning watch on Christmas Day, we anchored just outside the harbour and spent the whole of Christmas day here, there is loads to eat and a fair amount to drink, we didn't go out to meet the opposition, no! we had a great time instead, the lads on our mess are a great bunch they all like to have a bit of fun, like my mate from Derby they have been on board the Woolwich for some time now, it shows what sort of ship this is when the Captain made a speech over the tannoy wishing everyone a very Happy Christmas, hoping this war will be over and that we will all be back home with our loved ones very soon, now that's the sort of message that makes a real Captain stand out from the others.

There was another thing that he stressed in his speech and that was great diligence on our part for the last part of our journey, it still looks as though we will have no escort according to the buzzes going around the ship and sailing in the Indian Ocean can be very dangerous as there are quite a few Japanese Submarines operating in these waters, this is a fact according to the signals that we have been receiving over the last few weeks with the amount of merchant ships being sunk. anyway we stayed here at anchorage off Aden for a week, during that time we did nothing but exercises mainly with the guns Director and the T.S. this was to prepare the ship for any action that we might have to face and I have got to say this, "some of these men have no idea of what real action is about so they really do need these exercises."

We finally sailed from our anchorage at Aden on the 1st January 1944 during the morning watch, at a steady speed now, the Woolwich is a very old ship and can't go at any rate of knots so it was all eye's on watch for what we already know is out there somewhere, and what do you know we actually received a signal a day out of Aden from an Oil Tanker only twenty miles away to say that a Japanese Submarine had surfaced ordering her to stop and she had received further orders to abandon the ship before they torpedoed her, now this was a bit of a surprise to most of us when we heard this because it didn't fit in with the usual practice of the Japanese when sinking ships and then machine gunning the survivors swimming in the sea then sinking the life boats, but despite this message we could do nothing about it except to pass the message on. So we sailed on day after day still at this steady speed, the only thing that we did see to cause us a bit of worry was a wreckage which is evidently from a sunken ship, I was certainly worried as any enemy be it a plane, surface craft or the deadly U-boats, we are certainly a big sitting duck.

Just imagine if we are attacked with torpedoes and we spotted a tin fish coming straight towards us on a big ship like this! The Coxon at the wheel would then try to slew her out of the way eh! we wouldn't stand a cat in hells chance I know that for sure, I have been used to ships that have had some speed under their decks and can run their way out of trouble but on the Woolwich at this speed it does become nervy, I needn't have worried though as on the tenth day out from Aden with no problems what so ever we arrived at the port of Trincomalee in Ceylon or 'Trinco' as it's known to us matelots. It's in a sheltered bay which is wide with some trees on the side, the first thing that I noticed when we dropped anchor is how very hot it is here.

And so H.M.S. Woolwich had made it on her own arriving on the 10th January 1944. Shore leave is granted and the lads all decided that we should have a run if only to test the beer, but when ashore we got a big surprise, for one thing there is very little of Trinco to see apart from the Navy club, we tasted the beer but I'm afraid that not many of the lads were impressed, then again I don't suppose we can expect too much as this place to me is very much like Freetown, there isn't much to see at all, I certainly hope that I am not here for very long although we might not of seen the real Trinco yet, after all we have only been in the harbour area and I don't know if there is more to this place. It does remind me though of Freetown because of all the trees (or is it a jungle) surrounding the place, after a while we decided to return to the Navy club as we called it as the real name of the place is not known to us yet, it also seems to be the only place where we can get any beer.

While we were sitting here drinking one of the other matelots came over to our table and asked us "why are you drinking that stuff" and pointed out the best bottled beer to drink here, when we tried it we found that it wasn't too bad at that. Back on board the verdict on the run ashore was that Trinco was definitely not Alexandria but maybe when we have been here a while and had a chance to really look around the place we might see it a lot differently although I have my doubts, but like me after their first run ashore the lads are all wondering when we are going home as most of us have now done our time out of the UK, but apart from that my first thoughts while sitting on the mess are of Irene who's all alone in far off Alexandria and I couldn't help but feel sad, I was determined at the first opportunity to write a long letter to her.

The second day here and I was beginning to settle back in to the old routine again which is just the same as it was in Alex, however I'm finding it a lot warmer below decks and certainly hot on the upper deck, at night there is a black out routine the same as there was at Port Said and Malta, although I wouldn't think that there would be anything worth bombing here apart from a few ships, but I was mistaken as one of the Petty Officers pointed out to me that there are some very big oil installations hidden amongst the trees just a short way from the harbour, of course the Army have a place ashore here as well so there must be quite a lot of military stuff in the area that we don't know about. Time moves on and it's now the 12th, it's our watch ashore again tonight and only one or two of the lads are going to try the place again, I thought well why not, so a couple of us decided that we would take a trip into the wilds as you might say and it turned out to be really something to remember, we also did a quick run into Trinco and I can only say that it's a bit on the primitive side but I think it is a little better than Freetown, however that's as far as it goes as there is still nothing that you can call a shopping area of any description.

I would describe Trinco at the moment as more like an open market, these are small places on the side of the road, you can stand and watch things being made by hand, from pots to Jewellery also marvel at the skill of some of these people and how they can make beautiful pieces of Jewellery out of metal with the tools that they have, there is some very beautiful silks and materials of all sorts, lots of it all in fantastic colours, when you ask the price of these things was when the surprise came, but there is one thing that is very plentiful and that is the tea, there is every kind of tea here that you can imagine but also very expensive, I did manage to buy some dust tea which I had never heard of before but was told that it was very strong, I thought that it would be OK to take some back home with me as it won't deteriorate.

We have been here a month now and things have got a little better for us, we even had a visit from a E.N.S.A. Party (these are entertainers who travel from England to these far flung places and give concerts to the troops) It's quite nice too, for in places like these there's no entertainment of any sort so it's moral boosting to have a good old sing song and a laugh, also meeting ordinary people who can tell us how everyone is coping back home, well today is what you might call a special day it's 11th February 1944, we are having a visit from Winston Churchill and Admiral Sommerville (I hope I have his name right) who is coming aboard to inspect the crew 'what a load of old red tape', now someone must have tipped off the Japanese too because only a short time after he arrived so did about six Japanese bombers, I reckon that they must have come off a Carrier, but the bombers met with some very heavy gun fire from all the Naval ships and the Army ack-ack guns onshore, although bombs were dropped no damage was done other than to a few trees.

A visit from Winston Churchill.

I have been told by one of the signalmen that the Woolwich is going to do a similar job here to what she did in Alexandria but it's going to be a tedious one for her crew as there's not much life here at all, as for me well I think it's a terrible place and I can't wait to get the hell out of here, on looking back I can only think of two places that are worse than this, that's

Freetown and Aden, there is just simply nothing to see or do, of course there are no girls except for the natives and as I have said before no amusements of any kind, how the other forces on shore here stick it well I really don't know, but then again they are a long way from any war here so I suppose that it would suit some of them if they are never moved, 'what a number' to stay here for the rest of the war with no action of any kind.

It has now been two months in this depressing place, I am really bored stiff and still doing the same job on board that I did in Alex, the only thing that brought me some cheer today is that amongst my mail is a lovely letter from Irene, It's a lengthy one saying how much she misses me and praying that somehow I could get back to Alexandria, also did I think that there will be a chance some time, well how do you answer a letter like that? It's really heart breaking and I have to admit that I have thought such a lot about her these last few weeks, how I've missed her so much also thinking of the lovely times that we had, those nights and weekends that we spent together, yet both of us knowing what an impossible situation we faced, I must admit that sitting here reading this I've got tears in my eyes I just can't help myself, now I must somehow answer this letter and It will hurt her even more when I tell her the truth which is I doubt very much that I will ever get back to Alexandria, surely my next move should be home to England.

The signals now coming in to the Woolwich have changed completely from war in the desert, Italy and Greece to war in the Far East but we don't seem to get any good news, a lot of the messages are now in code. e have been getting plenty of shore leave, most of it is spent in the Navy club where else, but looking at the situation as a whole and we now seem to be a long way from any war, we haven't had any air raids since the one when we first arrived here, I was only telling the lads a few days ago how I would willingly swap this sort of life just to be back in the thick of it again, It is so boring every day the same old routine I want to get back to sea again.

The morning of the 14th March, climbing out of my hammock as usual sitting down to have breakfast before going on duty just like every other morning for the past nine and a half months but this was not going to be a morning like every other, because half way through breakfast I could hear my name being piped, I had to wait until the Bosun's mate arrived on the mess decks before I got the message. I had to report to the Chief Buffers Office at once along with four other ratings so off I went, I just couldn't believe it 'I'm off home at last', I was handed my draft chit along with the other lads, I have certainly been waiting for this moment, apparently we are being drafted onto a Cruiser H.M.S. Emerald who is on her way home to England and we are to report on board Emerald on 15th March at 0945hrs which is tomorrow, so the four of us are going ashore tonight to celebrate, we will probably get plastered that's if we can with the beer they sell here, the lads on the mess are real pleased for me they have been great although I haven't known them very long, once again I am going to miss some fantastic lads, the main people I will miss are 'Barker' he is a seaman bugler and ginger he's a wee Scots laddie 'a real bundle of fun' then there is his mate 'Scouse' well you don't ever forget mates like these in a hurry, they made me so very welcome when I first came on board and with tears in my eyes I say that I don't expect to see them again but I won't ever forget them.

The first thing that I have to do after my last duties as S.D.O.'s runner is to get all my things packed ready to go in the morning and if I get the chance I'll write to Irene one more time. So we all went ashore for the last time and we had a real good time, although most of the lads are the worst for wear now I reckon they will be feeling a bit sorry in the morning. I decided that I wanted to write that letter to Irene though I couldn't actually tell her that I was going home to England I had to try and put something into this letter that would tell her that I wouldn't be coming back to Alexandria and try somehow to explain that she might not hear from me again but that I do love her very much and I would never forget her.

I am now writing the letter on board my new ship H.M.S. Emerald, I left the Woolwich this morning with the other three lads. My three mates on the Woolwich were on the upper deck leaning over the guard rails waving and shouting, I looked back to watch them with a lump in my throat while we transported kit bags and hammocks by boat across to H.M.S. Emerald, once on board it was the usual routine, I will soon find out what mess and part of ship I'll be working also my role in defence, action stations and all the stuff that you want to know when you are joining a ship, I can tell you it's not all that easy because apart from the fact that you are on a new ship with new mess mates who are complete strangers and being a bigger ship with a much larger crew, some of them might take to you straight away yet others not speak at all, yes it's hard at first. To start off I am once again on the port watch and we fell in to start provisioning ship right after dinner, this job completed we moved alongside a Tanker to refuel then we anchored in the harbour, for the next three days I am working part ship which is something that I have not done for well over twelve months but it's the same routine as every other ship so no problem. 19th March on a bright sunny morning "hands to stations for leaving harbour" was piped over the tannoy just after we had finished breakfast while we were about to fall in for part ship duties, we weighed anchor and sailed from Trincomalee harbour, all hands fell in is general practice when a ship leaves harbour, they fall in the waste on both sides of the ship standing to attention in the rig of the day, I was still looking back at the old Woolwich until she was out of sight and I bet those three mates of mine were doing just the same, watching us.

That's the Navy in war time you make some great mates during your travels then in just a moment of time they are gone and you may never see them again, some may have been killed in action and some like my old mate Walt off the Dorsetshire, Tom, Robbo, Smithy and Fletch off the Javelin, now the three that I have just lost and lots more, you can go through life with all it's big wonders but there's nothing that can compare with the war time comradeship of your old ship mates. Well we sail on and arrive at Colombo on 20th March, shore leave is given, now this is a good run ashore I've been here quite a few times before and one thing I know is that the beer here is not too bad at all, you can buy anything in Colombo if you have the money to pay for it, there are some beautiful things such as trinkets, jewellery and silks of all kinds It's all really lovely stuff that you want to buy now that we are on our way home but as I have mentioned quite a few times a matelot doesn't get that kind of money.

Emerald sailed out of Colombo on the 21st during the first dog watch and we were closed up at defence stations, during the forenoon watch on 22nd two boats were sighted in the far distance, on a steady approach it we found that there is thirty two seamen alive in the two boats, after rescuing them we found that their ship a Freighter had been torpedoed by a Japanese Submarine five days ago, our Skipper had to be very wary as a favourite trick of these U-boat Skippers is to sink a ship and once the crew have taken to their lifeboats they hang around within sight of them waiting for someone to come along and pick them up, then torpedo them, so doing anything like this it has to be completed in very quick time, as soon as they are rescued we push off.

Now today the 23rd March I have only just realize that it is exactly two years since I left England, I never thought then that two years on I would have seen so much action, while I was pondering over this a couple of us wandered over to the Freighter skipper and got into a conversation with him, he got talking about the Japanese Submarine that sank their ship and how the U-boat had surfaced twice quite close to them in the five days after they were torpedoed, it seemed that this same U-boat could possibly be responsible for the two lots of wreckage that we sighted and despite searching around we found no signs of any survivors, bodies and no lifeboats, just lots of wreckage, sure signs that two Merchant ships had met their fate here in the last few days.

Sailing on and we arrive at Mauritius on the 27th, once again this is a place that I have visited a few times before, it's a beautiful place but unfortunately we are not staying here for very long so we're not given shore leave. We left within a couple of hours and for the next four days we sailed on not seeing anything at all not even a flying fish until land was eventually sighted, a few hours later we sailed into one of my most favourite places of all 'Durban and the Lady in White' once again she gave us that very famous reception. Our first job was to disembark the survivors who are none the worse for their five day ordeal in the lifeboats, they all gave us a wave as they got into their transport, I reckon they are very lucky and thankful that they are not lost like the other poor souls from the wrecks that we found, I wonder what happened to them.

It's more than likely that this will be the last time I will see Durban again so I intend to seek out some of my old civilian friends to see how they are getting on then make the most of my time ashore that is when leave is piped. Our watch is going first but I have part ship work to do and it's washing down paint work, never changes does it, the pipe comes over the tannoy loud and clear that leave is granted to the port watch from 1800hrs until 2300hrs, this is great news as it gives me plenty of time to find my old civilian friends ashore who I have known during my time on the Dorsetshire, when I tell them that I am on my way back to England they will ensure that I have a great send off. Durban is a lovely place and like Cape Town there is so much to see and do like visiting the old places again, of course the beer here is pretty good and now I'm off ashore and am really looking forward to it.

Once again here I am back on board and writing this in my diary, I can honestly say that I've still got a bad head after that run ashore, but it was great to see some of my old friends again. I am now moving on from that first night ashore just to say that I have had five fantastic days here, I think I crammed everything possible into those days, yes I will most certainly remember Durban and the times that I've spent ashore here, not forgetting the friends that I have made and will soon be leaving behind, here I am being morbid again when I should be feeling very happy now that we are on our way home, as always all good things must come to an end sometime, we sailed out of Durban on the 5th April 1944.

We are escorting a Troop ship, sailing on with no problems what so ever for four days when we arrive at the port of Mombasa on the 9th, we are staying here if I've heard the buzz right, I know this place and it's not a bad run ashore, it does have everything a sailor wants but then again it's not the sort of place to make you want to stay here for very long. The buzz was right shore leave has been piped and it's the Starboard watch that is doing the run tonight so I sling that hammock for an early night. We stayed in Mombasa for five days and although I went ashore twice I am very pleased that we sailed out on the 13th during the first watch and finally arrive at the port of Aden on the 16th, now I've already stated my views on this place before so in a few words 'It's a Hell Hole', I am very pleased that we didn't stay here as we sailed straight out again into the Red Sea.

Now, we all know where we are heading and very soon we are sailing through the Suez Canal, I never cease to marvel at the journey along this canal, the sights are really some thing worth seeing, at last we arrive at Port Said on the 19th, well I don't think that I shall lose any sleep if we leave Port Said but it looks as though we will be staying as we have gone alongside the jetty, shore leave has been given to the starboard watch, I have skipped the shore leave that port watch has had here in the past and being so close to Alexandria brought back very happy memories of someone very special so I just sat down on our second day here and wrote what I know will be my final letter to her, I know it makes sense now and it's a long letter, some of it she will like very much but some she wont, it's no good holding back any more I am on my way back home and it's almost a certainty that I will not be coming back this way again.

When we talked the last time I was in Alexandria I told her that there is not much chance of me getting back this way again but I will write to her when the time came that I was sure I wouldn't be back, I knew she had the idea that I will try to get back to Alex even if I did go home but she didn't seem to realize that the Navy doesn't work like that, she wanted us to have a life together and if things had turned out some other way it could have happened, but there was nothing I could think of that would get me a fixed posting in Alexandria, especially as all the Naval forces were now being moved to the Far East. I do still love her and I know that she loves me but the time has come when I know that the inevitable has happened and there is nothing I can do about it, I know that she will be heart broken when she receives this letter but I think it best that we let go now, I cannot say too much in this letter as the censor will cut it out but I don't want her to carry on believing that I will be coming back and cause her to suffer any longer, I know I will never forget her.

Here we are sailing out of Port Said for the last time on the 22nd and unescorted sailed all the way through the Mediterranean and we didn't see a thing until arriving at Malta on the 24th and my how things have changed in the last few months, we only stayed here for a few hours so no chance to see the place once more but it will always be remembered by every sailor who entered the famous Grand Harbour on that day when the first convoy from Alexandria got through, the sight of hundreds of people lining the walls of Valletta waving and cheering with flags flying every where, the noise of the sirens and that band playing on the jetty as we sailed into the harbour was something special, that is one day above all others that I will never forget for as long as I live I am really proud to have been a part of it, then again despite the dangers

I've had some great runs ashore even with the lack of food, when I look back in years to come I will have the knowledge that I was among those that helped save Malta, then strike back at the enemy from Malta to take some revenge for what they have suffered in those terrible times, when we started those operations from this place the Javelin certainly saw plenty of action she deserved to go home when she did, I don't think that many ships had done the sea time that she did and I reckon that her engines must be about worn out.

That is now all in the past as we sail out of Malta for the last time and after two days sailing we arrive at Gibraltar on the 26th April, after going alongside to refuel we sail straight away so it's England here we come. With an uneventful journey it was Scotland where we dock not England. The port of Greenock was where I sailed from on the 22nd March 1942, with that massive convoy we headed for Madagascar, now here we are back again in May 1944 more than two years later after having traveled thousands of miles on different seas and oceans around the world, I have seen so many famous things and places, the sort of life that some people live, survive and suffer, and most of all I have seen death in it's most horrifying form, also I found love in a lovely dark haired girl which was fated from the very beginning, and so what I have brought back with me? 'I will cherish in all the years to come my memories.' Back to the present though and the first thing that we are greeted with is no shore leave granted! now why the hell not? surely we are entitled to our leave, but no and we soon find out why after we go alongside the jetty, the Captain speaks over the tannoy and tells us "all leave is cancelled until further notice, the reason for this is that the invasion of France is imminent and that leave for all Naval personnel has been cancelled."

Now, how about that then for timing and here I was thinking that there would be no more action for me, I did think that maybe I wouldn't see any more for a bit but 'no' another big one or should I have said the biggest, well, I just can't believe it . . . what rotten luck or will I once again be able to say I am proud to have been there. I was so looking forward to going on leave but we should have suspected that something is coming up by the amount of shipping that we passed on our way up the Irish sea and the huge amount that was in this harbour when we arrived 'it began filling up even more since we have come alongside this jetty the activity and the number of Yanks that are walking about the place, it's alive with them and their Jeeps. Our first job is to provision ship taking on supplies of all kinds and this our first day in harbour we are not being allowed on to the jetty at all, I reckon the reason for that is to stop us from making use of the phone and in doing so tell our folks at home that we are going to invade France, further to this all mail is stopped from going on shore so nobody is going to know anything, 'now what a load of rubbish' people are not blind or daft, all this activity going on Army wise and all this shipping coming into Greenock it's pretty obvious that there must be a heck of a lot going on ashore too, and by that I don't mean the dockyard if there is going to be an invasion the surrounding area of Greenock and most other ports in England should be alive with troops in there thousands, anyway things here begin to get very hectic as the days pass into weeks and it is noticeable that ships are beginning to gather outside the harbour now as there is not much room inside here, we eventually also had to give up our berth alongside the jetty to make way for Troop ships that are coming in in two's and three's as well as big Merchant ships. We are into the month of June and we are outside Greenock harbour which is now a real sight to see with ships of all sizes, the weather at the moment is not being very kind to us, it's beginning to blow up a bit, my thoughts begin to turn to June 11th once again and the Malta convoy, surely this isn't going to be on the same date as well, but no, I don't think so this time because the ships begin to organize themselves into some sort of formation on the 4th June. Lots of Destroyers and Corvettes have arrived, they all start to take up their positions.

This is going to be a massive screening job for the Destroyers and the Corvettes. All the Naval craft have now moved out of the harbour as well and are getting into positions amongst all this lot and I must admit that I have never seen so many ships together in all my days in the Navy, there are scores of them, they must have come from other ports to join up with this lot, there are Troop ships all loaded with soldiers, big Supply ships, American Liberty ships, big Tank Landing Craft even one or two Tankers, oh I could go on, you name it and it's out here, one amazing thing that I have never seen before is that nearly every ship has a Barrage Balloon attached and flying overhead, I wouldn't like to be the person who gets this lot into some sort of order for convoying down the Irish Sea, it's certainly going to be a big job.

Finally just as it is getting dark the signal is given to move off and this massive fleet of ships got under way, into what is worsening weather and getting rough, we haven't been sailing down the Irish Sea very long when we are ordered to heave too, nobody has a clue what is going on, of course the Officers will know but not the crews. Pitching and rolling about, it must be playing hell with the troops. 'but what the hell is happening'? It's morning now and the weather still isn't very good, here we are with this great fleet of ships waiting for some orders so we are told. Now at last, during the forenoon watch our Skipper has spoken over the tannoy and he has told us that "due to the bad weather there is been a hold up in the plans to land the troops on the Normandy Beaches, but the invasion is still on."

So here we are stuck in the Irish Sea as the hours pass by, we are just waiting for the weather to improve, there is some sign that the wind is dropping as it gets towards evening, then sure enough it came during the second dog watch! the signal to carry on was passed to all ships and slowly this vast number of ships with all it's Naval unit's began to get under way once more. In the English Channel we join up with the invasion force in the dawn light, a massive array of ships of every description. It is early morning on the 6th June 1944, we are all heading towards the French coast, it is yet another sight that I will always remember in this war. As the morning light improved the sight of this vast fleet is even more fantastic and I can not imagine how it could have been put together! as far as the eye could see there is nothing but ships. By now the weather has improved quite a lot but it is still not ideal conditions for the small boats to be in. As we get nearer to the coast which I can see clearly now, all the big warships, Battle ships and Cruisers (that includes us) move to the front of the convoy and get in some form of a line, standing off shore we wait until our aircraft flies in and starts bombing the coast line, then at a signal all the big warships began the bombardment of the shore batteries and the coastline defence, it was as though all hell broke loose, then the small craft joined in with their smaller guns! then the rockets, I was standing there watching history being created as the shells fell on shore and exploded, with debris flying into the air all along the line, it was a real hammering, I certainly wouldn't like to be anywhere near that lot . . . 'it must be terrible.' This bombardment carried on for some time, It was a terrific sight to watch as the big shells that the Battle ships and Cruisers including us were firing! 'it was awesome.'

Emerald opening fire on 'D.' Day

I was watching through my binoculars as the shells began to burst onshore and in no time at all the shore batteries were silenced, although they did manage to hit one of our Destroyers and I saw one ship on fire over on our port side, but with being closed up at action stations I didn't get much chance to look around on my side of the ship after the bombardment ended because we moved to another position so as to allow the Troop ships and the Tank Landing Craft to move in closer, after the smaller ships close to shore had finished firing, the landing craft started to go in, I was watching some of the troops going down the rope ladders and scrambling nets from the Troop ships into the waiting craft down below, and they were really having a tough job because as I mentioned before the conditions were far from ideal as the small landing craft were bobbing about like corks.

Emerald opening fire on Normandy.

Somehow they managed, soon there were hundreds of landing craft all making for shore, this seemed to go on for hours and then the supplies were being unloaded and this carried on all day, only once did I see any planes that was two enemy planes and they were being chased by a few of our fighter planes. (recognizing our planes from theirs is quite easy, all Allied Planes are marked with black and white markings on them). As the day wore on we began getting the news of how our lads are getting on ashore and it is pretty good, but alas not for the Americans who had landed over on our right, it appears that they had met with some stiff opposition! they are bogged down and still on the beaches.

Night came after a very hectic day and everyone was waiting for the big air attack from the enemy, however it never came, when morning arrived all that I can see is some ships moving closer to shore and there is quite a lot of activity going on.

Now, it seems, on looking through my binoculars, that they are making some sort of landing bay where both boats and ships can get into for the purpose of being unloaded, also very noticeable this morning are the bodies that are floating about in the sea and there is quite a lot of them, from what I can see they are mostly Americans, still in full dress, so obviously they have had it hard in their sector. Although it seems very quiet in our sector at the moment we have heard that another of our Destroyers has been sunk during the morning, that's the second one so we have now been ordered to keep a sharp lookout as it's believed that the enemy are using some under water craft, probably midget submarines, these are very active at night time which could explain the loss of a Merchant ship, which was sunk by an explosive device during the night.

We received the news of the sinking of the Destroyer and Merchant ship when the Captain spoke over the tannoy to give us a progress report on the landings and how our troops are doing ashore, the landings have been a complete success except for the Americans who are still meeting with some stiff opposition, troops in our sector have also met with some pockets of resistance but are now slowly pushing inland, there is still lots of activity going on all around us and one very noticeable thing has begun to take shape over on our port side, it seems as though the beach parties are making progress in building a small harbour for the safety of the ships while they unload their cargoes, it appears to be like a boom made using sunken ships or old wrecks, that's what it looks like to me through my binoculars but I may be wrong, I have also noticed some small crafts towing something long behind them going into this area, as I have said it's all activity now.

I think though, what is on everyone's mind aboard Emerald is when are we going to get our leave, but on this second day after the landing I wouldn't think that it will be for a while yet, it does look as though we are preparing for a lengthy stay although this day has now passed off reasonably quiet with our fighter planes sweeping over the entire beaches now and again, it does look as though there is not much chance of the enemy making any show. but then night came and with it the enemy Bombers, there is a warning that mines could possibly be dropped and these planes were not being fired on because no flares were coming down, opening fire would have given away our position, but one of the randomly dropped bombs hit the Emerald, only in the light of day did it reveal how very lucky indeed this ship had been. For the previous day 'Y' Magazine which is right aft had been having some work done inside and the hoist on the upper deck had been in use, this hoist is used to lower the ammunition down into the magazine and works backwards and forwards so that it can swing the ammo off the deck down into the Magazine, now whoever had finished working on that job had left the hoist in position over the top of the hatch and that bomb hit the top of the hoist (which is actually in the shape of a letter 'f' without the dash part) and glanced off down the starboard side of the ship then exploded causing some considerable damage, now I was just about to go down the forward side of the gun deck when that bomb struck, the force of it made the ship lurch over to starboard and I just managed to grab the hand rail to stop myself from going head first down those steps, I can say this now, if that bomb had not hit the top of that stanchion the magazine could have gone up . . . well, I might not be writing this in my diary now.

They do say that the ship could have gone up and with it most of the crew, well that was a very close thing. The damage caused by that bomb had to have a patch put over it and we stayed here for another couple of days before being forced to return to England for repairs, so we sailed from the Normandy coast and arrived back at Portsmouth going straight into dry dock, then the questions started "What was it like? and how are we getting on?" Oh, all sorts of questions. We were still not allowed on shore and here's me not been home for more than two years, I hadn't even stepped foot on English soil yet unless you can call this dry dock England, but it was just great being here and knowing that the war couldn't last much longer now, since the invasion was well on it's way and things are going OK. Listening to the news on the radio it sounds as if the Americans had landed in the wrong place but are now making headway, "Marvelous."

They did a quick job of patching us up and we sailed out of Pompy on our way back to Normandy with the dockyard workers giving us a cheery send off. So here we are back again at our station off the beaches of Normandy, things don't seem to have changed a lot except that there doesn't seem to be quite so many ships here now, I can see that all the big Troop ships have gone as well as a lot of the Supply ships, I can also see that they have finished the job of screening the Supply ships while they unload their supplies, they do have a landing stage for them to go alongside, evidently the long things that I saw being towed by the small craft were parts of this landing stage, so I reckon that things are going along more smoothly now as far as I can gather there have been no more air raids but there has been one or two ships damaged by mines! of all things.

But it seems as though Hitler has still not given up all hope, as two nights after we arrived back there was an attack by our old enemy the E-boats, star shells were going up all over the place and nobody seemed to know what was happening until we heard a loud explosion, we immediately saw the flames shoot up into the night sky and a ship could be clearly seen on fire. We stuck it out here for ten more days until things had quietened down a lot and it was thought that we wouldn't be needed any more, by then the army was well inland and the entire landings had been a success apart from the American section. So off we sailed back at last to England and Pompy for the last time. We arrived at Portsmouth going straight alongside the jetty, here we stayed for two days working the ships routine, then surprisingly we moved into the dry dock again for more repairs, and at last that news that everyone was waiting for was piped over the tannoy "leave to both watches for 14 days." I had only been given just fourteen days leave when I was really entitled to twenty eight days after my service time abroad, but the Emeralds crew got fourteen days as well so I suppose that I've just got to get on with it, this fourteen days is the normal leave given before you go on foreign service, there is nothing that I can do about it anyway, I am going on leave that is all that mattered. With my railway warrant and my small suitcase I'm now off on leave which I think that I deserve.

I'm writing this short piece at home just before I turn in, I arrived here to the surprise of everybody who thought that I was thousands of miles away, yes, home and the feeling is great. I have no girl friend waiting for me, the one at the Nestles factory who I went out with a couple of times has managed to get herself in trouble with an Army chap, so I was very relieved about that. didn't write her a single letter while I was away, as I said at the time when I went out with her that it was only something to do to pass the time away, 'I'm free' so it's pubs pubs and more pubs and plenty of real beer for me, fortunately for me one of my old mates was on leave but only for a long weekend so we soon got together, off we went to the nearest big town of Burton-on-Trent, we were soon doing the rounds of the public houses, we called in at one that I have never been in before, it was a very small quiet pub, as soon as we walked in there sitting in the corner were two girls, but straight away I only had eyes for one, she had lovely dark hair and was really nice looking, well you know what sailors are! so we tried it on but they didn't seem interested at all no matter how hard we tried. Apparently the two girls were only passing the time away in the pub as they were waiting for a bus to take them home, but when they got up to leave they said goodnight and walked out, but Jack doesn't give up that easily and we followed. To cut a long story short we walked them to the bus station, I got her name and address and we arranged to meet, the outcome is that I saw her for most of my remaining leave and I do like her very much. My fourteen days leave passed far too quickly but I'd had a smashing time and found myself a new girlfriend, now talking of girlfriends I got a very big surprise when I arrived back at the ship off leave, I had received a letter from Irene, it was really heart breaking to read, in fact I was very pleased to be on the mess deck at a time when there were only a few men cleaning because reading this letter brought those tears back, I just couldn't help myself, she now realizes that we will not be seeing each other again and knows that I am a long way from her now.

It was a very long letter which I don't wish to disclose the remaining contents except to say again that I will never forget her and that she made my life a lot easier during those very hard times in the Mediterranean. We are still in dry dock and there is very little work being done, apart from the usual working part ship painting, by the looks of things I reckon that the Emerald will be here for some time and will be lucky if she ever goes to sea again. I wasn't far wrong, for after some weeks of this messing about she paid off and I don't think that anyone was surprised at all, ('Paid Off' comes from the old Navy, it's used when a ship had done a period of service at sea and arrives back into port, all of her ships company are drafted back to their respective Depots then after a time she is re-commissioned and gets an entirely new crew.)

The date I leave H.M.S. Emerald is 22nd September 1944 to R.N. Barracks.

Anyway that's how it works, so with kit bag and hammock I am down that gangway, into a lorry with just three more lads and a short journey brought us back to Pompy Barracks where it all started from. Without much to write about now it is a wait and see what happens next. It was a long wait working part ship when I got another draft chit to Whale Island on the 10th November. I was ships company again and soon got back into the old guard duties, a real good number and with being a watch keeper also plenty of shore leave. I really like Pompy with all it's pubs and there are no longer any air-raids to bother about like there used to be, as for the girls well there again I'm not interested any more now I've got a lovely one of my own who I am writing to regularly. I've got everything that I have ever wanted now someone who loves me and is not interested in any pleasure without me, I can only hope that we get lots more time together and that the draft onto another ship never materializes.

The Whale Island job is great, it's just Guard duties, the routine is exactly as it was before. At the moment there is very little to write about but I am really enjoying myself here with the regular shore leave. I had been here only a few weeks when it happened again, I got another draft chit and it's back to the Royal Naval Barracks in Pompy on the 25th January. Once again back into the old routine but I don't mind really as long as I keep on getting that long weekend leave to see my girlfriend, it looks as though I will be here for some time because we have started to work down in the dockyard, there is certainly plenty of work to do down there, but I don't mind this sort of work because it takes me away from the Barracks and all it's discipline. The weeks pass by. It is now the 29th March 1945 and I have just been handed another draft chit to H.M.S. Attack in Portland.

This base is for small boats such as the Motor Torpedo Boats, Motor Launches and Landing Craft, it's a small Naval base not all that far from Weymouth, the only problem with this base is distance, I know that my girlfriend will be very pleased about this because she doesn't want me to go to sea again as she is really worried because I've told her that there is always a chance that I may be drafted onto a ship again, there is an added problem now, this place is a lot further to travel than Pompy, the long weekend if I get any here is going to be shortened somewhat. I fell in on my first morning and got the cushiest number of all.

How about this, for a special duty job here . . . what a laugh 'Commanders Gardener' I just couldn't believe it (What did you do in the war dad sink ships? No son I was a Commanders head gardener) joking apart, I didn't ask for the job, 'really.' We fell in to work part ship as expected and the Chief Petty Officer started to read out the special duty jobs firsts, the gardening job came up second, then he asked "Now does anyone know anything about gardening?" I stuck my hand up and being I was the only one. The job is mine, anyway it is better than having a leading hand standing over you all day long, also I do know a lot about gardening. I was told to report to the Commanders Office where he took me into the garden behind the offices, we had a long chat then he left me too it, now I only had one man over me, he only occasionally told me what he wanted doing.

I love this place where I do my gardening, it is so quiet and peaceful and well away from the Naval establishment, it's a job that I enjoy doing, I reckon that I can just about manage it until the end of the war. Weymouth as I have mentioned is not far from Portland, it's is a great place for a run ashore, but being war time there is not much in the way of amusement, we can get a decent drink of beer though, but Portland, well, it's not a bad place but there is very little of what you call night life, unless you go into the pubs (these are always full of matelots), there is always the old sing songs, where ever there's a group of sailors in a pub you will find that there is plenty of singing going on. I have managed in the last couple of months to get in a few long weekend leaves. Another thing that I will always remember Portland for, I have got my marriage banns read out in the local church . . . Yes, I am going to marry the girl I walked with to the bus station in Burton-on-Trent.

Why not? I love her, I can't wait for the big day and the date is fixed, I have got to work it so I am on leave when the day comes, that will mean I need save my leave, which will mean missing out on some of the long weekends. I would have loved to have remained here at H.M.S. Attack until my demob, yes, I think I can talk about demob because the war is going well, that's for sure, it will soon be over as we are now well into the year 1945.

The news came sooner than I expected the prime minister has made an announcement today on the radio to the effect that at 3pm Tuesday 8th May 1945 Germany surrendered, so now the "WAR IN EUROPE IS OVER," but the far east one goes on.

Now, all good things come to an end and mine came on the 16th June when I was handed yet another draft chit back to Pompy Barracks after only a few months, the Commander got me a relief but this was only until the 16th July. So off I go back to Pompy Barracks once more. Back with the same routine, day in day out just the same old job, the leave you get here always offsets the boredom, you can get to London from Pompy in a very quick time, you learn the way to use the underground station from Waterloo to St Pancras off by heart so as not to miss your connections to Derby.

My big day came and I got 72hrs leave, I had arranged it nicely right up to the very day and that was my Wedding day, I got married in Derby, it was a Church wedding and I married a very lovely Edith Perry, it was a lovely wedding and despite the fact that it was war time everybody had a great time. So you see I'm not minding at all being in Pompy Barracks and here I stayed for just over a month then the usual happened once more I was handed a draft chit on falling in for duty on the morning of the 30th August, I have to be outside the drafting office at 09.30 with my kit bag and hammock, I am jotting this down in my note book as I sit here with one other rating while waiting for lorry transport to take the two of us to H.M.S. Tormentor, a long run to Warsash which is another shore base in Hampshire.

After a fairly smooth journey we arrived at what was definitely a school before the war, my first impressions are, well, there doesn't seem to be much pusser about this place, although there is a guard on duty at the gates when we arrived, I've found out that this place is the end of the line for most sailors, It is is one of the places that the Navy send ratings awaiting their demob. So it looks as though my sailing days are nearly over as like most of the lads here who have been in the Navy from almost the start of the war, as the war in the far East is not expected to last much longer there is no chance of us going to sea again, so here we stay until they think that enough is enough.

My first job here is sweeping up and keeping the place tidy, I've been doing this now for a couple of weeks, then this morning I was detailed off for another job and once again they don't come much cushier than this! 'Billiard room sweeper attendant' (I told you it was cushy,) my job apart from keeping this place neat and tidy is to look after the full size billiard table which is only used at night by the lads after all the day jobs have been done, part of my job is at night and that is to book in the people who want to use the table, also to take a small fee for each hour that they play including making sure that there isn't any trouble, then close the place up after the games have finished. During the day I have to keep the table in perfect condition by brushing it down regularly and press the cloth. we do have quite a lot of leisure time, this is spent mainly playing football between each others mess which is great fun, as for the rest of the lads well, there is not much to do during the day apart from cleaning and the occasional sentry duties on the gate, on the odd occasion we watch the great liner Queen Mary sailing down Southampton water.

Public houses in Warsash, well, I only went into one, apart from that there is no night life, in fact I think Warsash is a very boring place so roll on the Armistice let's get out of here.

So the weeks rolled by and you will notice that I have not mentioned anything about leave, the reason is, this place is a long way from any real connections (by railway), the journey would take far too long for there to be any chance of weekend leave from here, but I do write to my new wife fairly regular and can't wait for the day when we can be together for always, she is looking forward to that too. here is some relief when the news came though that there is to be a certain number of releases this week, after falling in on parade names are read out and the dates that these ratings would be released, mine is the second name out but my release date is the 6th January 1946, that is a couple of weeks away yet some are going in a couple of days time.

So it is decided that all of us who are being demobbed are going to have a last night booze up which is tonight, I can tell you now the beer flowed freely with quite a few bad heads the next day. It wasn't long before my turn came round, on the morning of the 6th January I handed in all my kit except my old hammock blanket which is my own, I then had to wait a further day to get my discharge papers including gratuities and change our uniforms for civilian suit including hat and our railway warrants, and with that my service in the Royal Navy ended.

I was released from the Royal Navy on the 7th January 1946, so after my life in the Navy I returned to civilian and married life. My first job as a civilian was a Derbyshire County Police Constable.

This is a true story of my war exactly as it happened, (which are the main things), there was a lot more I could have mentioned that were personal, looking back, also lots of things not fit to mention, obviously I have missed them out deliberately, these are the things I saw that were really Horrible and heart breaking, if I had included all these it would have made this a very long story, so I have written my account of the war which I feel very proud to be a part of. I end by saying I was only a young man of 17 years of age when I joined the Royal Navy but they were the best years of my life, the dangers well, I was one of the very lucky ones, I came back but a hell of a lot of my old shipmates didn't. My only hope is that the young people of tomorrow appreciate their freedom and don't ever forget what we went through, but for me I wouldn't change a thing.

PS. Just for anyone interested I received a Letter from Irene to say that she had now got another Boy Friend and is very happy and hoping that I am too, "but please not to answer this letter." I received this letter weeks after I arrived back here in England.

SOME LOWER DECK PHRASEOLOGY

Buffer-Bosuns

Bubbly-Rum

Buzz-Rumour

Jimmy The One-First Lieutenant

Bootneck-Royal Marine

Corned Dog-Tinned Meat

Fanny-Round Utensil For Carrying Rum

Flea Bag-Hammock

Ki-Cocoa

Killick-Leading Seaman

Nelsons Blood-Rum

Oppo-Pal

Pipe-Bosuns Call

Dock yard Matey-A man working on
board ship

Dhobing-Clothes Washing

Tiddly-Neat, Smart, Tidy

Tot-Daily issue of Rum

Mate Skint-No money

Matelot-Sailor

Pusser-Admiralty

Tin Fish-Torpedo

Sippers-Less than a tot of rum

Scran-Food

pongo's @Swaddies-Soldiers

H.M.S. JAVELIN
1942.

Lightning Source UK Ltd.
Milton Keynes UK
UKOW03f0641110614

233202UK00001B/89/P